KU-774-225

Cakes & Biscuits

Cakes & Biscuits
Margaret Wade

Editor **Sarie Forster**
Designer **Roger Hammond**
Editorial assistant **Lesley Toll**

Hamlyn
LONDON · NEW YORK · SYDNEY · TORONTO
in association with Phoebus

Strawberry Cream Buns.

Contents

The cover picture shows: background from left to right, Special Chocolate Gâteau, Meringues, and Fruit Tartlets; foreground from left to right, Refrigerator Cookies, Brownies, Vanilla Cookies, Raisin Cookies, Peanut Flapjacks, and more Vanilla Cookies.

Published 1977 by
The Hamlyn Publishing Group Limited
London New York Sydney Toronto
Astronaut House, Feltham, Middlesex, England

ISBN 0 600 31984 9

Made and printed in Great Britain by
Waterlow (Dunstable) Limited

Half and Half, Almond Crunchies, Cherry Rosettes, Little Coffee Meringues, Little Chocolate Sp

·read Swirls and Ginger Petits Fours.

Introduction

The baking of cookies and cakes is an art which is often neglected today, even by those who consider themselves to be good cooks. This book sets out to rectify that sad situation and reintroduce homemade cookies and cakes to the tea table.

Nothing is as appetizing as the aroma in the kitchen when baking is in progress, nothing more mouthwatering than the taste of shortbread still warm from the oven. Home baking does require a little more time and effort, but once you have mastered the essential skills you will find cookies and cakes a pleasure to make and to eat.

Build up your repertoire with old favourites such as Brownies and Macaroons; then, with the help of step by step pictures, move on to Eclairs and Cream Horns. As well as the familiar family cakes like Madeira Cake and Gingerbread, you will find elaborate cakes for special occasions – try Gâteau St Honoré, a delicious confection of choux pastry, chantilly cream and caramel on shortcrust pastry.

There are also ideas on making candies and petits fours, icings and cake decorations, and plenty of professional tips which both beginner and experienced cook will find helpful.

Gâteau St Honoré.

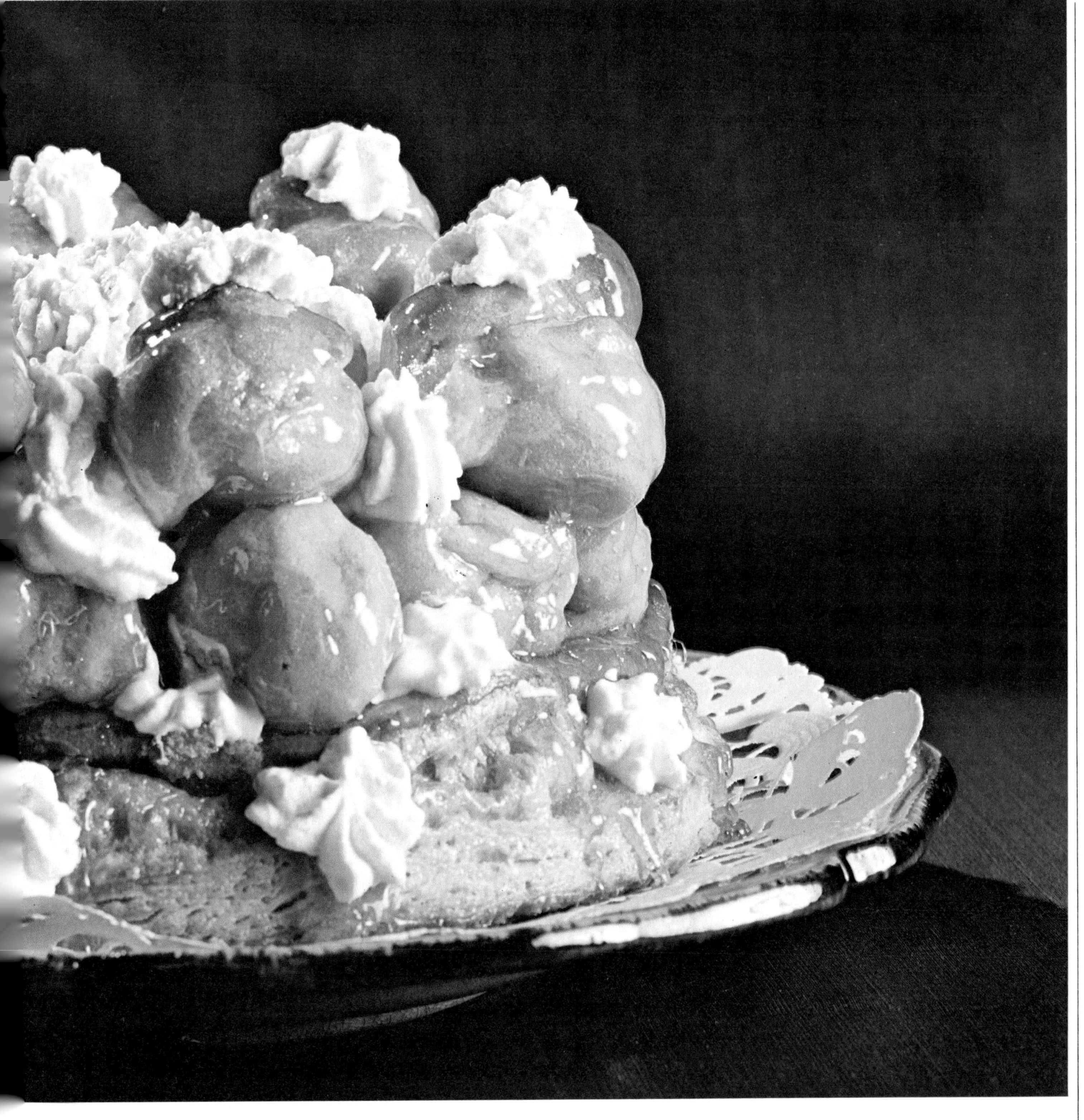

Cookies and biscuits

Once you have tried some of the recipes in this chapter you will agree that store bought cookies cannot compare. Make a variety of cookies from one batch of dough by dividing it into portions and flavouring and decorating each portion differently. Many of the recipes yield large quantities and you may find it efficient to use two or more baking sheets so that one batch is baking whilst others are shaped and arranged on the second sheet. Alternatively, instead of baking all the cookies at once, store some of the dough, well wrapped, in the refrigerator or freezer, and bake fresh cookies as you need them.

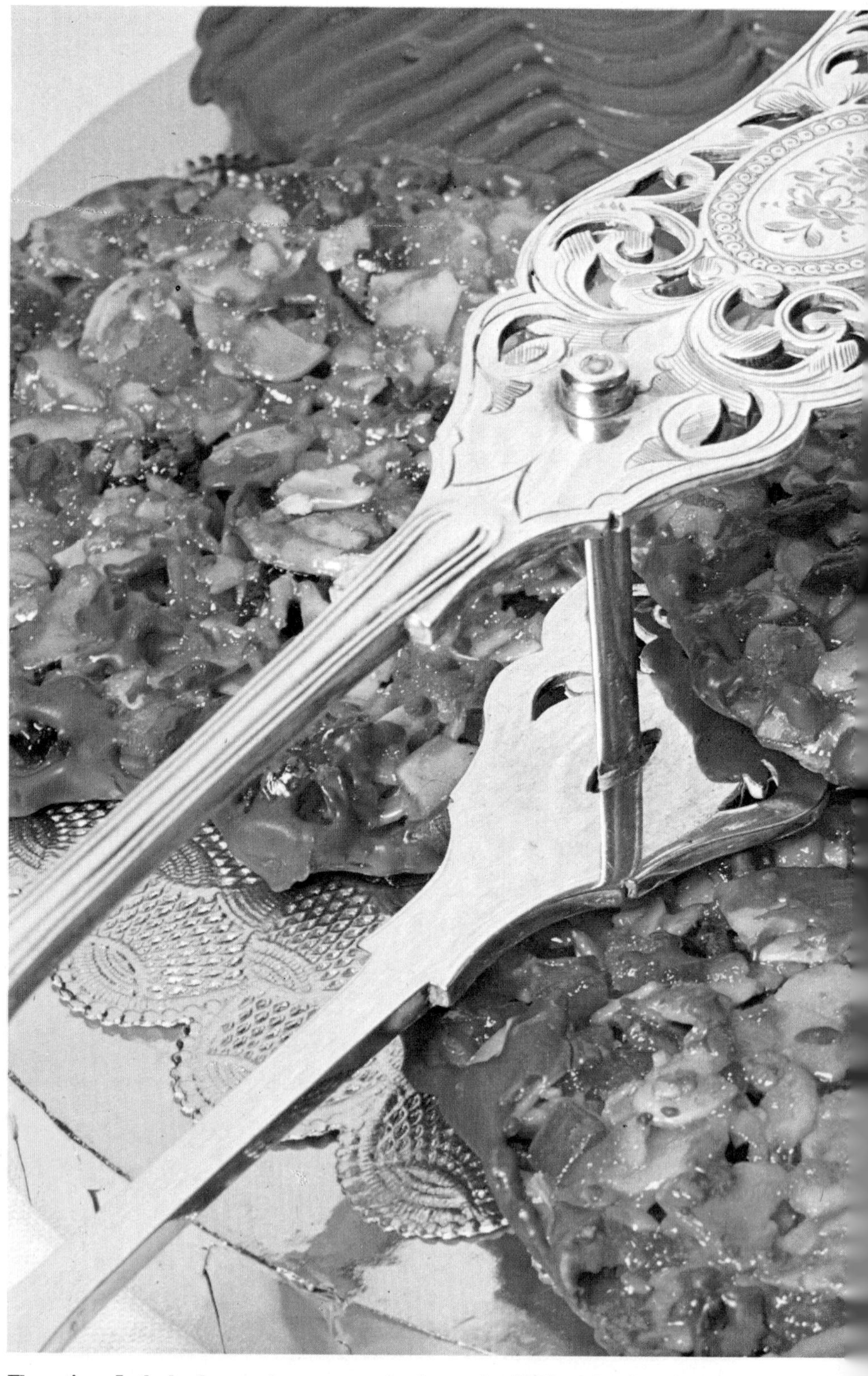

Florentines. In the background you can see the decorative finish on the chocolate side.

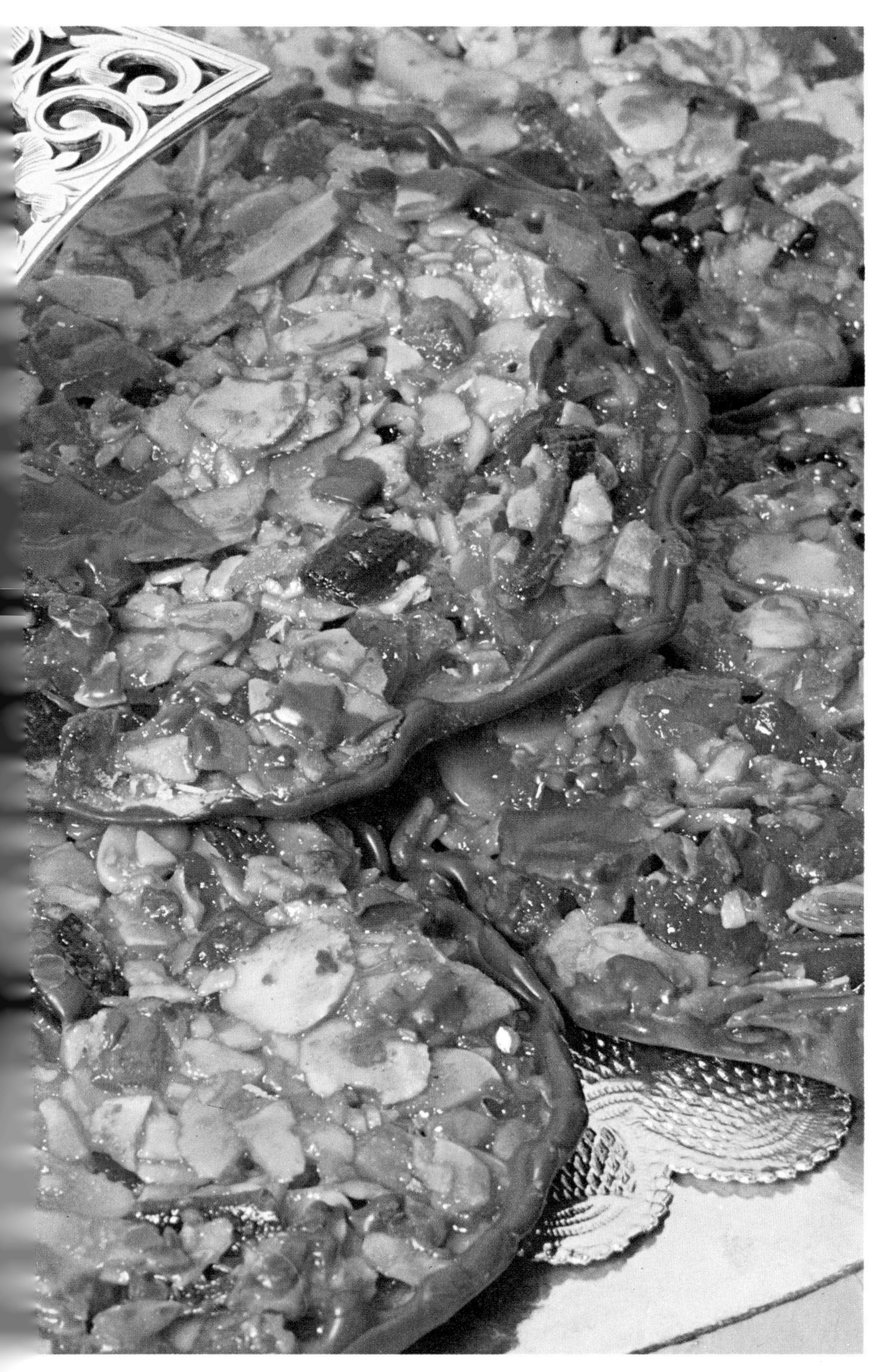

Florentines

3½ oz (80 g) unsalted butter
4 oz (100 g) castor sugar
1 oz (25 g) coarsely chopped glacé cherries
3½ oz (80 g) chopped, blanched or nibbed almonds
1 oz (25 g) flaked almonds
3½ oz (80 g) mixed, chopped candied peel
1¼ fl oz (3 cl) double cream
4 oz (100 g) grated plain dessert chocolate

Set the oven at 350°F (180°C) or Mark 4.

Melt the butter in a pan over a very low heat, then stir in the sugar and let the mixture just start to bubble. Stir in the remaining ingredients except for the cream and chocolate. As soon as the mixture starts to bind together, take the pan off the stove and beat in the cream. Turn into a basin and leave to thicken and cool.

Line a baking sheet with buttered and floured greaseproof paper. Use a teaspoon to drop good scoops of the cooled mixture onto the prepared baking sheet leaving sufficient room between each one for them to spread during baking. Put on the middle shelf in the pre-set oven and bake for 12–15 minutes, or until florentines have spread and set. Take out and set aside.

Meanwhile gently heat the grated chocolate until just liquid. When florentines are cold and firm, ease away the paper, turn over the cookies and, using a small knife, spread with softened chocolate. Mark in wavy lines with the back of a fork as the chocolate begins to set, to give a decorative finish.

Cookies and biscuits

Date Cookies

1 lb (450 g) dates
1 lemon
1 orange
4 eggs
1 lb (450 g) soft brown sugar
8 oz (225 g) plain flour
1 tsp (5 ml) coffee powder
1 tsp (5 ml) baking powder
1 tsp (5 ml) cinnamon
6 oz (175 g) walnuts
¼ pt (15 cl) orange juice
icing sugar
1 oz (25 g) butter or margarine

Set the oven at 375°F (190°C) or Mark 5.

Grate the peel of the lemon and orange and extract juices. Cut the dates into small pieces, place in a bowl and pour over the juice and grated peel. Cover the bowl and allow to stand for at least 10 hours.

Beat together the eggs until light, then add the brown sugar by degrees, taking care not to overbeat. Sift together the flour, coffee, baking powder and cinnamon and mix in with the sugar and eggs. Chop the walnuts, add to the date mixture and stir into the main mixture.

Turn the entire mixture into a buttered dish and bake in the pre-set oven for about 45 minutes and allow to cool.

Pour the orange juice into a separate bowl and gradually add enough sugar until the mixture is thick enough to spread. Melt the butter or margarine and stir in. Pour over cookies and cut into squares.

Melt in the Mouth Cookies

4 oz (100 g) plain flour
2 oz (50 g) ground almonds
2 oz (50 g) icing sugar
2 oz (50 g) unsalted butter
1 egg
salt
grated rind of 1 orange

To serve (optional)
icing sugar
jam, glacé icing or butter cream for filling

Set the oven at 350°F (180°C) or Mark 4.

Sift the flour in a mixing bowl, then add the ground almonds and the icing sugar and blend together. Make a well in the centre and add the butter, egg, a pinch of salt and the grated orange rind. Combine together, using 2 knives, until a soft but not sticky dough is reached. Wrap in foil and put in the refrigerator for about 2 hours to rest.

Take dough from wrappings and cut into small pieces. Mould these into shell tins or fancy cookie moulds. Bake in the pre-set oven for about 7 minutes, then allow to cool slightly in tins or moulds before cooling completely on a wire rack. Serve plain, or sprinkle with icing sugar, or sandwich together with jam, glacé icing or butter cream.

Apple Cookies

8 oz (225 g) plain flour
1 tsp (5 ml) bicarbonate of soda
½ tsp (2.50 ml) salt
1 tsp (5 ml) cinnamon
1 tsp (5 ml) nutmeg
1 tsp (5 ml) ground cloves
4 oz (100 g) butter or margarine
4 oz (100 g) soft brown sugar
3 oz (75 g) granulated sugar
1 egg
½ pt (30 cl) apple purée
3 oz (75 g) raisins
2 oz (50 g) walnuts

Set the oven at 425°F (220°C) or Mark 7.

Sift the flour, bicarbonate of soda, salt and spices into a bowl. Cream the fat and both types of sugar until light and fluffy, then stir in the lightly beaten egg and the apple purée. Fold in the flour mixture and stir in the raisins and walnuts.

Drop spoonfuls onto a greased baking sheet and bake in the pre-set oven for 10 minutes or until lightly browned.

Chocolate Crispies

4 oz (100 g) plain chocolate
½ oz (12 g) butter or margarine
3 oz (75 g) cornflakes or rice crispies

Place the chocolate and butter or margarine in a bowl over a pan of hot water. Stir until melted, then add the cornflakes or rice crispies.

Mix well and place spoonfuls of the mixture onto a sheet of greaseproof paper. Leave to set.

Storing in an airtight container is essential for keeping them crisp.

German Christmas Cookies

4 eggs
14 oz (400 g) sugar
grated rind of 1 lemon
1 tbsp (15 ml) brandy
1 lb (450 g) plain flour
4-6 oz (100-175 g) aniseed

Beat the eggs well, then beat in sugar a little at a time and continue beating for 15 minutes or until the mixture is thick and light and leaves a thin trail on itself when the whisk or beater is lifted. Beat in the grated lemon rind and brandy.

Sift flour into the egg mixture, then using your hand draw the flour and egg mixture together to make a smooth but not sticky dough (add more flour if necessary until correct consistency is reached). Turn onto a floured work surface and knead for about 10 minutes or until it is shiny, working in a little extra flour if the dough starts to stick. Cover and leave to rest for 1 hour.

Roll out dough to ⅜ inch (8 mm) thickness. Sprinkle springerle moulds with aniseed and flour, giving a sharp tap to free them of excess flour. Cut pieces of dough to match the size of the rectangular moulds and press firmly in or, using a rolling pin, roll large pieces of dough onto cylindrical moulds so the patterns are impressed.

Place dough, pattern side facing up, on 2 greased baking sheets and leave to dry uncovered, for 24 hours.

Set the oven at 250°F (130°C) or Mark ½. Bake cookies in the pre-set oven for 20–25 minutes or until firm. The tops should be white and the bottoms lightly browned. Cool on a wire rack. Store in an airtight tin for 1–2 weeks to mellow.

Wooden springerle moulds are of German origin and come in a wide variety of sizes and patterns. They are available in many cooking equipment shops and department stores and make attractive as well as practical kitchen decorations.

. plate of traditional, lemon and aniseed flavoured, German Christmas Cookies, which should prove especially popular with children. ›elow the plate is an assortment of wooden springerle moulds showing a variety of patterns.

Cookies and biscuits

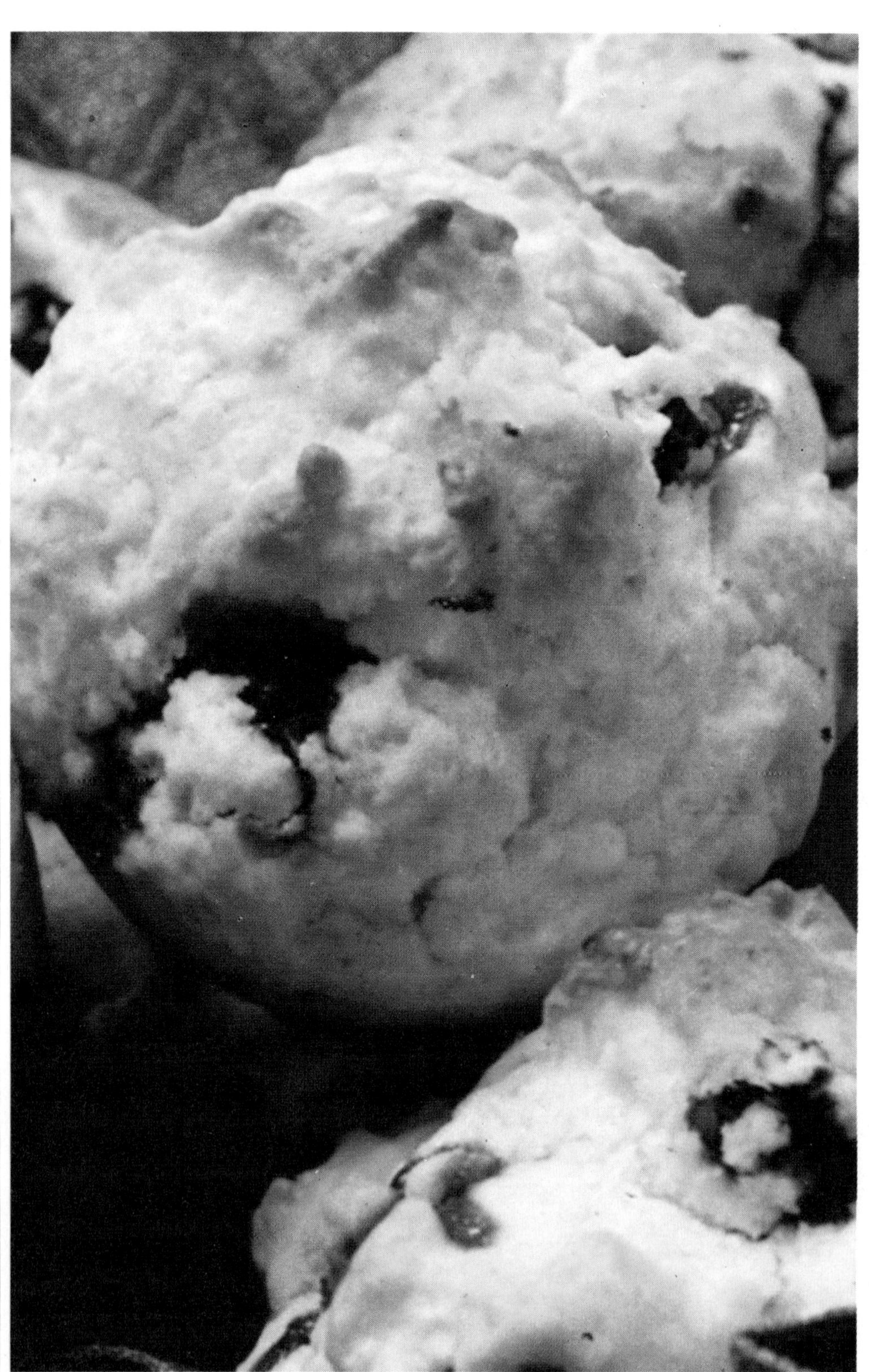

Bilberry Muffins. Try serving them well browned, still hot from the oven and generously buttered. Bilberries are usually available during the summer months.

Bilberry Muffins

8 oz (225 g) frozen bilberries
8 oz (225 g) plain flour
1½ oz (35 g) sugar
1 tbsp (15 ml) baking powder
salt
1 egg
1 fl oz (25 ml) melted butter or margarine.
4 fl oz (10 cl) milk

Set the oven at 425°F (220°C) or Mark 7.

Defrost and drain the bilberries thoroughly. Sift the flour, sugar, and baking powder and a pinch of salt into a mixing bowl. Beat egg and butter or margarine together and stir in the milk.

Make a well in the centre of the flour, lightly stir in the milk mixture until just blended, adding the bilberries half way through. The mixture should look lumpy.

Spoon the mixture into a greased bun tin, filling each one about two thirds full and bake in the pre-set oven for 25 minutes, or until well browned. Coo slightly in tin, then turn out onto a wir rack to cool completely.

Chocolate Fruit Meringue Cookies

2 oz (50 g) cooking chocolate
2 oz (50 g) almonds
2 oz (50 g) raisins
2 egg whites
4 oz (100 g) icing sugar

Set the oven at 300°F (150°C) or Mar 1–2.

Melt the chocolate in a bowl over a pan c hot water and allow it to cool slightly Blanch the almonds and chop into sma pieces. Beat the egg whites stiffly and ad the icing sugar by degrees, beating con tinuously. Fold in the chocolate and mos of the almonds and raisins. Spoon sma balls of the mixture onto a well grease baking tray and sprinkle over the rest c the fruit.

Bake in the pre-set oven for about 4 minutes.

te and Nut Triangles.

Date and Nut Triangles

b (450 g) quantity puff pastry
z (100 g) cream cheese
bsp (15 ml) thick honey
z (100 g) chopped dates
bsp (30 ml) fresh orange juice
ated rind of 1 orange
gg white
z (100 g) flaked almonds
stor sugar for dusting

t the oven at 375°F (190°C) or Mark 5.

end together the cream cheese, honey, tes, orange juice and rind.

Roll out the pastry to ¼ inch (6 mm) ickness, and with a knife, cut into an equal number of triangles measuring 4 inches (10 cm) along the sides by 2 inches (5 cm). Spread half the pastry triangles with cheese mixture and set aside. Dampen edges on one side of the remaining triangles with a little cold water and place on top of each of the cheese covered triangles. Brush the top and sides with a little beaten egg white, then sprinkle with almonds and castor sugar and transfer cookies to a baking sheet. Cover with a piece of greased greaseproof paper.

Bake in the pre-set oven for 15 minutes until well risen and the topping has started to bubble.

HOW TO CUT PASTRY TRIANGLES

1. When making large quantities of pastry triangles use a cutting wheel for speed. Roll out the pastry thinly and press the wheel down firmly on the pastry.

2. Lift the wheel up so that the triangles fall back onto the work surface. If any fail to fall or stay joined up, use a knife to finish off the job.

3. Thus in one easy movement you can cut 14 evenly sized pastry triangles.

Cookies and biscuits

For the busy cook Coconut Crisps are the perfect cookies to serve for afternoon tea, as they are easy to make as well as delicious. They are shown here lightly browned and decorated with glacé cherries.

Coconut Crisps

12 oz (350 g) desiccated coconut
7 oz (200 g) sugar
2 oz (50 g) plain flour
½ tsp (2.50 ml) vanilla essence
2 egg whites

To finish
few whole blanched almonds split in half, or glacé cherries cut in half

Set the oven at 350°F (180°C) or Mark 4.

Sift the flour. Blend together desiccated coconut, sugar and flour. Add vanilla essence and enough egg white to bind the mixture. Beat for about 5 minutes, then leave to rest for a further 5 minutes.

Cut a sheet of rice paper into 2 inch (5 cm) squares and place, shiny side down, on a baking sheet, or line a baking sheet with silicone paper.

Beat cookie mixture again until thick and white, then fill into a piping bag and pipe into 2 inch (5 cm) rounds on the prepared baking sheet. Place halved almond or cherry in the centre of each cookie and bake in the pre-set oven for 15–20 minutes or until lightly browned. Turn onto a wire rack to cool and remove paper only when cold. (Rice paper need only be trimmed as it is edible.)

Fly Biscuits

3 oz (75 g) butter or margarine
3 oz (75 g) castor sugar
6 oz (175 g) plain flour
alt
egg
oz (50 g) currants

et the oven at 375°F (190°C) or Mark 5.

ream the butter or margarine with the ugar until light and fluffy. Sift the flour. eparate the egg. Beat the yolk and add to he butter and sugar mixture together with little of the flour and the currants.

Knead into a firm dough and roll out to inch (12 mm) thickness. Cut into quares and place on a greased baking heet.

Bake in the pre-set oven for 10 minutes. rush with a little of the egg white, and ust with more castor sugar.

Brownies

2 oz (50 g) chopped plain dessert chocolate
4 oz (100 g) butter or margarine
8 oz (225 g) sugar
2 eggs
4 oz (100 g) plain flour
salt
4 oz (100 g) chopped pecans or shredded blanched almonds
½ tsp (2.50 ml) vanilla essence

Set the oven at 350°F (180°C) or Mark 4.

Melt chocolate in a basin over a pan of hot water. Cream butter or margarine until soft, then gradually stir in sugar and beat until mixture is light and fluffy. Stir in eggs, one at a time, beating after each addition. Sift the flour with a pinch of salt and stir into butter mixture. Stir in nuts, melted chocolate and vanilla essence.

Pour mixture into a greased 8 inch (20 cm) square baking tin, spreading it evenly. Bake in the pre-set oven for 25–30 minutes or until a light crust has formed. Take out of oven, cool slightly and cut into squares to serve.

Butterscotch Brownies

2 oz (50 g) butter or margarine
7 oz (200 g) dark brown sugar
1 egg
1 tsp (5 ml) vanilla essence
4 oz (100 g) plain flour
salt
1 tsp (5 ml) baking powder
4 oz (100 g) desiccated coconut or 4 oz (100 g) chopped dates

Set the oven at 350°F (180°C) or Mark 4.

Melt butter or margarine in a pan over a very low heat, stir in brown sugar and heat gently until completely melted. Cool slightly, then beat in egg and vanilla essence.

Sift the flour with a pinch of salt and the baking powder into a mixing bowl, then stir into butter mixture together with coconut or dates. Using a knife spread the mixture in a greased 11 by 7 inch (30×20 cm) cake tin and bake in the pre-set oven for 25 minutes or until a light crust has formed. Cool slightly before cutting into bars or squares while still in the tin.

Raisin Cookies

4 oz (100 g) self raising flour
½ tsp (2.50 ml) bicarbonate of soda
2 oz (50 g) castor sugar
4 oz (100 g) seedless raisins
2 oz (50 g) butter or margarine
3 tbsp (45 ml) golden syrup

Set the oven at 325°F (160°C) or Mark 3.

Sift into a mixing bowl the flour, bicarbonate of soda and sugar; add the raisins. In a pan over a low heat melt the butter or margarine, then stir in the golden syrup. Blend together for 1–2 minutes, then stir into the flour mixture and mix well to form a soft dough.

Shape the dough into small balls with your hands, then place them on a greased baking sheet, leaving plenty of space between them to allow for spreading during baking. Flatten each cookie slightly.

Bake in the centre of the pre-set oven for 10–15 minutes, then take out and cool slightly before transferring cookies to a wire rack. Store in an airtight tin.

Cats' Tongues

2 egg whites
2 oz (50 g) softened unsalted butter
2 oz (50 g) vanilla flavoured castor sugar
2 oz (50 g) plain flour

Set the oven at 375°F (190°C) or Mark 5.

Whip egg whites until stiff. Work the butter until white and creamy, then beat the sugar in well. Sift the flour and carefully stir in, then fold in the whipped egg whites.

Spoon some of the mixture into a piping bag fitted with a ¼ inch (6 mm) nozzle and pipe out short thin strips measuring about 3 inches (7 cm) long. Do not overfill piping bag. Leave sufficient space between each one to allow for spreading during baking.

Bake in the centre of the pre-set oven for about 5 minutes or until just beginning to turn pale brown at edges. Remove biscuits at once and carefully transfer to a wire rack to cool. The biscuits are fairly soft so use a palette knife to lift them – they will firm up on cooling.

Cookies and biscuits

Almond Cookies

6 oz (175 g) plain flour
6 oz (175 g) butter or margarine
3 oz (75 g) castor sugar
vanilla essence
1½ oz (35 g) ground almonds

Set the oven at 325°F (160°C) or Mark 3.

Sift the flour. Put all the ingredients into a bowl and work together to form a smooth dough. Roll small pieces of the dough into balls and flatten them into rounds.

Place the cookies on a greased baking sheet and bake in the pre-set oven for 25 minutes, or until golden brown.

Vanilla Cookies

4 oz (100 g) butter or margarine
3 oz (75 g) castor sugar
1 tsp (5 ml) vanilla essence
4½ oz (125 g) plain flour
baking powder

Set the oven at 325°F (160°C) or Mark 3.

Melt the butter or margarine in a pan over a medium heat until it just starts to brown. Remove it immediately from the heat and pour into a mixing bowl. Stand the bowl in cold water to cool the fat rapidly. When cool add the sugar and cream together until soft and fluffy. Beat in vanilla essence. Sift, then fold in the flour with a good pinch of baking powder.

Turn dough onto a floured work surface and roll out to about ⅛ inch (3 mm) thickness. Stamp out cookies with chosen cutters (stars, hearts, etc.) and place on a greased baking sheet.

Bake in the pre-set oven for 8–10 minutes until pale golden and crisp. Take out and cool on a wire rack. Decorate if liked with a little piped melted chocolate or glacé icing.

Almond Macaroons.

Almond Macaroons

approx. 14 almonds
6 oz (175 g) castor sugar
4 oz (100 g) ground almonds
1 tsp (5 ml) rice flour
1–2 egg whites
extra castor sugar for sprinkling

Set the oven at 350°F (180°C) or Mark 4.

Blanch the almonds to remove their skins, dry well and set aside.

Mix the castor sugar, ground almonds and rice flour together in a bowl. Lightly beat the egg whites. Gradually add sufficient beaten egg white to the dry mixture to form a firm dough.

Break off small pieces, each weighing about 1 oz (25 g), and roll them into balls. Place on a greased baking sheet, allowing plenty of room for spreading during baking.

Brush the tops with any remaining beaten egg white, press an almond into the centre of each macaroon, and sprinkle with a little castor sugar.

Bake in the pre-set oven for 15 minutes or until firm and lightly brown. Remove from the baking sheet whilst still hot.

Date Nut Bars

2 eggs
7 oz (200 g) sugar
8 oz (225 g) walnuts
1 lb (450 g) dates
4 oz (100 g) glacé cherries
1 tsp (5 ml) vanilla essence
2 oz (50 g) plain flour
1 tsp (5 ml) baking powder

Set the oven at 350°F (180°C) or Mark 4.

Beat the eggs and sugar together until light. Chop the walnuts, the dates and the glacé cherries, and add to the egg mixture with the vanilla essence. Sift the flour and baking powder together, and fold in, mixing well.

Spread in a greased baking tin and bake in the pre-set oven for about 45 minutes. Cut into bars whilst still warm.

Chocolate Spice Cookies

4 eggs
3 egg yolks
7 oz (200 g) soft brown sugar
8 oz (225 g) chocolate
10 oz (275 g) plain flour
1½ tsp (7.50 ml) baking powder
8 fl oz (175 ml) black treacle
1 tsp (5 ml) cinnamon
1 tsp (5 ml) salt
½ tsp (2.50 ml) allspice
¼ tsp (1.75 ml) nutmeg
4 oz (100 g) candied orange peel
8 oz (225 g) ground almonds
9 oz (250 g) icing sugar
lemon juice

Set the oven at 350°F (180°C) or Mark 4.

Beat the eggs and the extra yolks togethe until very light. Beat in the brown sugar Grate the chocolate, and sift the flour witl the baking powder and set aside. Stir in the egg mixture, the treacle, spices, salt orange peel, almonds, grated chocolate icing sugar, a little lemon juice, flour anc baking powder. Mix thoroughly.

Using well floured hands, spread th dough to a 1½ inch (3 cm) thickness on greased baking tin. Bake in the pre-se oven for 30 minutes. Cut into bars an keep for a week before eating.

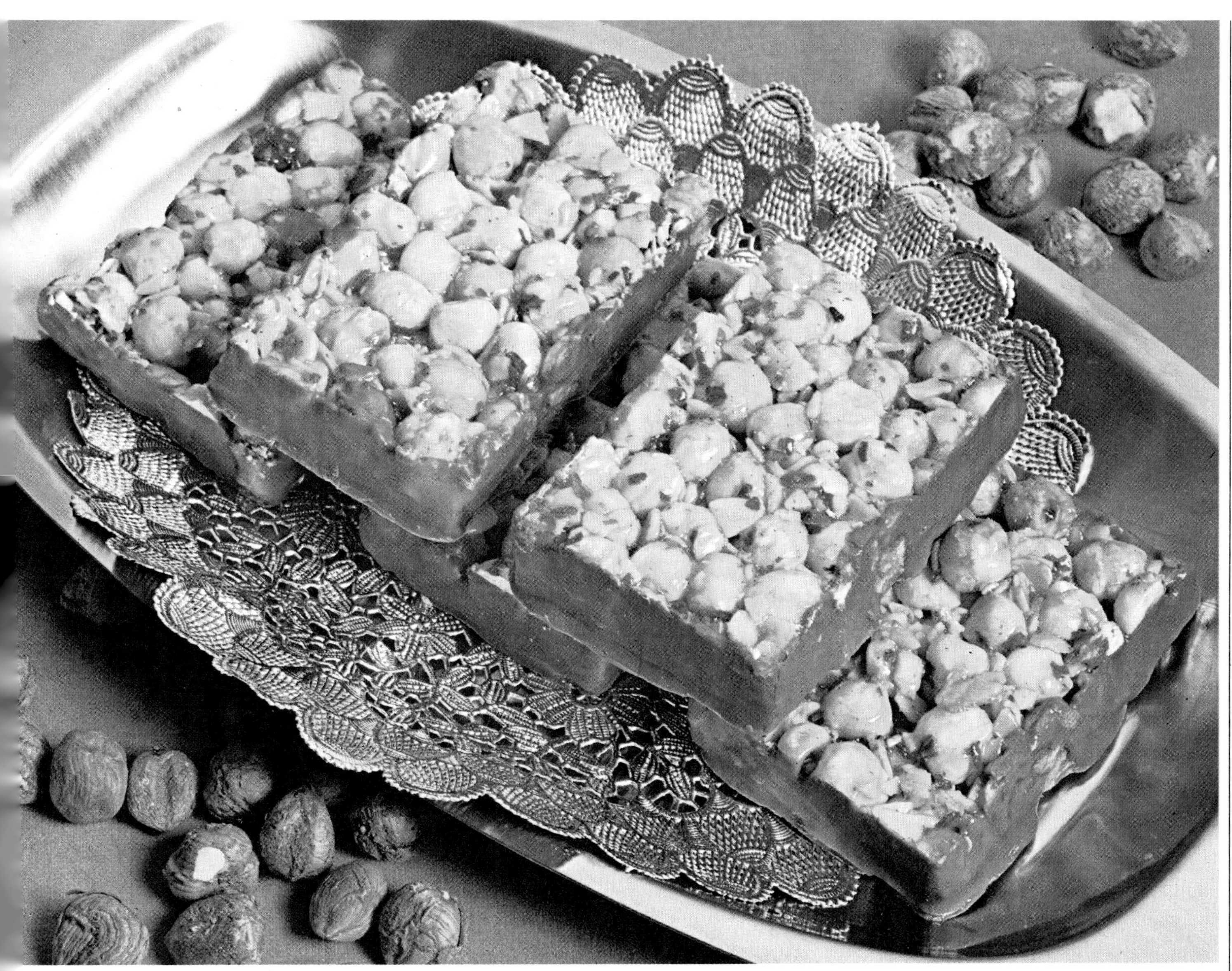

ocolate Nut Cookies cut into neat rectangles.

Chocolate Nut Cookies

z (225 g) hazelnuts
b (450 g) castor sugar
t (15 cl) water
z (225 g) plain dessert chocolate

t the oven at 350°F (180°C) or Mark 4.

t hazelnuts on a baking sheet and bake r 7–8 minutes. Rub them in a rough th to remove skins. Dissolve the sugar the water in a pan over a very low heat. hen completely dissolved, bring to boil slowly and cook until a light golden syrup is reached. Add hazelnuts and toss in syrup with a fork, off the heat. Pour mixture onto a greased baking sheet or tray and, with a sharp knife dipped in hot water, smooth out mixture to a neat rectangle, about ½ inch (1 cm) thick. Using the same knife, again dipped in hot water to prevent sticking, cut into equal squares or rectangles while mixture is still warm.

Melt the grated chocolate over gentle heat, stirring occasionally, until just liquid; remove from heat at once. Carefully dip each cookie into the pan to coat base and sides with chocolate. Place on greased baking sheet or tray and chill until chocolate is completely set.

Store in an airtight tin, interleaved with pieces of greaseproof or silicone paper.

Cookies and biscuits

Ginger Curls decorated with whipped cream and chopped pistachio nuts.

Ginger Curls

3 tbsp (45 ml) golden syrup
3½ oz (85 g) castor sugar
3 oz (75 g) butter or margarine
grated rind of 1 lemon
3½ oz (85 g) plain flour
ground ginger

To finish
¼ pt (15 cl) whipped double cream
2 oz (50 g) finely chopped pistachio nuts

Set the oven at 350°F (180°C) or Mark 4.

Gently heat the syrup, sugar, butter and lemon rind in a small heavy based pan until melted. Take the pan off the stove at once. Sift the flour and beat it in with a pinch of ground ginger. Set aside to cool for a few minutes until the mixture is of a dropping consistency.

Put 4–5 small spoonfuls of the mixture at a time on a greased baking sheet, leaving plenty of room between them to spread during baking. Bake just above centre shelf in the pre-set oven for 12 minutes. Take out at once, cool slightly but while still warm and pliable gently mould round a greased rolling pin.

When completely cool fill centre of each one with a little whipped cream and sprinkle with chopped pistachio nuts.

Almond Finger Cookies

8 oz (225 g) ground almonds
1 lb (450 g) icing sugar plus little extra for dusting
2 egg whites
4 oz (100 g) plain dessert chocolate

Blend together the ground almonds and icing sugar. Make a well in the centre and drop in 1 egg white. Begin to blend in the flour with a knife, working from the centre outwards, and add sufficient of the remaining egg white to make a firm paste.

Sprinkle work surface with icing sugar, turn out almond dough and knead until smooth and glossy. Divide into pieces each weighing about 2 oz (50 g). Roll out each one to make a long sausage measuring about 6 inches (15 cm) and round off the ends to give a neat finish.

Transfer fingers of dough to a sheet o waxed paper on a baking sheet, leaving a good 2 inch (5 cm) space between each one. Bake in the pre-set oven for 10 minutes, then cool for further 10 minute before lifting off to prevent them from splitting.

Meanwhile put the grated chocolate in a basin over a pan of hot water and hea until just liquid. Dip the ends of the cooki fingers in chocolate and leave on a wire rack to set.

Cornflake Surprises

4 oz (100 g) butter or margarine
3 oz (75 g) sugar
1 egg
vanilla essence
5 oz (150 g) self raising flour
crushed cornflakes

Set the oven at 375°F (190°C) or Mark 5.

Cream the butter or margarine and th sugar until light and fluffy. Beat in the eg and a few drops of vanilla essence. Sift th flour and fold in and work the mixture to smooth dough.

Using wet hands, divide the dough int small balls. Roll these in crushe cornflakes and place on a greased bakir sheet.

Bake in the pre-set oven for 20 minute

mond Finger Cookies showing chocolate coated ends.

HOW TO MAKE PALMIERS

½ lb (225 g) puff pastry
1 beaten egg

To finish
castor sugar
apricot glaze
few finely chopped walnuts

This recipe is also an ideal way of using puff pastry trimmings from other recip Roll out dough and cut into strips as giv in method below.

Set the oven at 400°F (200°C) or Mark

Roll out the puff pastry to ⅛ inch (3 m thickness and cut into lengths measuri 10 by 18 inches (15×45 cm). Brush w beaten egg, then sprinkle with cas sugar. Roll the shorter side of the pas into the centre, repeating on the oth opposite side so they meet in the cent Brush again with beaten egg, then tu over.

Using a sharp knife cut pastry roll ir ¼ inch (6 mm) pieces, then place, w apart, on a dampened baking sheet. Ba in the pre-set oven for 15–20 minutes, until lightly browned.

Remove from oven, brush with wa apricot glaze and sprinkle with nuts liked.

1. Roll out the pastry on a floured work surface, and brush the pastry all over wit a little beaten egg.

2. Take the shorter edges of the pastry a roll them tightly towards the middle unt they meet.

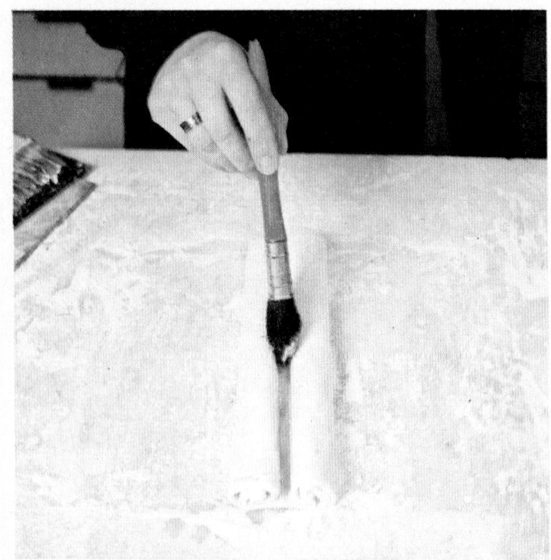

3. Brush the join with more beaten egg and roll the two sides together.

4. Thinly slice the twin roll of pastry with sharp knife.

Cocoa Balls

4 oz (100 g) butter or margarine
3½ oz (85 g) sugar
1 egg white
6 oz (175 g) self raising flour
salt
6 tbsp (90 ml) cocoa powder

For filling
5 oz (150 g) icing sugar
about 1 tbsp (15 ml) water

Set the oven at 375°F (190°C) or Mark 5.

Work the butter or margarine until it is soft, then cream with the sugar until the mixture is light and fluffy. Beat in the egg white.

Sift the flour, a pinch of salt and the cocoa onto a sheet of greaseproof paper, :hen stir thoroughly into butter mixture. Shape the paste into walnut sized balls and put on a greased baking sheet.

Bake in the pre-set oven for 8–10 min-ıtes or until cookies are just brown at the edges. Take out and cool for a few min-ıtes, then transfer to a wire rack to cool completely.

To make filling: sift icing sugar into a bowl and mix to a smooth, firm paste with he water, adding it 1 tsp (5 ml) at a time. Coat flat side of cookies with the icing and sandwich halves together.

Prune and Cornflake Drops

oz (225 g) prunes
oz (225 g) desiccated coconut
lb (450 g) cornflakes
2 tbsp (180 ml) condensed milk
tsp (2.50 ml) vanilla essence
alt

et the oven at 350°F (180°C) or Mark 4.

ut the prunes into small pieces and place ı a bowl. Mix in by degrees the ornflakes, coconut and a pinch of salt. our on the condensed milk and vanilla ssence, and mix all the ingredients well.

Shape the mixture into small balls and rrange on a well greased baking sheet. ake in the pre-set oven for about 10 ıinutes and allow to cool before serving.

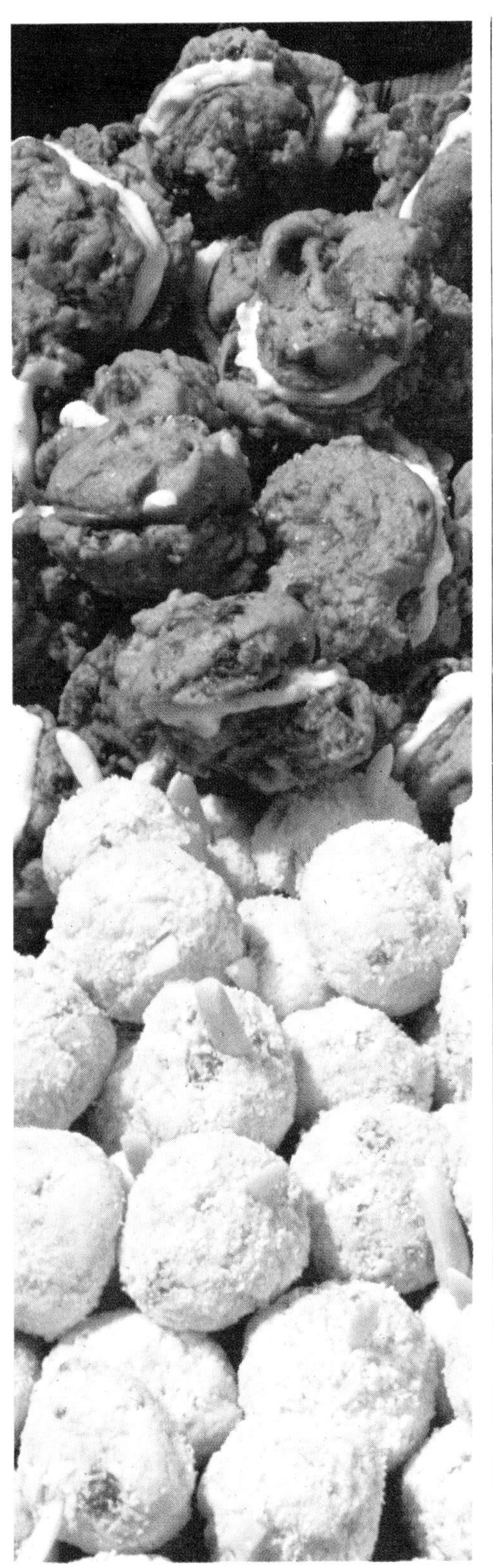

A plate of Cocoa Balls and Nutty Balls.

Nutty Balls

6 oz (175 g) shelled unsalted peanuts
12 oz (350 g) plain flour
salt
8 oz (225 g) butter or margarine
3 oz (75 g) icing sugar
2 tsp (10 ml) vanilla essence
2 tbsp (15 ml) slivered almonds

Set the oven at 400°F (200°C) or Mark 6.

Grind the peanuts in a blender and sift the flour with a pinch of salt into a mixing bowl.

In another bowl work the butter or margarine until soft, then cream with the sugar until the mixture is light and fluffy. Stir in vanilla essence, flour and ground peanuts.

Shape the dough into walnut sized balls, place on an ungreased baking sheet and top each cookie with a slivered almond.

Bake in the pre-set oven for 10–12 minutes or until cookies are just beginning to brown. Turn onto a wire rack to cool. Store in an airtight tin for up to 1 week, if liked.

Noëls

4 oz (100 g) shortening
vanilla essence
4 tbsp (60 ml) honey
1 large egg or 2 small eggs
6 oz (175 g) plain flour
salt
bicarbonate of soda
3 oz (75 g) almonds
3 tbsp (45 ml) mincemeat

Set the oven at 350°F (180°C) or Mark 4.

Cream the shortening well, then beat in a few drops of vanilla essence, the honey and the lightly beaten egg. Sift the flour, a pinch of salt and a pinch of bicarbonate of soda and fold into the mixture. Chop the almonds and stir in, then add the mincemeat and mix well.

Use a teaspoon to drop small heaps on a greased baking sheet and bake in the pre-set oven for 15 minutes.

Cookies and biscuits

Ginger Nuts

4 oz (100 g) self raising flour
½ tsp (2.50 ml) bicarbonate of soda
2 tsp (10 ml) ground ginger
1 tsp (5 ml) cinnamon
2 tsp (10 ml) castor sugar
2 oz (50 g) butter or margarine
3 oz (75 g) golden syrup

Set the oven at 375°F (190°C) or Mark 5.

Sift together the flour, bicarbonate of soda, ginger, cinnamon and sugar. Melt the butter or margarine and mix with the syrup. Stir into the flour mixture, blending well.

Roll the mixture into small balls and place on a greased baking tray, allowing plenty of room for spreading during cooking. Flatten each cookie slightly. Bake in the pre-set oven, on the centre shelf, for 15–20 minutes.

Allow to cool for a few minutes before removing from the baking tray.

Bourbon Biscuits

2 oz (50 g) butter or margarine
2 oz (50 g) sugar
1 tsp (5 ml) golden syrup
4 oz (100 g) plain flour
1 oz (25 g) cornflour
2 tbsp (30 ml) cocoa
½ tsp (2.50 ml) baking powder
1 egg

To finish
chocolate butter cream
castor sugar

Set the oven at 350°F (180°C) or Mark 4.

Cream the butter or margarine and the sugar until light and fluffy. Beat in the syrup. Beat the egg lightly. Sift the flour, cornflour, cocoa and baking powder together and add to the butter mixture alternately with the beaten egg. Knead until smooth.

Roll out the dough to about ¼ inch (6 mm) thickness, cut into fingers, and place on a greased baking sheet. Bake in the pre-set oven for 25 minutes.

When cold, sandwich together in pairs with a little chocolate butter cream, and sprinkle with castor sugar.

Fudge Squares

9 oz (250 g) plain flour
6 oz (175 g) butter or margarine
1½ oz (35 g) castor sugar

For topping
3 eggs
9 oz (250 g) dark brown sugar
3 tbsp (45 ml) plain flour
½ tsp (2.50 ml) baking powder
4 oz (100 g) walnuts
1 oz (25 g) desiccated coconut
vanilla essence

Set the oven at 375°F (190°C) or Mark 5.

Sift the flour into a bowl. Add the butter or margarine cut into small pieces and rub in with the fingertips until the mixture resembles breadcrumbs. Stir in the sugar and press the mixture into a greased square or rectangular baking tin.

Bake in the pre-set oven, on the centre shelf, for 5 minutes.

To make topping, whisk the eggs and sugar together until light. Sift the flour with the baking powder, and fold into the egg mixture. Coarsely chop the walnut and stir in with the coconut and a few drops of vanilla essence. Spread over the cookie mixture and return it to the oven to bake for a further 25–30 minutes.

Leave to cool in the tin before cutting into squares.

Shrewsbury Biscuits

4 oz (100 g) butter or margarine
4 oz (100 g) castor sugar
1 egg
8 oz (225 g) plain flour
2 tsp (10 ml) grated lemon rind

Set the oven at 350°F (180°C) or Mark 4.

Cream the butter or margarine together until light and fluffy. Beat the egg, and gradually add to the mixture, beating well. Sift the flour and fold into the mixture with the grated lemon rind. Knead lightly.

Roll out to ⅛ inch (3 mm) thickness and cut into rounds using a 2½ inch (6 cm) fluted pastry cutter. Place on a greased baking tray and bake in the pre-set oven for 15–20 minutes, or until pale brown.

Plain Chocolate Cookies

4 oz (100 g) plain chocolate
4 tbsp (60 ml) butter or margarine
6 oz (175 g) sugar
1 egg
6 oz (175 g) plain flour
salt

Set the oven at 400°F (200°C) or Mark 6.

Break the chocolate into small pieces and put in a heavy based pan with the butter or margarine. Melt slowly over a very gentle heat. Meanwhile beat the egg lightly, then beat in a little of the sugar at a time. Stir in the melted butter and chocolate, and blend well. Gradually stir in enough flour to make a stiff dough. Using floured hands, roll the dough into small balls.

Place in rows on a greased baking sheet, allowing a little room for spreading during cooking. Bake in the pre-set oven for 8–10 minutes until they have a firm, but cracked appearance.

Brandy Snaps

2 oz (50 g) butter or margarine
2 oz (50 g) sugar
1 tbsp (15 ml) golden syrup
2 oz (50 g) plain flour
½ tsp (2.50 ml) ground ginger
1 tsp (5 ml) lemon juice

Set the oven at 375°F (190°C) or Mark 5.

Melt the butter or margarine with th sugar and golden syrup in a heavy base pan over a low heat. Sift the flour with th ginger and stir into the melted mixtur with the lemon juice.

Drop teaspoonfuls of the mixture, al lowing plenty of room for spreading dur ing cooking, onto a greased and floure baking sheet. Bake in the pre-set oven fo about 10 minutes or until golden brown.

Remove the baking tray from the over and when the cookies have stopped siz zling take them off the baking sheet with palette knife. Quickly curl each brand snap round the greased handle of wooden spoon. If any of the cookies ha den and stick to the baking sheet, retur the baking tray to the oven for a minut and this will release them.

HOW TO MAKE GINGERBREAD FIGURES

5 oz (125 g) soft brown sugar
4¾ oz (120 g) black treacle
1 tsp (5 ml) ground cinnamon
1 tsp (5 ml) ground ginger
ground cloves
1½ tsp (7.50 ml) baking powder
3½ oz (85 g) butter or margarine
1 lb (450 g) plain flour
salt
1 egg

To decorate
8 oz (225 g) quantity of glacé icing

Set the oven at 325°F (160°C) or Mark 3.

Dissolve the sugar with the treacle, cinnamon, ginger and a pinch of ground cloves, in a heavy based pan over a low heat, then slowly and carefully bring the mixture to the boil. Blend in baking powder at once. Put the butter or margarine in a large bowl then pour the sugar mixture over and stir well.

Sift the flour and fold in a third of it with a pinch of salt. Add the lightly beaten egg, then blend in remaining flour until a smooth but firm dough is reached. Turn out onto a floured surface and knead, then wrap in greaseproof paper and leave in the refrigerator for about 30 minutes.

Take out the dough and roll out to about $\frac{1}{8}$ inch (3 mm) thickness. Using assorted cutters stamp out people, animals, trees, etc. and place on floured baking sheet. Bake in the pre-set oven for 8–10 minutes, then remove and cool on a wire rack.

Finish gingerbread men by piping glacé icing around outlines and fill in noses, mouths, eyes, hats and buttons with more glacé icing.

1. Roll out the gingerbread dough thinly on a lightly floured cold work surface. Stamp out people, animals or any other shape with fancy pastry cutters. Place on a lightly floured baking sheet.

2. The next part of the operation is only necessary if you intend to hang your gingerbread figures from the Christmas tree in the traditional way. Take a skewer and make a little hole in the top of each figure. When the cookies are baked and cooled, thread a narrow ribbon through each hole and hang on the tree.

Cookies and biscuits

An inviting arrangement of cookies: Spicy Oat Cookies are piled in the glass bowl in the background, with Peanut Marbles, rolled in desiccated coconut, and Chocolate Marshmallow Cookies together in the glass dish.

Spicy Oat Cookies

8 oz (225 g) plain flour
1 tsp (5 ml) bicarbonate of soda
salt
1 tsp (5 ml) ground cinnamon
1 tsp (5 ml) grated nutmeg
6 oz (175 g) shortening
7 oz (200 g) brown sugar
2 beaten eggs
1 tbsp (15 ml) grated orange rind
2 tbsp (30 ml) fresh orange juice
2 oz (50 g) chopped walnuts
6 oz (175 g) seedless raisins
4 oz (100 g) porridge oats

Set the oven at 375°F (190°C) or Mark 5.

Sift the flour, bicarbonate of soda, a pinch of salt and spices into a mixing bowl. In another bowl soften the shortening, then gradually cream together with the sugar until soft and light. Beat in the eggs, orange rind and juice a little at a time, then when well combined, stir in the remaining ingredients and mix thoroughly.

Using a small spoon, drop mixture in little heaps onto 2 well greased baking sheets and flatten each one with a fork. Bake in the pre-set oven for 10–12 minutes or until the cookies are a light brown.

Peanut Marbles

5 oz (150 g) peanut butter
2 oz (50 g) chopped peanuts
10 oz (275 g) sugar
3 oz (75 g) plain flour
4 oz (100 g) butter or margarine
4 fl oz (100 ml) milk
5 oz (150 g) porridge oats
2 oz (50 g) desiccated coconut
1 tsp (5 ml) vanilla essence
salt

To finish
1 egg white for brushing
4 oz (100 g) desiccated coconut or
6 oz (175 g) finely chopped peanuts

Sift the flour. Blend together the sugar, flour, butter or margarine and milk. Heat gently until the butter or margarine and sugar are melted, then bring to the boil and cook for 3 minutes, stirring continuously. Remove the pan from the heat and stir in remaining ingredients, except egg white and coconut or peanuts for rolling.

While the mixture is still warm, roll small pieces of it into walnut sized balls between the palms of your hands. Brush peanut balls with a little beaten egg white, then roll in coconut or peanuts.

Chocolate Marshmallow Cookies

3 oz (75 g) plain flour
4 oz (100 g) shortening
3 oz (75 g) butter or margarine
baking powder
salt
2½ oz (60 g) sugar
2 tbsp (30 ml) cocoa powder
2 eggs
1 tsp (5 ml) vanilla essence
3 oz (75 g) chopped pecans or walnuts

For glaze
2 oz (50 g) cooking chocolate
2 oz (50 g) plain dessert chocolate
2 oz (50 g) butter or margarine
2 tsp (10 ml) honey
2 oz (50 g) miniature marshmallows

Set the oven at 350°F (180°C) or Mark 4.

Sift the flour. Melt fat over a low heat; remove pan from heat and stir in flour, a pinch of baking powder, a pinch of salt, sugar, cocoa, eggs, vanilla essence and nuts, and mix well.

Spread mixture evenly in a greased 9 inch (22 cm) square shallow tin and bake in the pre-set oven for 25–30 minutes, or until the mixture pulls away from the sides of the tin. Cool.

To make the glaze: in a basin over a pan of hot water melt both kinds of chocolate, the butter or margarine and honey and stir until smooth and blended. Remove from heat, cool slightly and stir in the marshmallows.

Cut cooled cake into 18 squares, stand on a wire rack over a baking sheet and spread glaze on each cookie. Chill until the glaze is set before serving.

Crunchy Oat Cookies

4½ oz (125 g) porridge oats
3 oz (75 g) soft brown sugar
4 oz (100 g) butter or margarine

Set the oven at 375°F (190°C) or Mark 5.

Mix the oats and the sugar in a bowl. Melt the butter or margarine and pour over the oat mixture, blending well.

Press the mixture evenly into a buttered, shallow baking tin, and bake in the pre-set oven for 15 minutes, or until golden brown.

Cut into squares or fingers whilst still warm and leave in the tin until quite cold.

Chocolate Crunchies

8 oz (225 g) plain biscuits such as
Petit Beurre or Marie
2 oz (50 g) butter or margarine
2 tbsp (30 ml) golden syrup
4½ oz (125 g) plain cooking chocolate

Gently heat the butter or margarine, golden syrup and grated chocolate pieces until completely melted and blended. Crush the biscuits and stir into the mixture until smooth.

Turn into a greased flan ring set on a greased baking sheet. Spread the mixture over evenly and then smooth surface with a palette knife, dipped in a little hot water, to make it run smoothly. Chill in the refrigerator until firm, then wrap in foil and store in an airtight tin for up to 4 weeks. Cut in wedges to serve.

Peanut Flapjacks

3 oz (75 g) butter or margarine
2 oz (50 g) demerara sugar
½ tbsp (7 ml) golden syrup
4 oz (100 g) porridge oats
4 oz (100 g) salted peanuts

Set the oven at 300°F (150°C) or Mark 2.

Melt the butter or margarine with the sugar and syrup in a pan over a low heat. Mix together the porridge oats and peanuts. Pour in the syrup mixture and mix well. Turn the oatmeal mixture into a greased 8 inch (20 cm) diameter sandwich cake tin and bake in the pre-set oven for 40–45 minutes.

Remove from the oven and cool in the tin on a wire rack. When cool, cut into wedges to serve.

Cookies and biscuits

Traditional Shortbread

8 oz (225 g) plain flour
4 oz (100 g) rice flour
8 oz (225 g) unsalted butter
4 oz (100 g) castor sugar

Set the oven at 350°F (180°C) or Mark 4.

Sift the flour twice, the second time incorporating the rice flour. Work the butter with 2 knives on a cool work surface until it is soft. Blend in the flour and sugar in the same way until a smooth dough is reached. Knead gently, then cut the dough into 2 equal pieces.

Roll out each piece to a round measuring about 6 inches (15 cm), transfer to a well greased and floured baking sheet and bake on the middle shelf in the pre-set oven for 10 minutes. Then turn down the heat to 325°F (160°C) or Mark 3 and continue baking until shortbread is a light golden brown – about 25 minutes.

Variation:
For a more decorative finish to the shortbread, bake in a greased and floured 9 inch (23 cm) diameter fluted flan ring set on a greased and floured baking sheet. Sprinkle with icing sugar to serve.

Simple Shortbread

11 oz (300 g) self raising flour
8 oz (225 g) unsalted butter, cut in tiny pieces
4½ oz (125 g) castor sugar

Set the oven at 350°F (180°C) or Mark 4.

Sift the flour into a mixing bowl, rub in butter until the mixture resembles fine crumbs. Blend in sugar and work to a smooth dough. Turn onto a floured work surface and knead well.

Roll or press out dough to about ½ inch (1 cm) thickness to fit a floured 8 inch (20 cm) flan ring. Bake in centre of the pre-set oven for about 15 minutes or until shortbread is almost firm to the touch and pale golden. Turn onto a wire rack to cool and sprinkle with a little extra castor sugar to serve.

Traditional Shortbread showing decorative finish.

Virginia Butter Shortbread

4½ oz (125 g) butter or margarine
7 oz (200 g) dark brown sugar
1 egg
vanilla essence
7 oz (200 g) plain flour
1 egg white
1 tbsp (15 ml) castor sugar
1 tsp (5 ml) cinnamon
2 oz (50 g) almonds

Set the oven at 325°F (160°C) or Mark 3.

Blanch and halve the almonds. Cream the butter or margarine until fluffy, then beat in the brown sugar. Beat in the egg and a few drops of vanilla essence. Sift the flour and fold into the mixture, blending thoroughly to make a smooth dough.

Press into a greased cake tin. Beat the egg white lightly and brush a little of it over the shortbread. Mix the castor sugar with the cinnamon, and sprinkle over the shortbread. Press halved almonds into the dough.

Bake in the pre-set oven for about 45 minutes or until pale brown.

Cut into slices whilst still warm, but leave in the tin until quite cold.

Chocolate Chip Cookies

4 oz (100 g) butter or margarine
4 oz (100 g) sugar
2 tbsp (30 ml) golden syrup
1 egg
vanilla essence
7 oz (200 g) plain flour
½ tsp (2.50 ml) baking powder
¼ tsp (1.75 ml) bicarbonate of soda
3 oz (75 g) chocolate chips

Set the oven at 375°F (190°C) or Mark 5.

Cream the butter or margarine with the sugar until light and fluffy. Add the golden syrup and beat well. Beat the egg and stir into the mixture with a few drops of vanilla essence. Sift the flour with the baking powder and the bicarbonate of soda, and fold into the cookie mixture with the chocolate chips.

Drop teaspoonfuls of the mixture onto a greased baking sheet, allowing plenty of room for spreading during cooking. Bake in the pre-set oven for about 15 minutes.

Mocha Fingers

6 oz (175 g) shortbread biscuits
4 oz (100 g) plain chocolate
4 oz (100 g) butter or margarine
2 tbsp (30 ml) golden syrup
2 oz (50 g) icing sugar

For icing
2 oz (50 g) butter or margarine
4 oz (100 g) icing sugar
2 tsp (10 ml) coffee powder
2 tsp (10 ml) boiling water

Crush the shortbread biscuits with a rolling pin. Break the chocolate into small pieces and place in a bowl over a pan of hot water to melt. When the chocolate has melted, add the butter or margarine, the syrup and the sugar, and stir until dissolved and well blended. Stir in the crushed biscuits and mix thoroughly.

Press mixture into a greased rectangular baking tin and leave to set.

To make icing, cream the butter and icing sugar until light and fluffy. Dissolve the coffee powder in the boiling water and beat gradually into icing. Spread over the cookie mixture and place in the refrigerator until firm. Using a sharp knife, cut into fingers.

HOW TO MAKE REFRIGERATOR COOKIES

5 oz (150 g) butter or margarine
3¾ oz (90 g) castor sugar
9½ oz (265 g) plain flour

Note: you can make a chocolate version by reducing the flour by 1 oz (25 g) and replacing by 1 tbsp (15 ml) drinking chocolate.

Set the oven at 350°F (180°C) or Mark 4.

Work the butter or margarine until soft and creamy, then cream with the sugar until fluffy and pale coloured. Sift the flour, then blend into butter mixture until a firm but smooth dough is formed. Turn out onto a floured work surface and roll out into narrow sausage shapes. Wrap in foil or waxed paper and store overnight in the refrigerator.

Unwrap and cut the dough into slices. Transfer to a lightly floured baking sheet. Bake in the pre-set oven for 8–10 minutes or until just firm, then cool on a wire rack.

Variation:
For a chequer effect, place one plain and one chocolate roll side by side, then top with 2 similar rolls in opposite positions; gently press together. Cut and bake as above. Alternatively, top each slice with half a glacé cherry or pecan nut before baking as above.

1. Take 4 long sausages of cookie dough – 2 plain and 2 chocolate. Place a plain and a chocolate roll side by side, then top with 2 similar rolls in opposite positions. Press lightly together.

2. Slice through the chequered roll and place cookies on a lightly floured baking sheet and bake.

3. The finished result ready to eat.

Cookies and biscuits

German Peppery Nut Cookies

7 oz (200 g) sugar
2 separated eggs
8 oz (225 g) plain flour
1½ tsp (7.50 ml) cinnamon
ginger
ground cardamom
allspice
white pepper
3 tbsp (45 ml) finely chopped candied citron
grated rind of 1 lemon
2 oz (50 g) ground almonds

To finish
3–4 tbsp (45–60 ml) rum
icing sugar for rolling
roughly chopped glacé cherries

Beat together half the sugar with the egg yolks until light and fluffy. Sift the flour and a pinch of each of the spices into the egg mixture and stir well. Whisk the egg whites until they hold a stiff peak and then beat in the remaining sugar until glossy. Gently stir the egg white mixture into the flour mixture, together with citron, lemon rind and almonds. Cover bowl and leave in the refrigerator overnight.

Set the oven at 375°F (190°C) or Mark 5. Carefully roll and press the mixture (it crumbles easily) into walnut sized balls, place on a greased baking sheet and bake in the pre-set oven for about 20 minutes, or until lightly browned. Sprinkle with rum and icing sugar while still warm.

Store cookies in an airtight tin for at least a week for the flavour to mellow; they keep well for several weeks. Before serving roll again in icing sugar and top with a piece of glacé cherry.

Polish Fruit and Nut Cookies

8 oz (225 g) plain flour
salt
4 oz (100 g) butter or margarine
7 oz (200 g) sugar
1 egg
3 tbsp (45 ml) single cream

For topping
8 oz (225 g) seedless raisins
8 oz (225 g) chopped dates
8 oz (225 g) chopped figs
4 oz (100 g) chopped almonds or walnuts
3 oz (75 g) sugar
2 eggs
grated rind of 1 lemon
grated rind of 1 orange
3 oz (75 g) chopped glacé cherries
3 oz (75 g) chopped candied orange peel

Set the oven at 350°F (180°C) or Mark 4.

Sift the flour with a pinch of salt into a mixing bowl and rub in the butter or margarine until the mixture resembles breadcrumbs. Stir in the sugar. Mix the egg with the cream and stir into the crumb mixture to make a smooth dough. Turn into a 16 by 10 inch (39×26 cm) swiss roll tin and pat out to fill it evenly. Bake in the pre-set oven for 20 minutes or until browned.

Meanwhile make topping by mixing together the fruit and nuts, sugar, eggs and fruit juices, then spread over the partially-cooked dough. Return to the oven and bake for a further 15–20 minutes.

Cool, then sprinkle over glacé cherries and orange peel. When nearly cold cut in 1 by 2 inch (2.50×5 cm) rectangles and store in an airtight tin.

Polish Honey Cookies

5 oz (150 g) honey
3¼ oz (85 g) sugar
2 whole eggs
1 egg yolk
8 oz (225 g) plain flour
bicarbonate of soda
cinnamon
grated nutmeg
ground cloves
ginger

For filling
6 oz (175 g) chopped plain dessert chocolate
4 fl oz (10 cl) double cream
1 tsp (5 ml) vanilla essence
5 oz (150 g) icing sugar
8 oz (225 g) ground browned almonds

Set the oven at 350°F (180°C) or Mark 4 unless leaving dough to stand overnight.

Make dough by warming honey in a pan and then stirring it into the sugar; add 1 egg and 1 egg yolk and beat until mixture is light and thick. Sift the flour, a pinch of soda and a pinch of each of the spices together, and stir into egg mixture to make a firm dough. Cover and leave for 1 hour or overnight. Beat 1 egg with a pinch of salt to make an egg glaze.

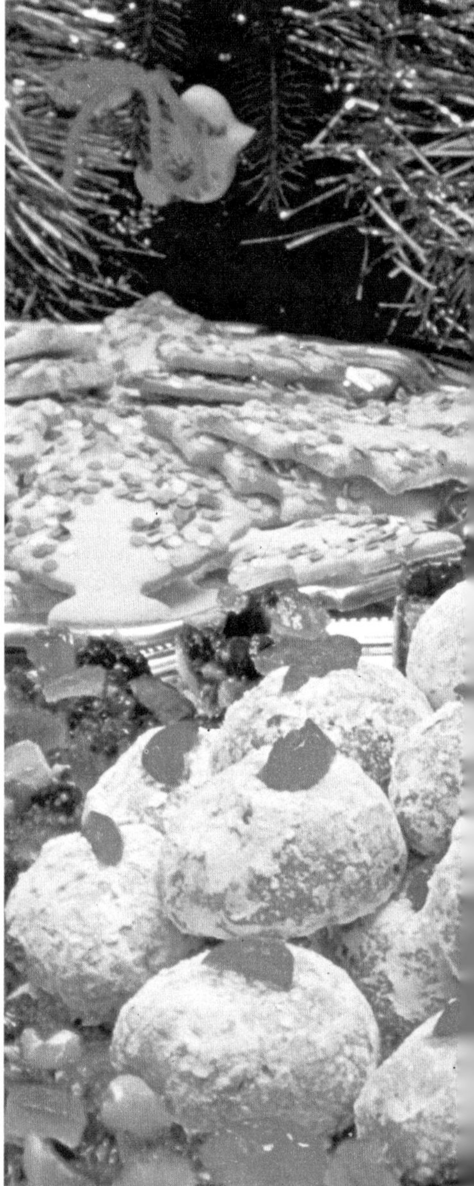

An array of cookies: German Peppery Nut Co Cookies, Dutch Spice Cookies, behind at righ

Roll out cookie dough on a lightl floured work surface to a 16 by 10 inc (40×25 cm) rectangle, then place on baking sheet and brush with egg glaze.

Bake in the pre-set oven for 15 minute or until the dough starts to brown. Coc slightly, cut in half lengthwise and trim th edges, then finish cooking on a wire rack

To make the filling: melt chocolate on heatproof plate over a pan of hot wate Cool slightly when just liquid, then mi

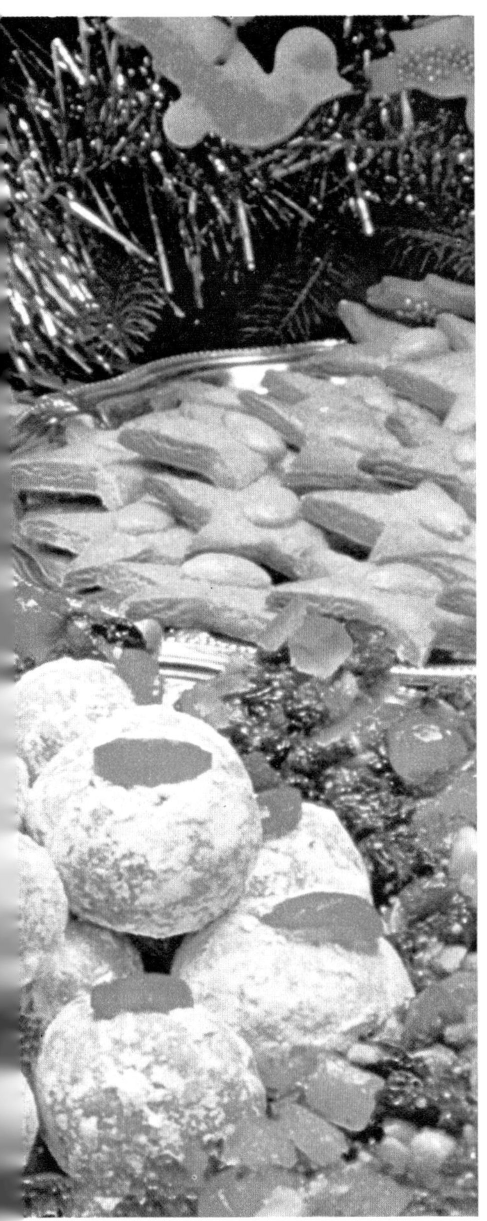

ont, surrounded by Polish Fruit and Nut rican Sugar Cookies.

/ith remaining filling ingredients. Spread ver one half of the dough, then place ther half on top, the unglazed side face .own, and press firmly with a wooden oard for 1–2 hours or until filling is firm nd set. Cut in 2 inch (5 cm) squares to erve. Store in an airtight tin for up to 2 ays before eating.

Dutch Spice Cookies

4 oz (100 g) butter or margarine
7 oz (200 g) light brown sugar
1 egg
8 oz (225 g) plain flour
salt
1½ tsp (7 ml) cinnamon
grated nutmeg
white pepper
ground cloves

To finish
2–3 tbsp (30–45 ml) milk
30 blanched almonds, split in half lengthwise
1 tbsp (15 ml) sugar dissolved in a little milk

Set the oven at 350°F (180°C) or Mark 4.

Cream the butter or margarine and sugar together until soft and fluffy. Beat in the egg. Sift the flour, a pinch of salt and a pinch of each of the spices into a mixing bowl and stir into the butter mixture. With your fingers, blend the mixture together until a smooth dough is formed, adding a little milk if it is very stiff. Chill for 1 hour.

Roll or pat out the dough to ¼ inch (6 mm) thickness, stamp out into rounds with a 1½ inch (3.7 cm) cookie cutter and place on a greased baking sheet. Press half an almond into the centre of each cookie and brush with a little milk and sugar if liked.

Bake in the pre-set oven for 15–20 minutes or until the cookies are lightly browned. Store in an airtight tin for 2–3 weeks to allow the flavour to mellow.

American Sugar Cookies

4 oz (100 g) butter or margarine
5 oz (150 g) sugar
1 egg
2 tbsp (30 ml) milk
1 tsp (5 ml) vanilla essence
grated rind of 1 lemon
12 oz (350 g) plain flour

For decoration
12 fl oz (35 cl) glacé icing
coloured sugar for sprinkling
silver sugar balls
few roughly chopped glacé cherries

Cream butter or margarine and sugar together until light and fluffy, then beat in egg, milk, vanilla essence and lemon rind. Sift together 8 oz (225 g) flour only and baking powder, stir into egg mixture and add enough of remaining flour to make a stiff but workable dough. Cover and refrigerate overnight.

Set the oven at 375°F (190°C) or Mark 5. Make glacé icing and cover.

Divide dough in half and roll out each half to ⅛ inch (3 mm) thickness. Using 3 inch (8 cm) fancy cookie cutters, stamp out shapes, place on greased and floured baking sheet and bake in the pre-set oven for 10 minutes, or until just beginning to brown. Cool cookies on a wire rack.

When cool cover cookies with glacé icing then sprinkle with coloured sugar or silver balls or decorate with a glacé cherry. Store in an airtight tin for 1–2 weeks for flavour to mellow.

Spice Island Cookies

2 oz (50 g) shortening
2 oz (50 g) butter or margarine
2 oz (50 g) soft brown sugar
1 egg
8 tbsp (12 cl) black treacle
¼ pt (15 cl) milk
8 oz (225 g) plain flour
salt
nutmeg
ground cloves
cinnamon
1 tsp (5 ml) bicarbonate of soda

Set the oven at 375°F (190°C) or Mark 5.

Cream the fats with the sugar. Lightly beat the egg, add to the fat mixture with the black treacle and milk, and stir well. Sift the flour with a pinch of salt, a pinch of each of the spices and the bicarbonate of soda. Beat in the dry ingredients, blending well.

Put spoonfuls of the mixture on a greased baking sheet and bake in the pre-set oven for 10 minutes.

Cookies and biscuits

Peanut Bars

6 oz (175 g) digestive biscuits
2 oz (50 g) butter or margarine
1 oz (25 g) castor sugar
2 tbsp (30 ml) golden syrup
4 tbsp (60 ml) crunchy peanut butter

For topping
2 oz (50 g) butter or margarine
1 tbsp (15 ml) lemon juice
9 oz (250 g) icing sugar
1 oz salted peanuts

Crush the digestive biscuits with a rolling pin. Melt the butter or margarine, the sugar and the syrup in a heavy based pan over a low heat. Stir in the peanut butter and the crushed biscuits and blend well.

Press into a greased rectangular baking tin and leave to set.

To make topping, place butter or margarine, lemon juice and icing sugar in a bowl over a saucepan of hot water, and stir until smooth and glossy. Allow to cool, then beat until thickened and then spread over the cookie mixture. Finely chop the peanuts and sprinkle over. Leave to set before cutting into bars.

Walnut Whirls

2 oz (50 g) plain flour
2 oz (50 g) cornflour
2 oz (50 g) castor sugar
2 oz (50 g) butter or margarine
1 egg yolk

To finish
butter cream
2 tbsp (30 ml) apricot jam
2 oz (50 g) walnuts

Set the oven at 350°F (180°C) or Mark 4.

Sift the flour and cornflour into a bowl. Add the sugar and rub in the butter or margarine until the mixture resembles breadcrumbs. Add the egg yolk and mix to a smooth dough.

Roll out onto a floured surface and cut into rounds with a 2 inch (5 cm) pastry cutter. Place on a greased baking sheet and bake in the pre-set oven for 15 minutes.

When cold, sandwich together in pairs with butter cream. Sieve the apricot jam. Chop the walnuts. Brush the cookies with jam and roll them in the walnuts.

Coffee Fingers

4 oz (100 g) butter or margarine
1 oz (25 g) icing sugar
1 tsp (5 ml) coffee essence
4 oz (100 g) plain flour
coffee butter cream
chocolate glacé icing

Set the oven at 375°F (190°C) or Mark 5.

Cream the butter or margarine and the sugar until light and fluffy. Add the coffee essence. Sift and fold in the flour.

Using a forcing bag fitted with a large fluted nozzle, pipe the mixture into fingers on a greased baking sheet. Bake in the pre-set oven for 10–15 minutes.

When cold sandwich together 2 fingers with a little coffee butter cream, and dip the ends in chocolate glacé icing.

Butterscotch Cookies

1 oz (25 g) walnuts
4 oz (100 g) butter or margarine
4 oz (100 g) soft brown sugar
2 egg yolks
vanilla essence
1 tbsp (15 ml) cream
5 oz (150 g) plain flour
salt
baking powder

To finish
extra butter

Set the oven at 375°F (190°C) or Mark 5.

Chop the walnuts and set aside. Melt the butter or margarine in a heavy based pan over a gentle heat. Stir in the brown sugar and continue to heat gently until well blended. Leave to cool, but do not allow the mixture to harden.

Add the egg yolks and a few drops of vanilla essence, and beat the mixture thoroughly. Stir in the cream. Sift the flour, a pinch of salt and a pinch of baking powder, and stir in, blending well.

Place teaspoonfuls of the cookie mixture on a greased baking sheet, allowing plenty of space for the cookies to spread during cooking. Bake in the pre-set oven for about 8 minutes.

Brush the still warm cookies with a little extra melted butter and leave to cool.

Iced Lemon Cookies

8 oz (225 g) plain flour
salt
4 oz (100 g) shortening
2 oz (50 g) sugar
grated rind of 1 lemon
2 egg yolks
1 tbsp (15 ml) sherry or 1 tbsp (15 ml) water and lemon juice mixed

For topping
4–5 oz (100–125 g) icing sugar
1–2 tbsp (15–30 ml) lemon juice
1 tbsp (25 g) chopped pistachio nuts

Set the oven at 350°F (180°C) or Mark 4.

Sift the flour and a pinch of salt into a mixing bowl. Rub in the shortening until the mixture looks like fine breadcrumbs. Stir in sugar and lemon rind. Mix egg yolks with sherry or water and lemon juice, then add to flour mixture and knead lightly with the hand to form a smooth dough.

On a floured surface, roll out dough to ⅛ inch (3 mm) thickness and cut out 3 inch (7.50 cm) rounds with a plain pastry cutter. Put cookie rounds on a greased baking sheet and bake in the pre-set oven for 8–10 minutes or until cookies just begin to brown.

To make topping: sift icing sugar into a small bowl and stir in enough lemon juice to make a stiff paste. Stand the bowl over a pan of hot water and heat icing until it is just tepid and thinly coats back of a spoon. If too thin, beat in a little extra sifted icing sugar.

Coat cookies with icing topping while still on wire rack, then sprinkle a few chopped pistachio nuts in the centre of each cookie.

ed Lemon Cookies are quick and simple to make. They are shown here arranged on a plate with a few chopped pistachio nuts rinkled onto the centre of each one for decoration.

Small fancy cakes

Treating family and friends to tea and cream cakes at a pâtisserie would be an expensive exercise, but with the help of this chapter you can provide a tea table groaning with goodies at a reasonable cost. Try making Cream Slices, Chocolate Eclairs or some of the iced fancies next time someone special comes to tea. You may feel that this area of cookery is beyond you, but the clear step by step pictures on how to make Choux Pastry and Puff Pastry, how to pipe Eclairs and shape Cream Horns, demonstrate that fancy cake making is not as tricky as it first seems.

Cream Buns filled with whipped cream and heavily sprinkled with icing sugar.

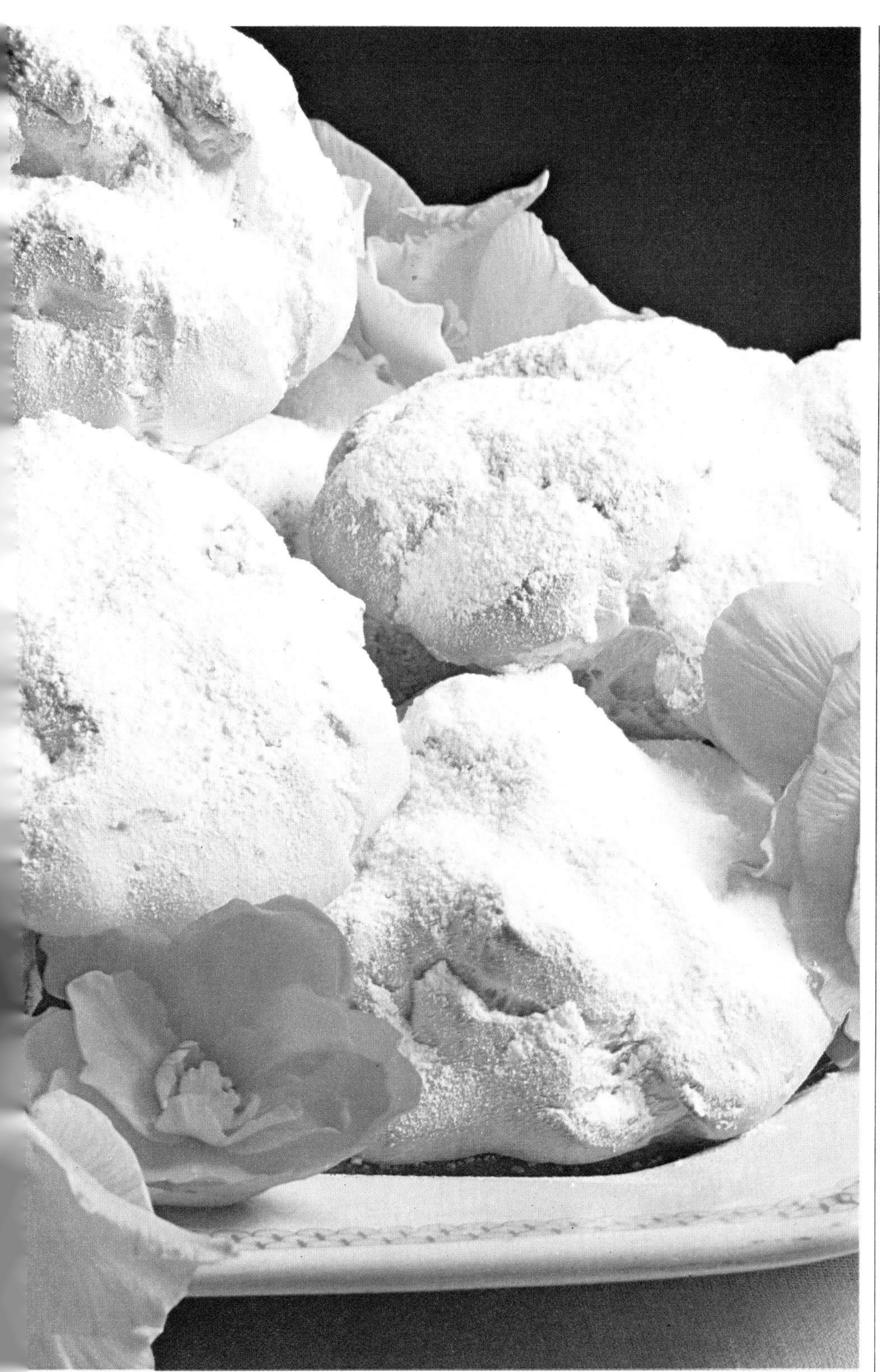

Cream Buns

5¼ oz (165 g) self raising flour
5 eggs
8 fl oz (20 cl) water
4 oz (100 g) butter or margarine
¼ pt (15 cl) whipped double cream
icing sugar for sprinkling

Set the oven at 400°F (200°C) or Mark 6.

Make the choux paste as for basic sweet choux pastry, extending the beating stages by a few minutes each time to give really light, puffy buns when baked.

Fill the paste into a piping bag fitted with chosen plain round nozzle and pipe onto a dampened baking sheet. Bake in pre-set oven for 15–20 minutes or until golden and well risen. Take out and cool on a wire rack.

Split buns in half and when cold fill with whipped cream; pile up on a plate and sprinkle with icing sugar.

Salambos

choux buns, made as for cream buns
8 oz (225 g) castor sugar
confectioner's custard
kirsch

Allow the choux buns to cool before making the caramel topping.

Put the sugar in a thick saucepan and heat gently until the sugar melts and forms a rich brown caramel. As soon as this happens dip the saucepan in a shallow pan of warm water – this will stop the caramel hardening. Dip each choux bun quickly into the caramel.

When the topping has set, split each bun and fill with confectioner's custard, lightly flavoured with kirsch.

Small fancy cakes

Strawberry Cream Buns filled with confectioners' custard and sliced strawberries.

Strawberry Cream Buns

2½ egg quantity sweet choux paste
¼ pt (15 cl) confectioners' custard
1 lb (450 g) wiped, hulled and sliced fresh strawberries
¼ pt (15 cl) chantilly cream
icing sugar
2 oz (50 g) toasted flaked almonds

Set the oven at 425°F (220°C) or Mark 7.

Fill choux paste into a piping bag fitted with 1 inch (3 cm) plain writing pipe and pipe out 3 inch (8 cm) diameter rings of paste onto a greased baking sheet.

Bake just above the centre of pre-set oven for 8–10 minutes or until buns are golden and well risen. Take out and cool on a wire rack, then cut in half.

When cold fill buns with confectioners' custard and strawberries, replace the tops and pipe over chantilly cream, using a small rosette nozzle. Sprinkle generously with icing sugar, scatter over browned almonds and place a half strawberry on top of each bun.

Confectioners' Custard

☆ Basic Recipe

½ pt (30 cl) milk
1 vanilla pod
1 oz (25 g) plain flour
3 egg yolks
4 oz (100 g) castor sugar

Gently heat the milk with the vanilla pod in a pan over a very low heat, until tiny bubbles just start to rise to the surface. Do not allow to boil. Immediately take the pan off the heat, remove the vanilla pod and reserve for future use, then set milk aside.

Sift the flour. Whisk together the egg yolks, flour and sugar. Stir in the vanilla flavoured milk. Pour the mixture into a bain marie or into a basin and stand in a pan of hot water over a gentle heat. Using a wooden spoon stir custard until it becomes thick and creamy and evenly coats the back of the spoon. Remove from the heat at once and use hot or cold according to recipe.

HOW TO PIPE ECLAIRS AND CHOUX BUNS

1. Pipe the choux paste onto a baking sheet. Use a knife as a break to ensure a neat end to each éclair. Dip the knife in cold water each time it is used.

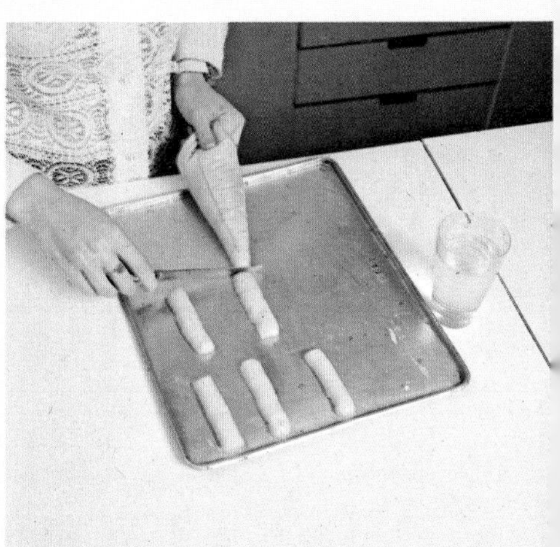

2. When each éclair is the required length, dip the knife in water again and lop off the other end neatly.

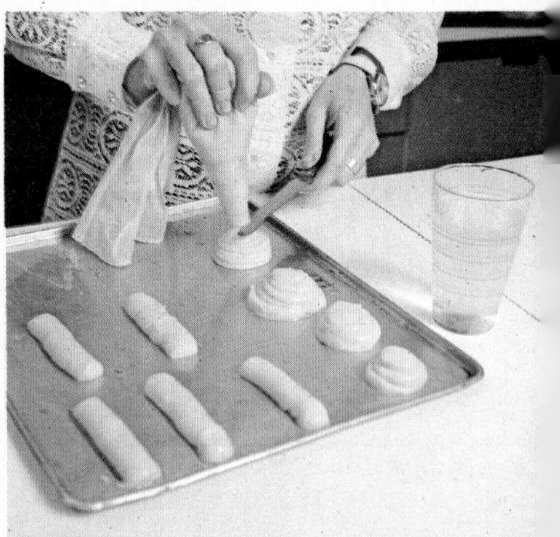

3. For buns, hold the pipe vertically above the baking sheet and press down to the required size, then lop off the tip with a cold wet knife.

HOW TO MAKE BASIC CHOUX PASTRY

Plain Choux Pastry

Basic Recipe

2 oz (50 g) unsalted butter
4¾ fl oz (13 cl) cold water
2½ oz (62 g) self raising flour
2 eggs

Set the oven to 425°F (220°C) or Mark 7 unless the chosen recipe specifies otherwise.

Melt the butter in the water in a heavy based pan over a moderate heat until dissolved and the mixture comes to the boil. Sift the flour and add at once, and as the mixture bubbles up turn off the heat immediately.

Using a wooden spoon beat until the mixture forms a smooth paste and comes away cleanly from the sides of the pan. Beat in 1 egg until the mixture becomes smooth again, then beat in the remaining egg.

Place a plate over the pan and leave at room temperature until the paste is completely cold. Use according to recipe. Bake in the pre-set oven.

Sweet Choux Pastry

1 oz (25 g) unsalted butter
¼ pt (15 cl) milk
1 sugar lump
3 oz (75 g) self raising flour
2½ eggs

Melt butter in the milk in a heavy based pan over a low heat until dissolved and the mixture starts to bubble. At once add the sugar and stir until it is dissolved, then bring to the boil. Sift the flour and stir in, letting the mixture bubble up as for plain choux pastry.

Remove from the heat immediately, then beat in eggs, one at a time, until the mixture forms a smooth paste and comes away cleanly from the sides of the pan. Use when cold and bake according to chosen recipe.

1. Melt the butter and water together in a pan until the butter is dissolved and the mixture comes to the boil.

2. Add the sifted flour, and as the mixture bubbles up, turn off the heat.

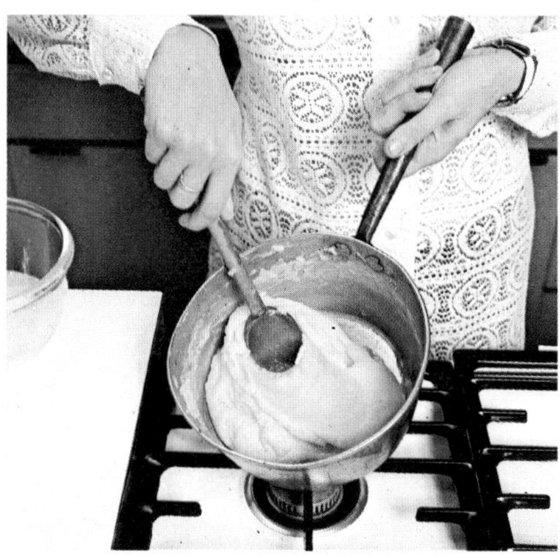

3. Beat with a wooden spoon until the paste is smooth and comes away cleanly from the sides of the pan.

4. Beat in the first egg.

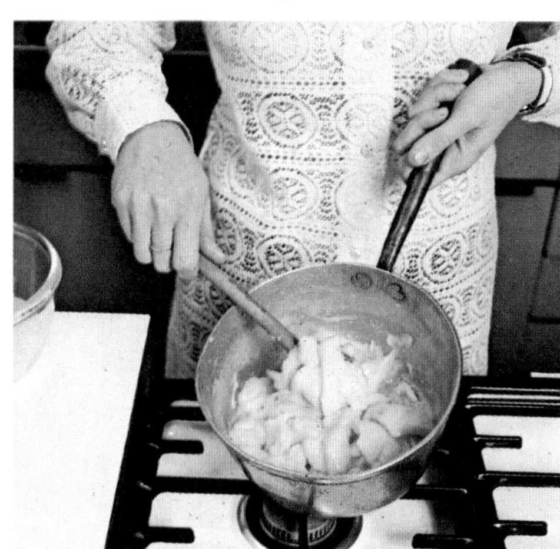

5. When the mixture is smooth again, beat in the second egg.

6. Keep beating until the paste is perfectly smooth then leave to cool.

Small fancy cakes

Strawberry. **Swans made entirely of choux pastry and decorated with chantilly cream, strawberries, icing sugar and finely chopped pistachio nuts.**

Strawberry Swans

2½ egg quantity sweet choux paste
¼ pt (15 cl) chantilly cream
1 lb (450 g) wiped, hulled and quartered fresh strawberries
icing sugar
¼ pt (15 cl) confectioners' custard
finely chopped pistachio nuts
pieces of angelica cut to resemble swans' tails

Set the oven at 425°F (220°C) or Mark 7.

Fill the choux paste into a piping bag fitted with a 1 inch (3 cm) plain writing nozzle and pipe 2 inch (5 cm) blobs of paste as for choux buns, using all but about one sixth of the paste, onto greased baking sheet. Leave space between them for expansion during baking.

Bake just above the centre of pre-set oven for about 15 minutes or until very crisp, dark brown and well risen.

Meanwhile pipe the remaining paste, using ¼ inch (6 mm) plain writing nozzle, into thin figure 2's on a second greased baking sheet, leaving plenty of space between them. These shapes will be the swan's necks.

Bake in the pre-set oven below choux buns for 8–10 minutes or until dark brown and very crisp.

Take out the buns and cool on a wire

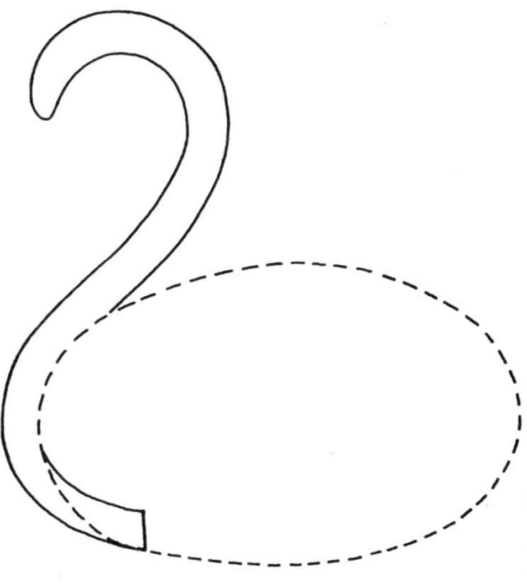

The dotted line indicates a bun cooked, split and filled with chantilly cream. Push the head through the bun and then affix the "wings" as explained in the recipe.

rack, split them in half just below the centre. Cool the neck shapes on the baking sheet as they are very fragile.

Spread confectioners' custard thickly over bottoms of choux buns, spoon in strawberries and sprinkle with icing sugar. Using a piping bag fitted with a large crown pipe, pipe a thick band of chantilly cream over strawberries. Cut remaining choux bun halves in two and push into the chantilly cream at an angle to form swans' wings. Secure them in position with a little more chantilly cream.

To fix the necks in position, pipe a small blob of chantilly cream at one end and push a neck shape into it. Sprinkle with more icing sugar if liked and with pistachio nuts; position angelica tails in the cream and decorate with more strawberries.

Horseshoe Buns

2½ egg quantity sweet choux paste
¼ pt (15 cl) confectioners' custard
¼ pt (15 cl) whipped double cream
icing sugar
crystallized rose petals

Set the oven at 425°F (220°C) or Mark 7.

Fill choux paste into a piping bag fitted with ½ inch (12 mm) plain writing nozzle and pipe rings of the mixture onto a greased baking sheet, stopping just before you complete the circle to give a horseshoe shape.

Bake just above the centre of the preset oven for about 8 minutes or until a rich brown and well risen. Take out and cool on a wire rack.

When cold cut horseshoes in half and fill bottoms with confectioners' custard combined with 2 fl oz (5 cl) whipped cream. Put tops on.

Fill remaining whipped cream into a piping bag fitted with ½ inch (12 mm) plain writing nozzle and squiggle cream over tops of horseshoes. Well sprinkle with icing sugar and put a crystallized rose petal at the end of each horseshoe.

Horseshoe Buns.

Choux Rings split and filled with chantilly cream.

Luxury Butter Cream

Basic Recipe

4 oz (100 g) sifted icing sugar
3 egg yolks
4 oz (100 g) softened unsalted butter
1 tbsp (15 ml) brandy
1 tbsp (15 ml) coffee syrup

Blend together the sugar and egg yolks in a mixing bowl, stand it over a pan of hot water and whisk until thick and creamy. Remove from the heat at once, stand bowl in a tray of ice and continue beating until it reaches blood temperature.

In another bowl cream the butter until soft and fluffy, beat in the egg yolk mixture, a little at a time, together with a few drops of the brandy and coffee syrup until completely blended. Use according to recipe.

Choux Rings

2½ egg quantity sweet choux paste
¼ pt (15 cl) chantilly cream
icing sugar
toasted flaked almonds

Set the oven at 425°F (220°C) or Mark 7.

Fill choux paste into a piping bag fitted with ¼ inch (6 mm) plain writing nozzle and pipe mixture into 3 inch (8 cm) diameter rings onto a greased baking sheet.

Bake just above the centre of the preset oven for about 8 minutes or until a rich brown and well risen. Take out and cool on a wire rack.

Cut rings in half and sandwich with chantilly cream. Using a piping bag fitted with a plain nozzle, pipe a ring of cream on top of each bun. Sprinkle with toasted almonds, then icing sugar.

Tiny Choux Buns and Eclairs decorated with butter cream.

Tiny Choux Buns and Eclairs

2 egg quantity plain choux paste
½ pt (30 cl) confectioners' custard
8 oz (225 g) quantity glacé icing, coloured and flavoured as required

Set the oven at 425°F (220°C) or Mark 7.

Fill choux paste into a piping bag fitted with a ¼ inch (6 mm) plain round nozzle and pipe assorted éclair and bun shapes on to a greased baking sheet.

Bake just above the centre of the preset oven for about 8 minutes or until golden and well risen. Take out and cool on a wire rack.

Cut shapes in half and sandwich with confectioners' custard.

Colour and flavour glacé icing in portions with orange, lemon, coffee or chocolate as liked; then cover buns and éclairs.

When icings are almost hard, decorate éclairs and buns with sugar rosettes, silver or sugar balls, split coffee beans or chocolate chips.

Snowballs

2½ egg quantity sweet choux paste
¼ pt (15 cl) chantilly cream flavoured with 1–2 tsp (5–10 ml) brandy
½ pt (30 cl) luxury butter cream (tinted with edible food colourings if liked)

Set the oven at 450°F (230°C) or Mark 8.

Fill choux paste into a piping bag fitted with 1 inch (3 cm) plain round nozzle. Pipe large rounds onto a greased baking sheet and bake just above the centre in the pre-set oven for about 35 minutes or until dark brown and well risen. Take out and cool on a wire rack.

When cold cut buns in half and sandwich with brandy flavoured chantilly cream. Fill luxury butter cream into a piping bag fitted with a small rosette nozzle and completely cover each choux bun in cream rosettes.

HOW TO MAKE PUFF PASTRY

1 lb (450 g) self raising flour
1 lb (450 g) butter or margarine
1 fl oz (2.50 cl) lemon juice
7 fl oz (20 cl) ice cold water

Basic Recipe

Sift flour onto a very cold work surface and make a well in the centre of the flour. Cut 3 oz (75 g) chilled butter or margarine into tiny pieces (keep remainder chilled) and place in centre of the well. With one hand, begin to draw the flour into the centre and rub in the butter until it resembles very fine crumbs. Make a well in the centre again, then pour in lemon juice and a little of the cold water.

Using 2 knives, work the mixture from the sides to the centre, adding a little water from time to time, until a firm but smooth dough is formed. Wrap in greaseproof or waxed paper or foil and chill in refrigerator for about 30 minutes.

Meanwhile shape remaining butter into a small rectangle and reserve. Lightly flour work surface again, then unwrap chilled dough and roll out to a narrow rectangle. Place the slab of butter in the centre of the dough.

Make a parcel of the dough by folding nearest pastry edge into the centre of the butter. Fold the sides up and over, pressing down gently as you do so. Complete by folding the edge furthest away into the centre. Half turn the dough on the work surface, then roll out again to the same sized rectangle. Wrap again and chill in refrigerator for about 30 minutes.

Return the dough to the floured work surface again, unwrap and roll out, repeating this once more and always giving the dough a half turn each time. Rewrap and chill finally before use according to the recipe. Puff pastry can be stored in the refrigerator for up to a week.

1. Place the sifted flour on a cold work surface – preferably marble. Put some of the ice cold butter or margarine in the centre of the flour.

2. Using really cold hands, draw a little flour into the butter and start rubbing in gently with just 2 fingers and thumb.

6. Take the remaining butter from the refrigerator.

7. With a knife, pat the remaining butter into a rectangle on the cold surface.

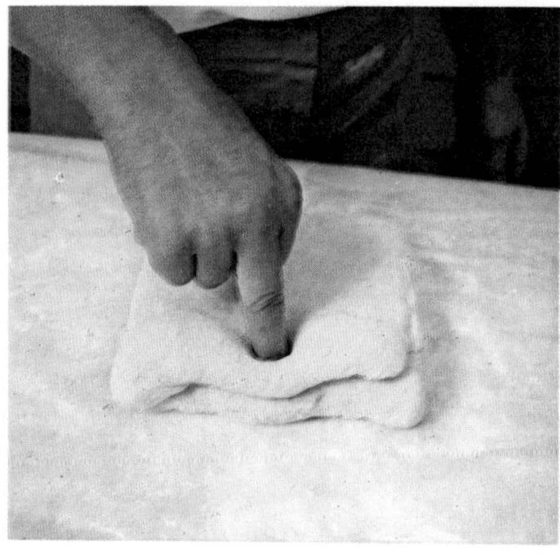

11. Make an indentation with your finger in the top fold of the pastry. This will help keep your place when rolling out.

12. Wrap in greaseproof paper and leave in the refrigerator for 30 minutes. Take out and place in the same position as

3. When all the flour is rubbed in and the mixture resembles fine breadcrumbs, shape into a pile with a well in the centre.

4. Pour the lemon juice into the well with a little ice cold water. Using 2 knives, work the liquid into the mixture. Gradually add enough water to bind the mixture together into a dough.

5. Work the dough into a smooth ball with your hands. Sift a little flour over the dough, fold it in a clean cloth and leave in the refrigerator to rest.

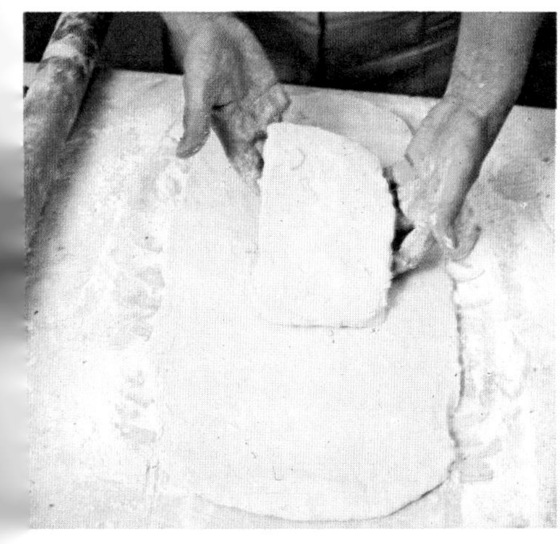

8. Take the dough from the refrigerator ınd roll out into a rectangle on the lightly loured work surface. Place the rectangle of butter in the centre.

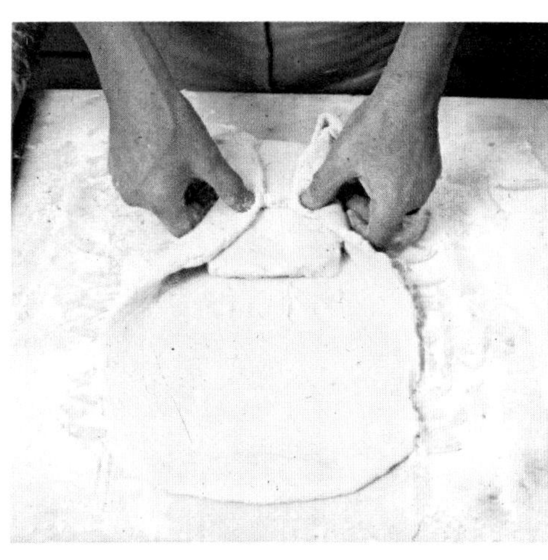

9. Carefully wrap the pastry round the butter to form a neat rectangular parcel.

10. Turn the pastry 90°. Roll out as before and fold up into a parcel.

ɔefore. Roll, fold and turn, then repeat the ɔrocess before refrigerating again. This ·olling, folding, turning and refrigerating ɔrocedure has to be done 5 times before ·he pastry can be used.

Small fancy cakes

Eccles Cakes heavily sprinkled with castor sugar.

Eccles Cakes

8 oz (225 g) puff pastry
8 oz (225 g) coarsely chopped seedless raisins
4 oz (100 g) chopped candied peel
4 oz (100 g) soft brown sugar
juice of 1 small lemon

To finish
1 egg white
castor sugar for sprinkling
1 tbsp (15 ml) rum or brandy

Set the oven at 400°F (200°C) or Mark 6.

Blend together the raisins, candied peel, sugar and lemon juice, in a pan over a moderate heat, stirring continuously until there's no likelihood of the mixture sticking. Turn the heat to low and cook gently for about 5 minutes.

Roll out pastry to a round large enough to cut 6 5 inch (12 cm) diameter circles. Stir the cold fruit mixture, then spread over half of each pastry round to within ¼ inch (6 mm) of the edges. Dampen the pastry edges with a little cold water, then fold over each round to form a half circle, pressing the edges together to seal them completely.

Transfer the pastry shapes to a bakin sheet moistened with cold water, brus them with egg white, sprinkle with suga then make a few slits in the top of each on with a sharp knife. Bake just above th centre shelf in pre-set oven for about 2 minutes or until golden and well risen.

Take out and cool on a wire rack. Drit ble a little rum or brandy through the sli before serving if liked.

HOW TO MAKE CREAM SLICES

8 oz (225 g) puff pastry
½ pt (30 cl) confectioners' custard
strawberry or raspberry jam
¼ pt (15 cl) whipped double cream
glacé icing
3 oz (75 g) melted plain dessert chocolate

Set the oven at 425°F (220°C) or Mark 7.

Roll out the pastry to a thickness of no more than ¼ inch (6 mm). Using a rectangular metal flan frame measuring 14 by 4½ inches (35 × 12 cm), cut out, inside the frame, a wide strip of pastry. Reroll remaining pastry and repeat this process until you have 4 equal pastry rectangles.

Lightly flour a baking sheet; place one pastry rectangle on prepared baking sheet, fit over flan frame and bake above the centre shelf in the pre-set oven for about 10 minutes or until the pastry is golden and well risen. Take out and cool, then carefully split in half lengthways. Repeat this process with remaining 3 rectangles to give 8 pieces in all.

Choose 7 of the neatest rectangles (the eighth piece isn't required for this recipe, so use up in another way), reserving the thickest and smoothest for the top piece.

Layer the first strip with confectioners' custard, the second with jam, the third with whipped cream, then repeat this layering with next 3 strips.

Top with the reserved strip of pastry, cover with glacé icing and before it sets pipe on melted chocolate, using a piping bag fitted with a fine writing nozzle, in 2 parallel lines. Feather the chocolate by drawing through it a skewer or needle, if you like. Leave to firm before cutting into slices for serving.

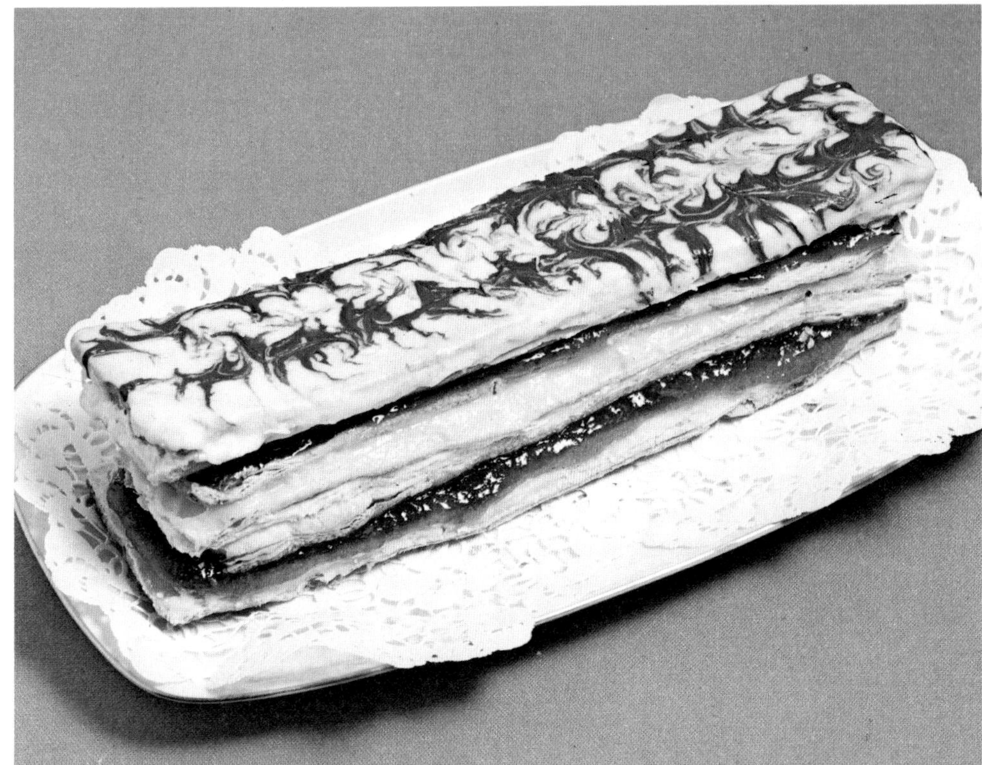

Cream Slice topped with glacé icing and piped chocolate.

1. Cut panels of pastry with a metal rectangular frame. Transfer each panel to a lightly floured baking sheet, leaving the frame in position whilst baking. This helps to keep the pastry's shape.

2. After baking, slice each panel horizontally in half so that you have 8 panels out of the original 4.

3. When you have assembled the layers of pastry, and filled and iced them, decorate with melted chocolate. Pipe 2 lines of chocolate along the length and, using a skewer, draw out branches.

Small fancy cakes

Maids of Honour

8 oz (225 g) quantity of puff pastry

For filling
6 oz (175 g) cottage cheese
2 oz (50 g) sultanas
1–2 drops of almond essence
2 oz (50 g) ground almonds
2 eggs
about 4 oz (100 g) jam of choice

For topping
4 oz (100 g) sifted icing sugar
a little water
2–3 drops of almond essence

Set the oven at 450°F (230°C) or Mark 8.

Lightly flour a cold work surface and knead the puff pastry dough. Roll out as thinly as possible to a large circle. Using a 3 inch (8 cm) fluted pastry cutter cut out 15–20 rounds to fit bun tins. Collect up the pastry trimmings and either bind gently together by layering and roll out again to make rounds, or shape into Palmiers.

To make the filling: work the cottage cheese through a sieve into a basin, then add the remaining filling ingredients except the jam. Beat well until smooth.

Line pastry rounds into the dampened bun tins and fill each one with a little blob of jam. Then top with a little of the cheese mixture. Bake tartlets in the pre-set oven for 10 minutes, then reduce the oven temperature to 350°F (180°C) or Mark 4 and bake for a further 15 minutes or until the pastry is well risen and the topping firm. Take out and cool in the tins.

Make the topping by sifting the icing sugar into a bowl and blending with just enough water to form a spreading consistency. Add the almond essence.

When the tartlets are completely cold, top each one with a little of the almond flavoured glacé icing and leave to set.

Variation:
Substitute the cottage cheese filling with the following: in a bowl beat together 4 oz (100 g) finely chopped blanched almonds, 2 oz (50 g) castor sugar, 2 egg yolks and the white of 1 egg. When blended stir in 1 oz (25 g) plain flour or cake crumbs, 1 tsp (5 ml) orange flower water or fresh orange or lemon juice, together with 1 tsp (5 ml) finely grated lemon rind. Fill into the jam-lined pastry cases and bake as above. Do not ice.

HOW TO MAKE CREAM HORNS

1 lb (450 g) puff pastry
1 beaten egg
¼ pt (15 cl) cold water
2–3 tbsp (30–45 ml) raspberry or other chosen jam
3 tbsp (45 ml) confectioners' custard
¼ pt (15 cl) whipped double cream
few finely chopped pistachio nuts (optional)

Set the oven at 400°F (200°C) or Mark 6.

Lightly flour work surface and roll out the pastry very thinly to a square large enough to give a trimmed square measuring 24 inches (60 cm). Cut this into 1¼ inch (3 mm) strips.

Grease and flour the outside of metal cream horn moulds. Take one strip of pastry per mould and carefully wind it around the mould, starting from the point and overlapping the pastry as you wind. Moisten the overlapping edges with a little cold water to help them stick together. Trim excess pastry from the top.

Place moulds, flat side down, on a floured baking sheet. Brush with beaten egg and bake just above the centre shelf in the pre-set oven for about 15 minutes or until the pastry is golden. Take out and transfer to a wire rack; holding a cloth in both hands, immediately begin to ease the pastry off the moulds. This is best done before the pastry cools.

Mix together the jam, confectioners' custard and about 3 tbsp (45 ml) whipped cream. Spoon this into each horn, then fill remaining cream into a piping bag fitted with a star nozzle and pipe a large swirl of cream over the end of each pastry horn. Sprinkle with a little of the chopped pistachio nuts if liked.

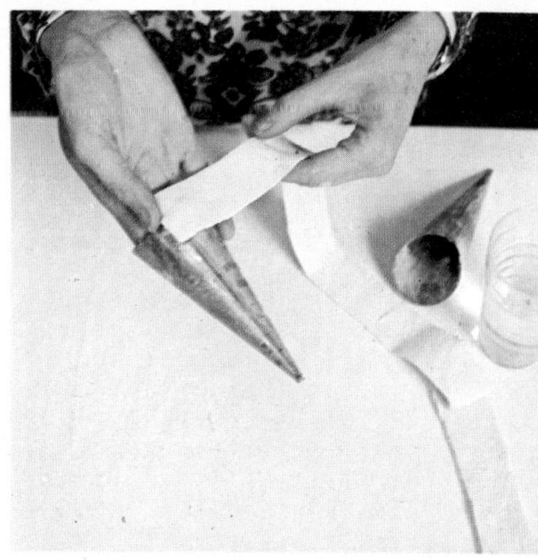

1. The traditional method of winding the pastry round cream horn moulds is to start at the top, leaving some surplus pastry over the edge, and wind downwards overlapping generously.

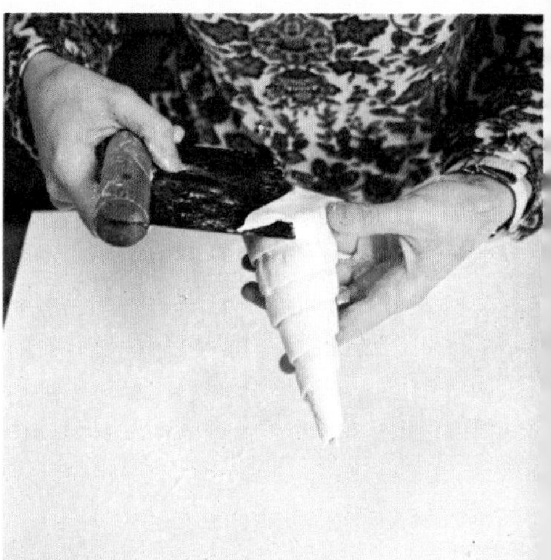

5. When you reach the top of the mould, trim away the surplus pastry making a sloping edge. Stick the top under edge to the upper edge with a little water, and dip the pointed end in cold water and pinch firmly together. This seals the pastry and holds the shape.

2. However, you may find it easier to start at the bottom and wind towards the top. Make sure that each overlapping strip is at least a third over the previous one.

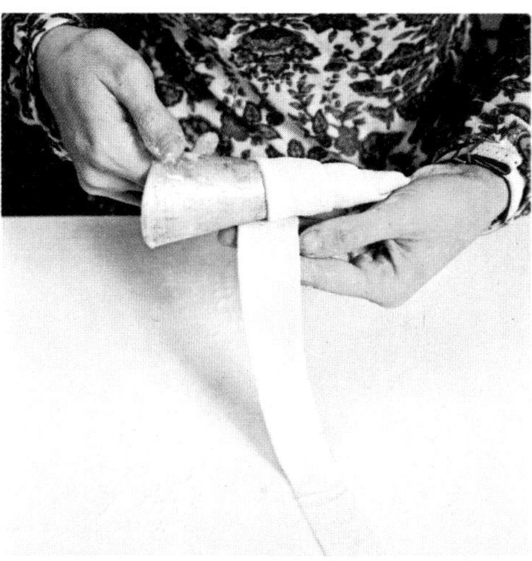

3. Continue winding round the horn mould, taking care not to stretch the pastry as this will spoil the finished shape.

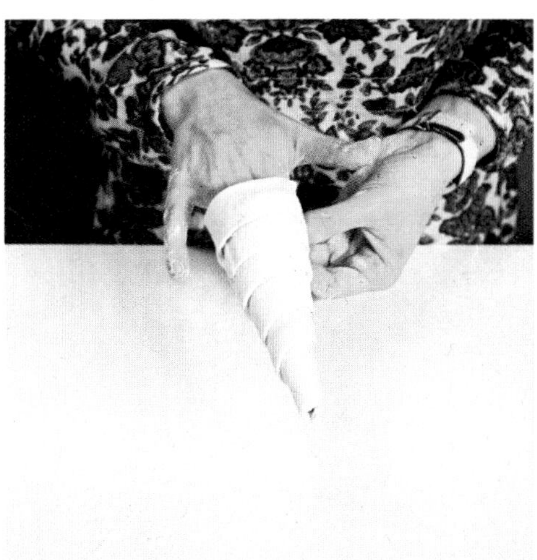

4. Wind the pastry right to the top of the horn mould, leaving some surplus. Make sure the winding ends at the shallow back part of the mould.

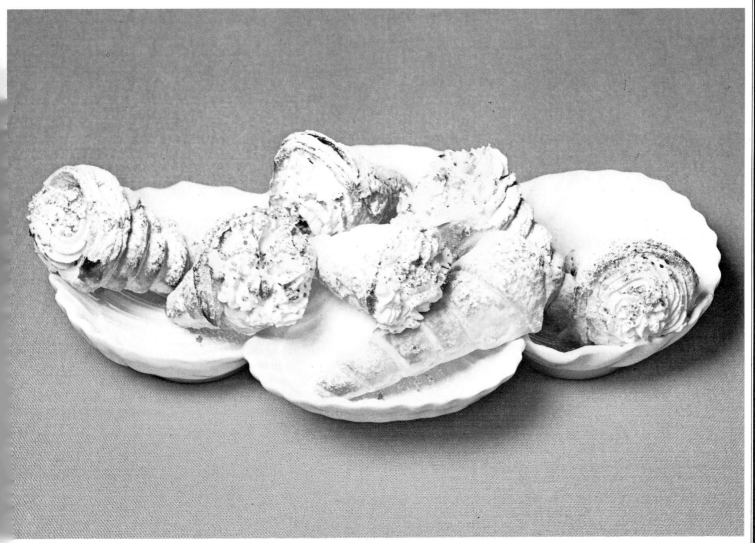

ream Horns.

'ariations:
:ream horns can also be filled simply with ·lain whipped cream, lightly flavoured 'ith vanilla. Add fresh raspberries or strawberries, if in season, for a special treat.

For another alternative filling using whipped cream, add sugar and a dash of rum instead of vanilla, and stir in a little grated chocolate before filling the cream horns.

Small fancy cakes

Almond Boats

4 oz (100 g) quantity sweet shortcrust pastry
apricot glaze
2 oz (50 g) Madeira cake crumbs
½ tsp (2.50 ml) apricot brandy
juice of 1 large orange
6 oz (175 g) almond paste
pink and blue edible food colourings
butter cream

Set the oven to 375°F (190°C) or Mark 5.

Roll out the pastry thinly, then lift on to a rolling pin. Put metal boat moulds close together so rolled out shape of pastry covers them easily. Gently unroll the pastry over the moulds, ease in, pressing down lightly, then roll over the whole to trim off the excess pastry.

Bake blind on a baking sheet in the pre-set oven for about 10 minutes or until a light brown colour.

Remove from the oven, cool on a wire rack, then turn out and brush inside each pastry case with apricot glaze.

Combine cake crumbs, apricot brandy and orange juice. Fill this mixture into the pastry cases rounding it up in the centre to form a ridge lengthways. Brush with more apricot glaze.

Cut the almond paste in half. Colour one half a soft pink, roll out very thinly, then cut out 12 petal shapes by inverting a boat mould and cutting around its base. Place a pink petal on one side of each tartlet, trimming off excess where it meets the pastry edge. Repeat the process with the plain almond paste, placing the petals on the other side of each tartlet.

Colour the butter cream pale blue and fill into a piping bag fitted with a rosette nozzle. Pipe rosettes along the centre.

Sweet Shortcrust Pastry

Basic Recipe

1 lb (450 g) self raising flour
8 oz (225 g) softened unsalted butter or margarine, or half of each fat together
4 oz (100 g) castor sugar
2 egg yolks
9 fl oz (27.50 cl) cold water

Sift the flour onto a cold work surface, make a well in the centre of the flour and put into this the fat, the sugar and the egg yolks. Using 2 flat bladed knives, gradually blend the ingredients together, adding a little water from time to time, to help form the mixture into a soft, slightly sticky dough. Not all the water may be required so use it sparingly.

With well floured hands, lift the dough onto a piece of non-stick (silicone) paper and chill in the refrigerator for about 30 minutes before rolling out.

Almond Boats with rosettes piped along the centre of each one.

Fruit Tartlets

1 lb (450 g) quantity sweet shortcrust pastry

For filling
1 well drained can mandarin oranges, or red or white cherries, fresh raspberries or strawberries
redcurrant jelly glaze for red fruit, or apricot glaze for yellow fruit

Set the oven to 350°F (180°C) or Mark 4.

Roll out the pastry very thinly, stamp out rounds with a 3 inch (7 cm) pastry cutter and line into tartlet tins. Bake blind in the pre-set oven for about 10 minutes or until light brown. Take out, cool slightly then remove paper and dried beans or rice. Stand pastry cases in cooling oven for about 3 minutes to harden off. Then cool completely on a wire rack.

When cold fill tartlets with chosen fruit and cover with plenty of glaze.

Apricot Glaze

8 oz (225 g) apricot jam
½ pt (30 cl) water
6 oz (175 g) castor sugar

Gently heat together the jam, water and sugar in a heavy based pan over a low heat until all are completely dissolved. Increase the heat until the mixture just starts to bubble gently and becomes fairly thick but still of a pouring consistency. Work through a sieve, and use the glaze while still warm. Store in clean, dry jars if not using immediately.

Redcurrant Jelly Glaze

Basic Recipe

12 oz (350 g) jar redcurrant jelly
2½ fl oz (6 cl) water

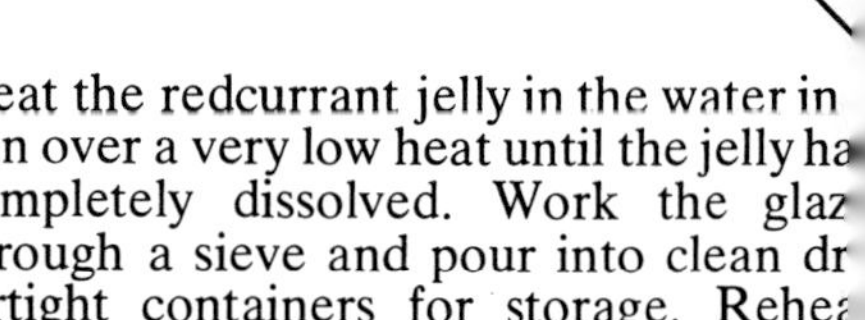

Heat the redcurrant jelly in the water in pan over a very low heat until the jelly has completely dissolved. Work the glaze through a sieve and pour into clean dry airtight containers for storage. Reheat gently before use.

lmond Bull's Eyes.

Almond Bull's Eyes

lb (450 g) quantity sweet shortcrust pastry
oz (100 g) almond paste
-3 tbsp (30–45 ml) fresh orange juice

ɔ decorate
oz (100 g) sifted icing sugar
little tepid water
? chocolate chips

ɛt the oven at 350°F (180°C) or Mark 4.

Roll out the pastry to a thickness of ¼ inch (6 mm) and cut out 12 rounds with a 3 inch (8 cm) diameter fluted pastry cutter. Place rounds on a greased and floured baking sheet.

Blend almond paste with sufficient orange juice just to make it fluid enough to pipe, and fill into piping bag fitted with a rosette nozzle. Pipe rings of almond paste mixture on top of each other around the edges of the pastry rounds, leaving the centre hollow. Bake in the pre-set oven for about 15 minutes or until pastry bases are just cooked and pale brown. Take out and cool on a wire rack.

In a basin combine icing sugar with just enough water to make a flowing paste. Thinly cover centres of pastry rounds with icing. When almost set place a chocolate chip in the centre of each one. These small cakes will keep for up to 1 week in an airtight tin.

Birds' Nests with blue icing piped over the tops to represent the nests.

Small fancy cakes

Birds' Nests

2 oz (50 g) softened butter or margarine
2 oz (50 g) vanilla flavoured castor sugar
2 oz (50 g) self raising flour
2 oz (50 g) cornflour
2 eggs
1–2 tbsp (15–30 ml) milk

For icing
2 oz (50 g) softened butter or margarine
4 oz (100 g) icing sugar
4 oz (100 g) vanilla flavoured icing sugar
1 egg yolk
edible blue food colouring

Set the oven to 350°F (180°C) or Mark 4.

Make the sponge by creaming the butter or margarine in a mixing bowl until soft and light, then cream with the castor sugar. Sift the flours together, then beat into the creamed mixture a little of the flour. Beat in 1 egg carefully, then add the rest of the flour and remaining egg and blend together. Stir in enough milk just to make a smooth mixture. Turn into a greased and floured 8 inch (20 cm) diameter sandwich tin and bake in the pre-set oven for about 25 minutes or until golden and just firm to the touch. Cool, then turn out of the tin and stamp out ovals with a small oval pastry cutter.

To make the icing: Cream the butter in a bowl, then beat in the plain icing sugar together with the egg yolk. Spread two thirds of the butter cream over the sponge ovals and chill in the refrigerator. Tint the remaining butter cream a pale blue and fill into a piping bag fitted with a small plain nozzle.

When firm, smooth chilled butter cream with a knife which has just been dipped in hot water.

Blend vanilla flavoured icing sugar with sufficient water to make a thick paste in a small pan over a low heat. Heat gently until the icing reaches blood heat and is fairly runny. Using a large spoon trail a little of this icing over each sponge cake to cover evenly and leave to firm.

When set, pipe blue butter cream over the tops, just like a doodle, to represent birds' nests.

Small fancy cakes

Sponge Cake

Basic Recipe

8 oz (225 g) butter or margarine
8 oz (225 g) castor sugar
7 oz (200 g) self raising flour
1 oz (25 g) cornflour
4 eggs
3½ fl oz (9 cl) milk

Set the oven at 350°F (180°C) or Mark 4.

Cream the butter or margarine and sugar until pale coloured and fluffy. Sift the flour and cornflour together. Using a metal spoon fold in a quarter of the flour mixture, then carefully beat in one egg, a little at a time to avoid curdling the mixture. Continue folding in portions of flour, followed by an egg each time, until all are incorporated.

Beat in the milk to make a smooth batter then pour into either 2 8 inch (20 cm) diameter sponge tins or one 12 inch (30 cm) diameter shallow sponge tin, greased and lined with greaseproof paper.

Bake in the pre-set oven for 30 minutes for the large tin, 20 minutes for the 2 smaller tins, until golden, well risen, firm to the touch, and just pulling away from the sides. Turn out and cool on a wire rack.

Blackberry Sweetheart Cakes decorated with chantilly cream and blackberry leaves.

Chantilly Cream

Basic Recipe

¼ pt (15 cl) double cream
2 tsp (10 ml) castor sugar
½ tsp (2.50 ml) vanilla essence
1 egg white

Whisk the chilled cream until just thick – don't overwhip or it will become too firm to use properly. Stir in the sugar and vanilla essence. In another bowl, stiffly whip the egg white and lightly fold into the whipped cream mixture. Use according to recipe.

Blackberry Sweetheart Cakes

4 egg quantity basic sponge
chantilly cream, made with ¼ pt (15 cl) double cream
1 lb (450 g) fresh blackberries – reserve a few leaves for decoration if liked
redcurrant jelly glaze

Set the oven to 350°F (180°C) or Mark 4.

Make and bake the sponge and cool on a wire rack. Using a small heart-shaped cutter, cut out heart shapes, then with a sharp knife carefully cut away the centres to make a case. Coat inside each heart with a little chantilly cream, then fill with blackberries and coat with melted redcurrant jelly glaze.

Put the remainder of the chantilly cream into a piping bag fitted with a rosette nozzle and pipe tiny rosettes of cream around the top edges of the hearts. Add a blackberry leaf to decorate if liked.

Domino Cakes

4 egg quantity basic sponge
glacé icing
chocolate butter cream
4–6 oz (100–175 g) chocolate chips

Make and bake the sponge and cut int rectangles measuring 1 by 2 inche (2.50×5 cm). Make glacé icing and choco late butter cream.

Split sponge rectangles in half and sand wich with chocolate butter cream. Plac on a wire rack with a sheet of greaseproo paper underneath. Coat each rectang with glacé icing and when almost firm arrange chocolate chips on top to repres ent the dots on the face of a set o dominoes.

Melt about 1 oz (25 g) of chocola chips in a pan over a low heat, then sprea thickly on a sheet of greaseproof pape Before chocolate becomes too firm, c into very thin strips and place in centre rectangles to represent the dividing line o dominoes. Put the cakes into paper cas to serve.

Chocolate Boxes

5 oz (150 g) plain dessert chocolate, broken into small pieces
chocolate butter cream
3 eggs plus 1 extra egg yolk
5 oz (150 g) castor sugar
$2\frac{1}{4}$ oz (55 g) self raising flour

For chocolate squares
12 oz (350 g) plain dessert chocolate, broken into small pieces

Set the oven at 325°F (160°C) or Mark 3.

In a small pan over a low heat gently melt the 5 oz chocolate until just liquid. Make the chocolate butter cream.

Make a sponge by whisking together in a bowl over a pan of hot water the eggs, egg yolk and sugar until thick and foamy. Remove from heat, cool slightly, whisking all the time. Sift, then fold in the flour, melted chocolate and blend together. Turn mixture into a greased and floured 8 inch (20 cm) square cake tin and bake in the pre-set oven for 25–30 minutes or until risen and just firm to the touch. Cool, then turn out of the tin.

Cut sponge cake into $1\frac{1}{2}$ inch (3 cm) squares, then cut them in half and sandwich with chocolate butter cream, spreading a little of the butter cream around the sides so that chocolate squares will stick. Fill piping bag fitted with a small rosette nozzle with the remaining butter cream.

To make the chocolate squares: gently heat the chocolate in a pan over a low heat until it is just liquid enough to pour. Pour thinly onto a sheet of foil or greaseproof paper and when almost set cut into $1\frac{1}{2}$ inch (3 cm) squares. When hard, lift off the foil or paper and stick squares on to sides of each cake. Then decorate the top of each one with rosettes of chocolate butter cream.

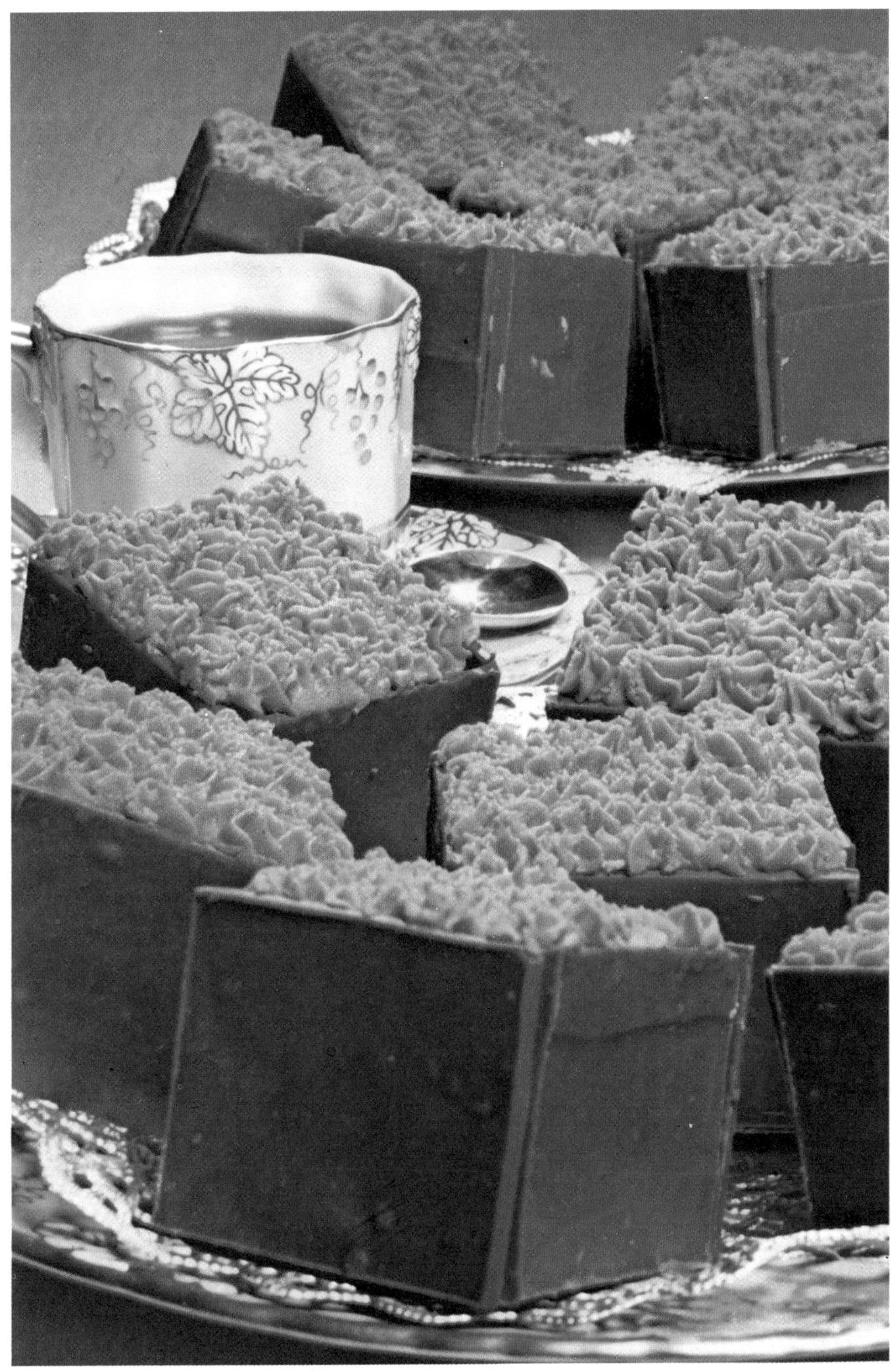

Chocolate Boxes. These small cakes can be kept for several days as the sponge is kept fresh and moist surrounded by the hardened chocolate rectangles stuck on each side and the piped butter cream rosettes on the top.

Small fancy cakes

Madeleines rolled in coconut and decorated with glacé cherries and angelica.

Madeleines

4 oz (100 g) self raising flour
3 eggs
4 oz (100 g) castor sugar
1 oz (25 g) butter or margarine

To finish
redcurrant jelly
desiccated coconut
few glacé cherries, cut in half
few thin strips of angelica

Fill a steamer with water and bring to a constant boil. Sift the flour.

Whisk together the eggs and sugar in a bowl stood over a pan of hot water until the mixture is light and creamy and the beater just leaves an outline of itself for a few seconds. Take off the heat and cool for a few moments, whisking all the time, then carefully fold in the flour and stir in the melted butter.

Spoon mixture into the greased and loured dariole moulds, cover with greased greaseproof paper and foil, pleating both to allow for expansion during steaming. Place in steamer and cook for 1 hour. Then remove from steamer, discard wrappings and turn cakes out of the moulds.

While still warm, brush each cake with a ittle melted redcurrant jelly, then toss in esiccated coconut, spread on a large sheet of greaseproof paper. Place a half lacé cherry and 2 or 3 angelica strips on op if liked.

Coconut Cakes

egg whites
oz castor sugar
oz desiccated coconut
anilla essence
tsp (10 ml) lemon juice

et the oven at 200°F (100°C) or Mark ¼.

'hip the egg whites until very stiff. Beat the castor sugar by degrees and fold in e remaining ingredients. Spoon balls of e mixture onto a greased and floured aking sheet and bake in the pre-set oven r ¾–1 hours.

Coconut Cones.

Coconut Cones

8 oz (225 g) desiccated coconut
4 oz (100 g) vanilla flavoured castor sugar
1 egg
edible pink food colouring

To decorate
halved glacé cherries or thin strips of angelica

Set the oven to 350°F (180°C) or Mark 4.

Mix together the coconut and sugar, then blend in the beaten egg until the mixture just forms a sticky dough. Divide mixture in 2 and colour one half pink with the food colouring.

Cut mixture into small pieces, each weighing about 2 oz (50 g), and shape into cones with your hands. Place on a baking sheet lined with non-stick (silicone) paper and bake in the pre-set oven for 15–20 minutes. Take out and cool, then decorate with glacé cherries or angelica if liked.

Vanilla Sugar

Basic Recipe

This is simply made by adding 2–3 split vanilla pods to a jar of sugar and keeping it for several weeks/months so the sugar absorbs the vanilla flavour.

Vanilla pods used to flavour milk, custards or creams can be used again many times after drying well.

Small fancy cakes

Sponge Buns

4 oz (100g) softened butter or margarine
4 oz (100 g) castor sugar
8 oz (225 g) self raising flour
2 eggs
1 tbsp (15 ml) milk
2½ oz (60 g) fruit (sultanas, currants, seedless raisins, chopped glacé cherries), desiccated coconut, or flavouring (finely chopped orange or lemon rind, cocoa or coffee powder)

Set the oven at 375°F (190°C) or Mark 5.

Cream together the fat and sugar until light and pale coloured. Fold in 2 oz (50 g) flour and 1 egg, then beat well. Do the same with another 2 oz (50 g) flour and remaining egg. Then beat in remaining flour a little at a time until a stiff mixture is formed. Stir in the milk.

Fill mixture into greased bun tins and bake just above the centre of the pre-set oven for 15 minutes or until golden and just firm to the touch. Cool on a wire rack.

Queen Cakes

4 oz (100 g) softened butter or margarine
4 oz (100 g) castor sugar
4 oz (100 g) self raising flour
2 eggs
salt
2 oz (50 g) sultanas or seedless raisins

Set the oven at 375°F (190°C) or Mark 5.

In a mixing bowl beat the fat until light and creamy. Add the sugar and cream with the fat until pale and fluffy and the mixture drops easily from the spoon. Sift the flour. Beat the eggs, one at a time, into the cake mixture with a portion of flour. When well blended, fold in the remaining flour with the sultanas or raisins. Spoon a good blob of the mixture into 12 greased and floured bun tins. Bake in pre-set oven for about 10 minutes or until pale golden. Take out and cool on a wire rack.

Variations:
Cherry Cakes: substitute 2 oz (50 g) chopped glacé cherries for fruit.
Chocolate Cakes: substitute ½ oz (12 g) cocoa powder for ½ oz (12 g) of the flour.
Orange or Lemon Cakes: add 2 tbsp (30 ml) finely grated rind and cream with the fat before adding the sugar.

Cherry Fairy Cakes

4 oz (100 g) self raising flour
salt
2 eggs
4 oz (100 g) shortening
4 oz (100 g) castor sugar
2 oz (50 g) roughly chopped, glacé cherries

Set the oven at 350°F (180°C) or Mark 4.

Sift the flour with a pinch of salt. Put all the ingredients into a mixing bowl and beat hard for about 1 minute or until well combined. Put spoonfuls of the mixture into 18 greased and floured bun tins and bake in the pre-set oven for 15 minutes or until golden. Turn out and cool on a rack.

Variations:
Coconut Buns: add 1 oz (25 g) desiccated coconut to the mixture.
Date and Nut Buns: add 2 oz (50 g) chopped dates and 1 oz (25 g) finely chopped nuts to the mixture.
Iced Fairy Cakes: cover with plain or lemon flavoured glacé icing and top each cake with half a glacé cherry.

Raspberry Buns

8 oz (225 g) self raising flour
salt
4 oz (100 g) butter or margarine
4 oz (100 g) castor sugar
1 lightly beaten egg
1 tbsp (15 ml) milk
2 oz (50 g) raspberry jam

Set the oven at 425°F (220°C) or Mark 7.

Sift the flour and a pinch of salt into a bowl, then rub in the fat until the mixture resembles fine crumbs. Stir in the sugar. Make a well in the centre, then stir in the egg, followed by the milk, and blend to form a smooth dough.

Turn the dough onto a floured work surface and knead for a few seconds. Then press out a little with your hand and cut dough into 12 pieces. Shape each piece into a round bun and place on a greased and floured baking sheet.

Using the handle of wooden spoon make a small hole in the top of each bun and spoon in a little of the jam. Put the buns into the pre-set oven and bake for about 10 minutes or until well risen and golden. Take out and cool on a wire rack.

Sponge Buns with some of the ingredients y

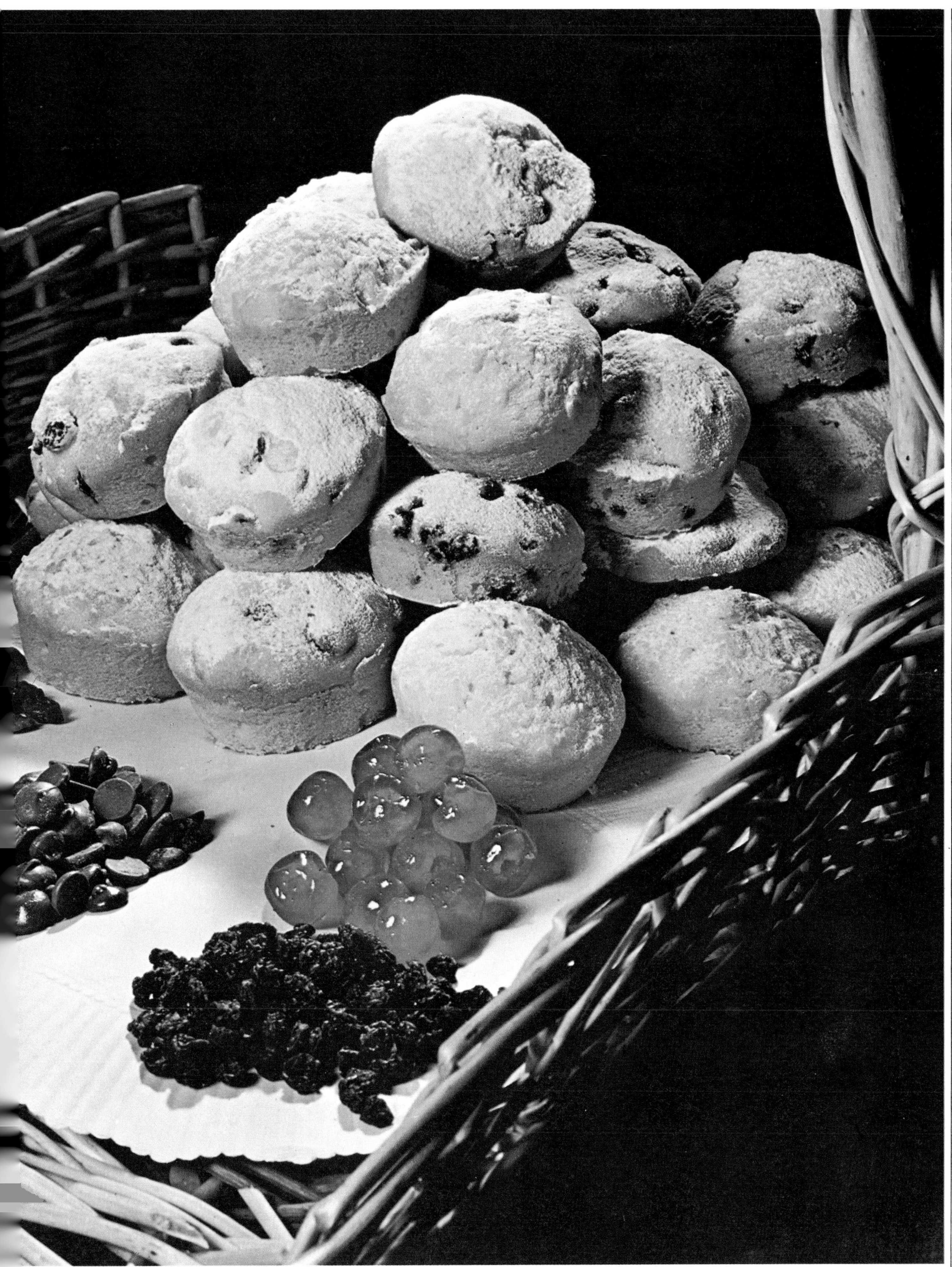

vary the original recipe.

Small fancy cakes

Little Flower Cakes

4 egg quantity basic sponge
butter cream
glacé icing

To decorate
coloured sugar flowers
angelica

Make and bake the sponge and cool. Cut two-thirds into 1 by 2 inch (2.50×5 cm) lengths. Use a 1½ inch (3 cm) plain cutter to stamp out rounds from the remaining piece of sponge. Make butter cream and glacé icing in chosen colourings.

Cut the sponge shapes in half, then sandwich with a little butter cream. Cover them completely except for the bases with more butter cream. Chill them in refrigerator until butter cream is firm, then using a knife dipped in hot water, smooth butter cream. Chill again, then place sponge shapes on a wire rack stood over a sheet of greaseproof paper. Coat with glacé icing and when firm decorate with sugar flowers and angelica to resemble green stems and leaves.

Glacé Icing

Basic Recipe

8 oz (225 g) icing sugar
2 tbsp (30 ml) cold water or flavoured liquid such as fresh orange or lemon juice or other fruit juice, or black coffee

Sift the icing sugar into a mixing bowl. Gradually add the water or other preferred liquid and mix until the icing is smooth but fairly stiff. If too much liquid is added, the icing will become too runny and more sieved icing sugar will have to be added until it returns to the required stiffness.

If not using the icing immediately, cover the bowl with foil or a damp cloth, or stir in a little lemon juice if not already used to prevent the icing hardening.

Variation:
Use a few drops of edible food colouring to give pink, blue, mauve etc coloured icing. Add colourings sparingly to avoid the result being too garish or dark.

Butter Cream

Basic Recipe

6 oz (175 g) softened, unsalted butter
12 oz (350 g) icing sugar
½ tsp (2.50 ml) vanilla essence
3–4 tbsp (45 - 60 ml) milk or warm water

Cream the butter until it is soft and fluffy and pale coloured, then gradually beat in the icing sugar, together with the vanilla essence and enough milk or water to blend to a smooth mixture. Use according to recipe.

Variations:
Orange, lime or lemon butter cream: omit vanilla essence and add a little grated orange, lime or lemon rind plus about ½ tbsp (7.50 ml) juice. Beat well to prevent mixture from curdling.
Coffee butter cream: omit vanilla essence and add 1–2 tbsp (15–30 ml) instant coffee powder, according to taste.
Chocolate butter cream: omit vanilla essence. Add 1–1½ tbsp (15–22 ml) cocoa dissolved in a little hot water; cool before beating into butter mixture, or melt 1 oz (25 g) chocolate until just liquid and blend into icing sugar.

Little Flower Cakes decorated with sugar flowers and angelica.

Square Iced Sponges and Cherry Cream Cakes.

Cherry Cream Cakes

4 egg quantity of basic sponge
utter cream
pt (15 ml) double cream
oz (25 g) icing sugar
tsp(5 ml) kirsch or cherry flavoured liqueur
oz (50 g) coarsely chopped glacé cherries
oz (50 g) coarsely chopped angelica

Make and bake the sponge in the usual way. When completely cold, stamp out iny rounds using a 1 inch (2.50 cm) plain astry cutter.

Make the butter cream, and spread the ponge rounds with a little of it.

Whip the cream in a bowl until it is stiff, hen beat in the icing sugar and the kirsch r cherry flavoured liqueur. Using a metal poon, fold in three-quarters of the glacé herries and angelica, reserving the re-nainder for decoration.

Carefully spoon the cherry cream mix-ure on top of the butter cream covered rounds, then decorate with the rest of the glacé cherries and angelica.

Square Iced Sponges

4 egg quantity of basic sponge, baked in 12 inch (30 cm) shallow square baking tin
glacé icing
pink and blue food colourings
butter cream for piping

Cut the baked sponge into 2 inch (5 cm) squares and place on a wire rack. Make the plain glacé icing and divide into 2 portions and tint one a pastel pink, the other a pastel blue.

Holding a knife blade diagonally across the top of a sponge square, cover one triangular half (including the sides) with pink glacé icing. The icing must be fairly stiff to ensure it does not run out of shape. Repeat this process with the remaining squares and leave to set. Then cover the remaining triangles and sides with blue glacé icing in the same way and leave to set.

When completely firm, fill butter cream into a piping bag fitted with a small rosette nozzle and pipe a band of rosettes along the line where the 2 coloured glacé icings meet. If liked pipe a single rosette at the opposite corners and link the corners with a thin strand of butter cream.

Small fancy cakes

Chocolate and Pineapple Cakes

4 egg quantity basic sponge
6 oz (175 g) plain dessert chocolate, broken into small pieces

To decorate
1 can drained and halved, pineapple rings
redcurrant jelly glaze
8 glacé cherries
few thin strips of angelica
chocolate hundreds and thousands

Set the oven at 350°F (180°C) or Mark 4.

Make the sponge and pour into a greased 11 by 7 inch (30×20 cm) baking tin and bake for about 25 minutes or until golden and just firm to the touch. Cool slightly, then turn out of the tin onto the floured paper. When cold cut sponge into 8 equal rectangles.

Chocolate and Pineapple Cakes.

Heat the chocolate in a pan over a low heat until just liquid. Dip the sides of each piece of sponge into the chocolate, then stand them on a greased wire rack to drain. When almost set, carefully cut off excess chocolate.

To decorate cakes: brush cakes with a little melted redcurrant jelly glaze, then carefully roll the sides only in chocolate hundreds and thousands. Place 3 half rings of pineapple, slightly overlapping, on top of each cake, brush again with redcurrant jelly glaze, then finish with a glacé cherry and angelica strips set at one end in the centre of the pineapple ring.

Basic Swiss Meringue Mixture

Basic Recipe

5 egg whites
8 oz (225 g) castor sugar

Set the oven at 275°F (140°C) or Mark 1.

Stiffly whip egg whites until they stand in a peak. Sprinkle over 2 oz (50 g) of the measured sugar and whisk again for about 3 minutes. Sprinkle over remaining sugar and fold in carefully and as lightly as possible with a spatula.

Fill meringue mixture into a piping bag fitted with a large nozzle and pipe blobs of, or put spoonfuls of, meringue onto a baking sheet lined with a greased sheet of greaseproof paper, spacing them wide apart.

Bake in the pre-set oven for about 1 hour 20 minutes for large meringues or 55 minutes for smaller meringues; they should be crisp and completely dry.

Note: for a smooth finish to plain meringues, well grease 2 large spoons and using them like ice cream scoops, spoon up mixture with one and smooth off with the other.

eringues with pink, blue and pale lemon Chantilly Cream.

Chocolate Chip Meringues

egg white quantity basic meringue
oz (100 g) chocolate chips

et the oven at 275°F (140°C) or Mark 1.

arefully fold whole chocolate chips into asic meringue mixture after all the sugar as been added. Put spoonfuls of eringue onto a baking sheet lined with a reased sheet of greaseproof paper, spacg them well apart, and bake in pre-set ven for about 1 hour 20 minutes for large eringues, 55 minutes for smaller ones.

Meringues with Chantilly Cream

5 egg white quantity basic meringue
¼ pt (15 cl) chantilly cream
6 oz (175 g) butter quantity butter cream
blue, pink and yellow food colouring

Pipe and bake meringues as for basic meringues.

Colour chantilly cream by dividing into 3 equal portions. Using a cocktail stick or skewer, carefully add a few drops of the first colour until desired shade is reached. Repeat process with remaining portions. Do exactly the same for the butter cream.

Sandwich meringues with chantilly cream, then pipe matching coloured butter cream along the centres, using a piping bag fitted with a small crown nozzle.

Large cakes

Cake recipes are passed down from mother to daughter like heirlooms, and a reliable recipe is worth treasuring. This chapter deals with the familiar family cakes like Madeira Cake, Fruit Cake and Sponge Cake, and introduces some variations on a few well loved themes.

Apart from finding the right recipes, there are many factors which affect success in cake making: first of all, measure the ingredients with care; never bake in a crowded oven; follow the baking instructions exactly, but remember that no two ovens are the same and experience is the best guide for cake making.

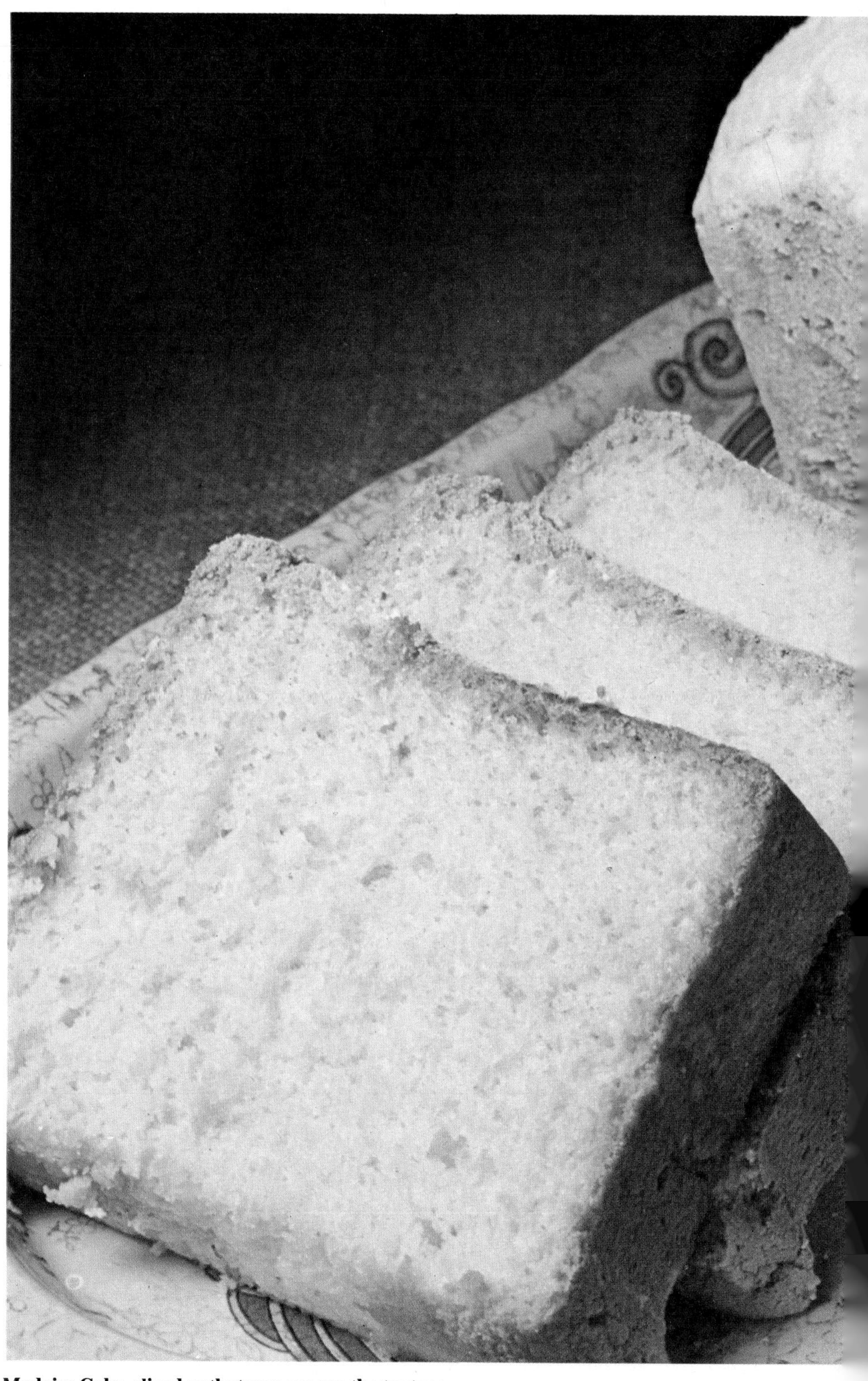

Madeira Cake, sliced so that you can see the texture.

Madeira Cake

7 separated eggs
4 oz (100 g) castor sugar
5 oz (150 g) self raising flour
1½ tbsp (25 ml) milk
salt
1 tsp (5 ml) vanilla essence
icing sugar for sprinkling

Set the oven at 350°F (180°C) or Mark 4.

In a large bowl stiffly whip the egg whites until they hold a peak. In another mixing bowl beat the egg yolks until they are doubled in volume and foamy. Add the castor sugar, milk and vanilla essence and beat the eggs again. Sift the flour with a pinch of salt and beat into the sugar mixture. Using a metal spoon, fold in the whisked egg whites, adding them a third at a time.

Grease and flour a loaf tin measuring 9 by 5 by 3 inches (22 by 12 by 8 cm) or an 8 inch (20 cm) diameter cake tin. Turn the cake batter into the prepared tin and three quarters fill.

Bake the cake in the pre-set oven for about 45 minutes, or until risen and golden. Cool on a wire rack, then sprinkle thickly with icing sugar to serve.

Special Iced Cake with completed trellis work.

Special Iced Cake

8 oz (225 g) softened butter or margarine
8 oz (225 g) castor sugar
4 eggs
8 oz (225 g) self raising flour
2 tbsp (30 ml) milk
6 oz butter quantity brandy flavoured butter cream
glacé icing
edible food colouring of choice

Set the oven at 350°F (180°C) or Mark 4.

Cream the fat and sugar in a mixing bowl until pale coloured and fluffy. Using a metal spoon fold in a quarter of the flour, then carefully beat in 1 egg, a little at a time to avoid curdling the cake batter. Continue folding in portions of flour, followed by an egg each time, until all are incorporated.

Well grease the sides of 12 inch (30 cm) diameter 1 inch (3 cm) deep cake tin and line with greased and floured greaseproof paper cut to fit.

Pour the cake batter into the prepared tin.

Bake the cake in the pre-set oven for 30 minutes or until it is golden, well risen, firm to the touch and just pulls away from the sides of the tin. Take out and cool on a wire rack.

With the bottom side up to give the smoothest possible surface for icing, cover with flavoured butter cream, and working it down the sides. Put the sponge into the refrigerator to chill until the butter cream is hard. Take out and smooth off the surface for icing by drawing a palette knife dipped in hot water over the butter cream; shake off the drops of water each time before applying the knife. Return the sponge to the refrigerator and chill again until the butter cream is hard.

Meanwhile tint the glacé icing to desired shade, then spread over butter cream covered sponge cake. Decorate the iced cake according to personal preference with crystallized fruit, sugar roses, finely chopped nuts etc.

Coffee Gâteau

8 oz (225 g) softened butter or margarine
8 oz (225 g) castor sugar
4 eggs
7 oz (200 g) self raising flour
1 oz (25 g) cornflour
2 tbsp (30 ml) coffee syrup
6 oz butter quantity coffee butter cream

Set the oven at 350°F (180°C) or Mark 4.

In a mixing bowl cream the fat and sugar until pale coloured and fluffy. Using a metal spoon fold in a quarter of the flour,

HOW TO PIPE A TRELLIS

1. Using a piping bag fitted with a small writing nozzle, practice drawing a series of straight lines in icing.

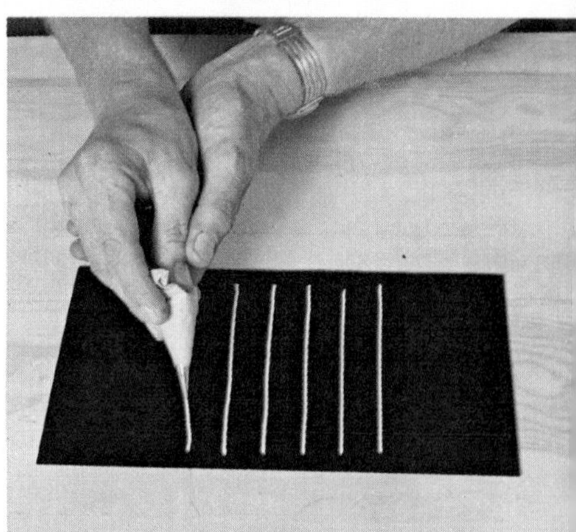

2. Note correct position of hands for piping. The second hand steadies the first.

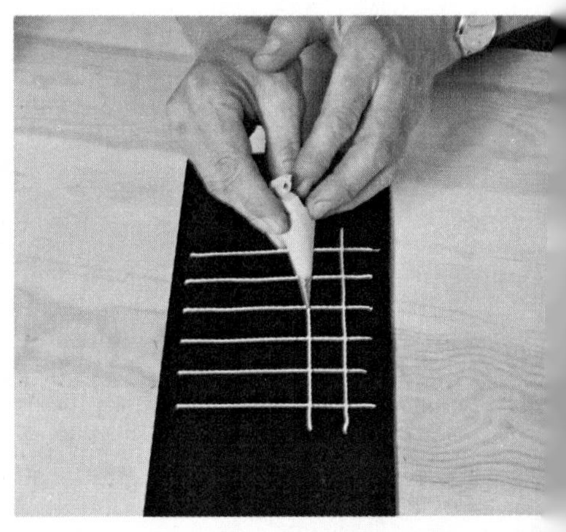

3. Pipe another series of lines across the first set. Try to keep the hands clear of the work surface so that the second line of piping does not pull the first line out of shape and ruin the effect.

then carefully beat in 1 egg, a little at a time to avoid curdling the cake batter. Continue folding in portions of flour, followed by an egg each time, until all are incorporated. Beat in the coffee syrup.

Well grease the sides of 12 inch (30 cm) diameter 1 inch (3 cm) deep cake tin and line with greased and floured greaseproof paper cut to fit.

Pour the cake batter into the prepared tin.

Bake the cake in the pre-set oven for 30 minutes or until it is golden, well risen, firm to the touch and just pulls away from the sides of the tin. Take out and cool on a wire rack.

With the bottom side up (this always has the smoothest and best looking surface) completely cover the sponge with a good half of the coffee butter cream, chill in the refrigerator, then smooth the top with a knife. Fill remaining butter cream into a piping bag fitted with a plain writing nozzle and pipe a trellis pattern on top of the cake. Change the nozzle to a small rosette nozzle and pipe rosettes all round the sides of the cake. Pipe a single small rosette at each point on the trellis where the lines cross each other.

Featherweight Jam Sponge

eggs
egg yolk
¼ oz (60 g) icing sugar
oz (50 g) self raising flour
aspberry, strawberry or blackcurrant jam for filling
cing sugar for sprinkling

et the oven at 375°F (190°C) or Mark 5.

eat the eggs, egg yolk and sugar together a mixing bowl until thick and creamy. ift the flour and fold into the egg mixture, sing a metal spoon.

Grease and flour 8 inch (20 cm) diame-r deep cake tin, then line with greased reaseproof paper cut to fit. Turn into the repared cake tin and bake in the pre-set ven for 30 minutes or until pale gold and p of cake springs back when gently pres-d with a finger.

Cool on a wire rack, then turn out of tin d cut in half; sandwich with chosen jam d sprinkle the top generously with icing gar.

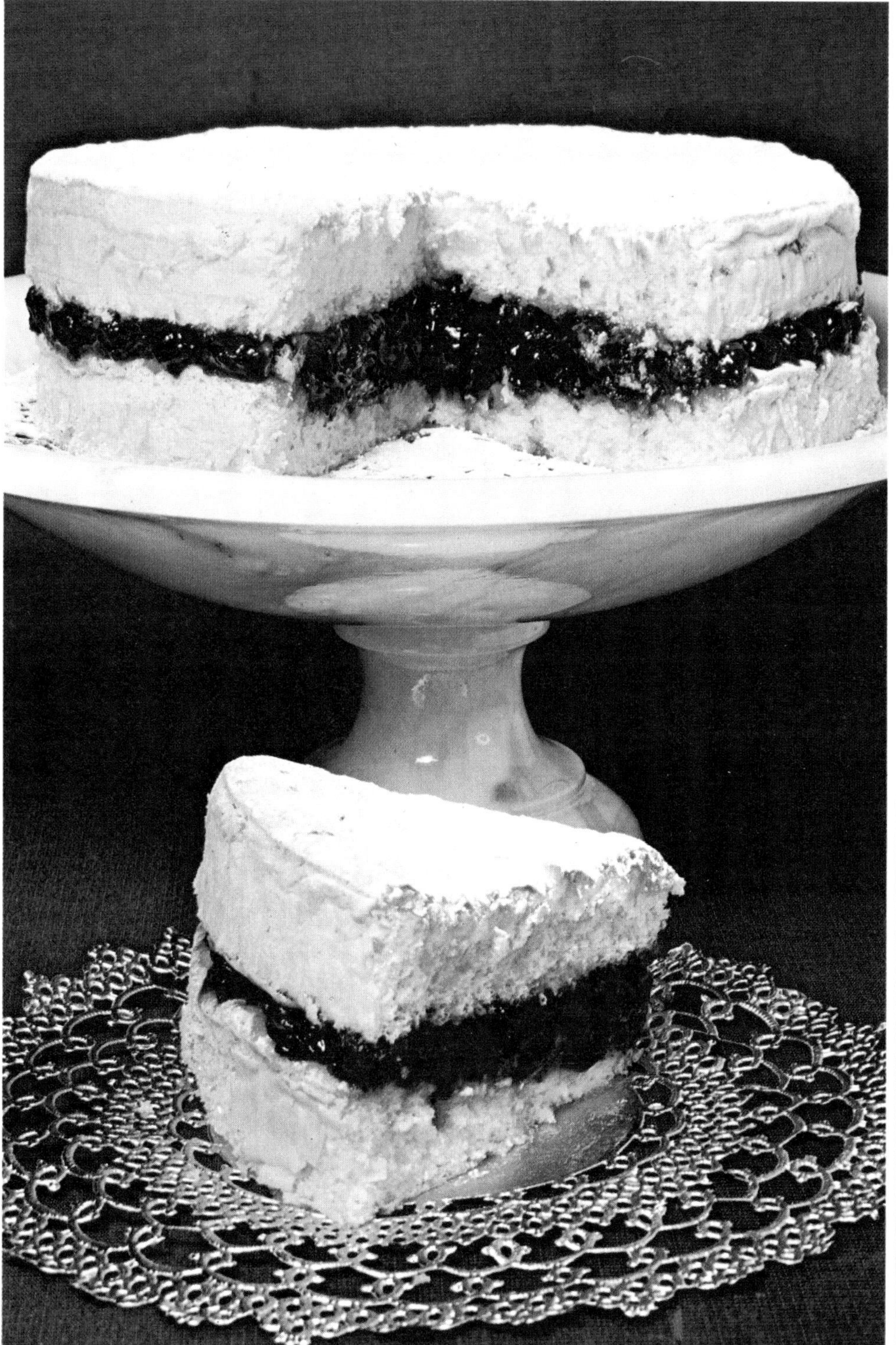

Featherweight Jam Sponge. Fill this lighter than air fatless sponge with plenty of homemade jam and sprinkle the top of the cake with a generous dusting of icing sugar. Sponges are not intended for storing and are at their best for only a day or two.

Angel Cake. Another fatless sponge, this one is truly food fit for angels, with a topping of flaked, browned almonds and a sprinkling of icing sugar. You can see the texture from the slice which has been cut out. Serve the day after baking.

Angel Cake

5 egg whites
1 tsp (5 ml) cream of tartar
5 oz (150 g) castor sugar
salt
2 oz (50 g) self raising flour
2 oz (50 g) cornflour

To decorate
4 oz (100 g) flaked almonds
icing sugar for sprinkling

Set the oven at 325°F (160°C) or Mark 3.

Stiffly whip the egg whites in a large bowl until they stand in a firm peak; there should be no liquid egg white at all. Sprinkle over the cream of tartar, then gently draw them to the sides of the bowl to make a well in the centre.

Pour the sugar and a pinch of salt into the well, then fold in carefully with a metal spoon or spatula to retain as much beaten in air as possible. When the sugar is completely combined, make a well again. Sift the flour and the cornflour together and repeat the folding in process with the flours.

When combined turn at once into an ungreased 6 inch (15 cm) loose bottomed cake tin. Cut through the mixture a few times with a knife to break up any air bubbles present, then cover the top thickly with flaked almonds.

Bake in the pre-set oven for 45 minutes or until light and fluffy. Do not be tempted to open the oven during the cooking period because the mixture is very delicate and cannot survive sudden changes of temperature or knocks caused by opening and shutting the oven door or moving the tin. Cool in the tin until cold, then turn out on to a wire rack. Sprinkle with icing sugar.

Genoese

$4\frac{1}{2}$ oz (125 g) sifted icing sugar
4 eggs
salt
$4\frac{1}{2}$ oz (125 g) self raising flour
$4\frac{1}{2}$ oz (125 g) butter or margarine, melted but not oily

Set the oven at 350°F (180°C) or Mark 4.

n a mixing bowl stood over a pan of hot vater beat the sugar, eggs and a small inch of salt until the mixture is thick, oamy and almost doubled in volume. Remove the bowl from the heat and continue eating until the mixture cools to about lood temperature. Sift the flour over the gg mixture and carefully fold in; then stir n the melted butter.

Line either a 12 inch (30 cm) diameter ound or square deep cake tin, or 2 8 inch 20 cm) diameter sandwich tins, with reased greaseproof paper cut to fit. Turn nixture into the prepared tin(s) and bake n the pre-set oven for 40 minutes for a arge sponge, 20 minutes for a smaller ne, or until golden and the cake springs ack when gently pressed with a fingertip. ake out and cool on a wire rack.

ariation:
or chocolate iced genoese, cover plain enoese made as above, with chocolate osting made by bringing 4 oz (100 g) astor sugar and $1\frac{3}{4}$ fl oz (4 cl) water to the oil, then simmering until the sugar syrup oes a very light yellow, remove from the eat and cool until tepid. Melt 4 oz (100 g) lain dessert chocolate, broken into ieces, in a pan until just liquid, remove om the heat and add the sugar syrup to it, gether with 1 drop olive oil. Stir connuously until the frosting cools and ickens to a spreading consistency.

Using a palette knife, dipped in hot ater, spread three quarters of the frostg over the genoese, taking it just over e edges. Have ready 2 packets of chocote finger biscuits, trimmed so they stand bout $\frac{1}{2}$ inch (12 mm) above the cake. ress these firmly onto the sides, securing em with the remaining chocolate frostg. Leave to firm in a cool place.

Orange or Lemon Gâteau

8 oz (225 g) softened butter or margarine
finely grated rind of $\frac{1}{2}$ orange or lemon
8 oz (225 g) castor sugar
4 eggs
8 oz (225 g) self raising flour and cornflour, mixed
crystallized orange or lemon slices for decoration
juice of 1 orange or lemon

For vanilla frosting
5 oz (150 g) sifted icing sugar
$1\frac{1}{2}$ tbsp (22 ml) vegetable oil
1–$1\frac{1}{2}$ tbsp (15–22 ml) milk
2–3 drops of vanilla essence

Set the oven at 350°F (180°C) or Mark 4.

Put the softened fat in a mixing bowl together with the orange or lemon rind. Add the sugar and cream with the fat until pale coloured and fluffy. Using a metal spoon fold in a quarter of the flour, then carefully beat in 1 egg, a little at a time to avoid curdling the cake batter. Continue folding in portions of flour, followed by an egg each time, until all are incorporated. Beat in the orange or lemon juice.

Well grease 2 8 inch (20 cm) diameter sandwich tins and line with greased and floured greaseproof paper cut to fit. Pour cake batter into the prepared tins.

Bake the cakes in the pre-set oven for 20 minutes or until golden, well risen, firm to the touch and they just pull away from the sides of the tins. Take out and cool on a wire rack.

Make vanilla frosting by beating together in a bowl the icing sugar, oil, milk and vanilla essence until very smooth. Sandwich the sponge rounds with vanilla frosting and decorate the top of the gâteau with crystallized orange or lemon slices.

HOW TO APPLY GLACE ICING

1. Stand the cake to be iced on a wire rack or cake board or any other flat surface. Pour all the icing into the middle of the cake, scraping every bit from the bowl with the spatula.

2. Dip the palette knife in the hot water, shaking off all the drips, and run the flat of the blade quickly through the glacé icing, working it from the centre to the sides and down to give an even layer overall.

3. Keep dipping the knife blade in and out of the hot water so that it runs freely, and smooth off any remaining ridges around the edges of the cake. Smooth the icing on the sides and leave to set until hard. Place chosen decorations for top of the cake on just before the icing sets completely.

HOW TO MAKE A SWISS ROLL

2¼ oz (62 g) self raising flour
4 oz (100 g) castor sugar
3 eggs
icing sugar for sprinkling

For filling
red jam or butter cream

Set the oven at 425°F (220°C) or Mark 7.

Line a swiss roll tin measuring 10 by 14 by ¾ inches (25 cm × 35 cm × 19 mm) with greaseproof paper, cut to fit. Brush the paper lightly with oil. Prepare a work surface of several layers of newspaper topped with a sheet of greaseproof paper. All papers should be about 3 inches (8 cm) larger than the swiss roll tin. Sift a little flour over the greaseproof paper.

Sift the sugar onto a piece of foil and heat in the pre-set oven for about 6 minutes. Sift the flour. Whisk the eggs with the hot sugar until pale and foamy. Fold in the flour quickly but gently so the air bubbles are not lost.

Pour the batter into the prepared tin, spreading it evenly, and bake in the pre-set oven, just above centre, for 8 minutes or until golden. Take out of the oven and flip the sponge over and carefully place on the prepared greaseproof paper. Leave to cool.

Trim the sides and spread with jam. To roll up, grip the ends of paper nearest you at either side, lift up and start to roll the sponge away from you. Put one hand behind the papers and push firmly on the sponge as you roll. Ease the paper away from the sponge, keeping it taut and at an angle above the sponge. Keep rolling until the swiss roll is completed. Brush off any surplus flour and sprinkle with icing sugar.

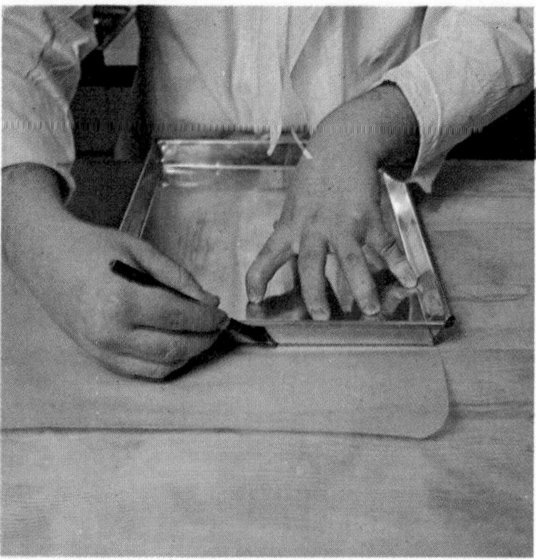

1. Make greaseproof paper fit your swiss roll tin by drawing round the tin onto the paper, cut through and place the pencilled side downwards.

2. Lay paper on the tin and brush all over – including the sides – with oil.

6. Stop whisking, then shake the sifted flour over the surface of the egg mixture.

7. Using a spatula, gently fold and cut the flour into the mixture until completely blended. Take care not to lose any of the air bubbles which you have just been whisking up.

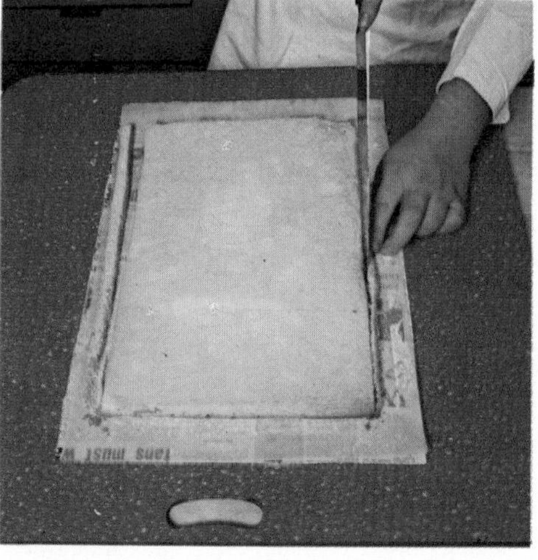

9. Trim the sides of the cooled sponge with a sharp knife. This gives a neat finish to the end result.

10. Pick up the papers nearest you and hold them in the way shown above. Press the edge firmly onto the jam.

3. Prepare a work surface with newspaper and greaseproof paper, then sift a little flour onto the greaseproof paper.

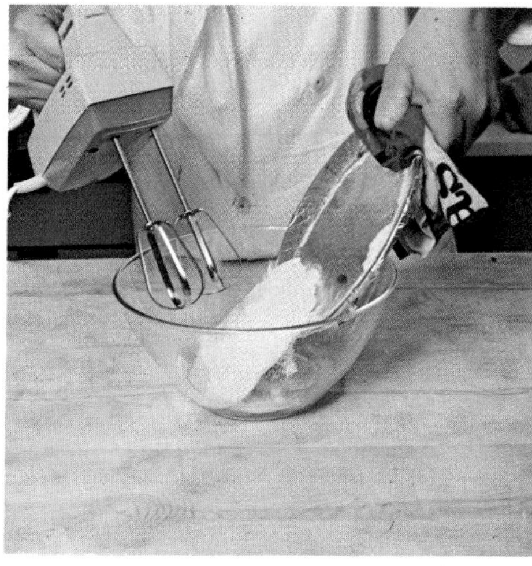

4. Heat the sifted sugar in the oven for 6 minutes. Break the eggs into a large bowl and when the sugar is really hot, quickly tip it onto the eggs and start whisking immediately.

5. Continue whisking until the mixture looks like this. It should almost have doubled its bulk and be pale and foamy.

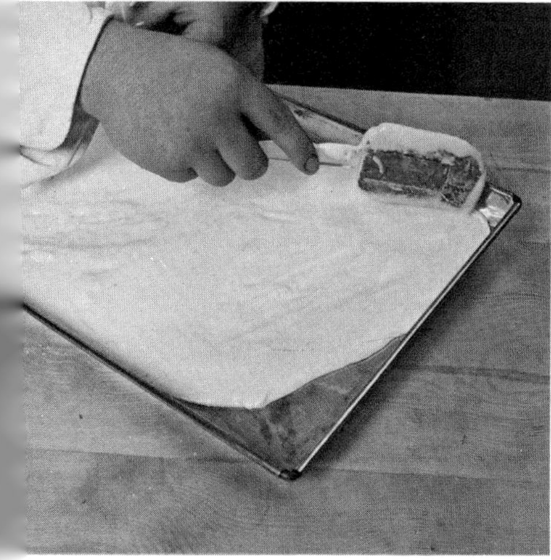

. Turn the mixture into the prepared tin nd spread with the spatula right over the urface, taking care to reach right into the orners of the tin.

. Roll up quickly, using one hand to ld the papers taut and the other to push m behind.

Swiss Roll filled with butter cream.

Large cakes

Raspberry or Strawberry Gâteau

1 lb (450 g) wiped and hulled fresh raspberries or strawberries
8 oz (225 g) softened butter or margarine
8 oz (225 g) castor sugar
4 eggs
7 oz (200 g) self raising flour
1 oz (25 g) cornflour
¼ pt (15 cl) double cream
icing sugar for sprinkling

Set the oven at 350°F (180°C) or Mark 4.

Reserve about half the fruit and work the remainder through a sieve to give 3 fl oz (7 cl) juice.

In a mixing bowl cream the fat and sugar together until pale coloured and fluffy. Using a metal spoon, fold in a quarter of the flour, then carefully beat in 1 egg, a little at a time to avoid curdling the cake batter. Continue folding in portions of flour, followed by an egg each time, until all are incorporated. Beat in the fruit juice.

Well grease 2 8 inch (20 cm) diameter sandwich tins and line with greased and floured greaseproof paper cut to fit. Pour cake batter into the prepared tins.

Bake cakes in the pre-set oven for 20 minutes or until they are golden, well risen, firm to the touch and they just pull away from the sides of the tins. Take out and cool on a wire rack.

In a bowl whip the double cream until almost stiff; stir in the reserved fruit, except for a few perfect ones for decorating the top, and sandwich sponges with the cream mixture. Arrange remaining fruit on top and sprinkle with icing sugar.

Sand Cake.

Sand Cake

8 oz (225 g) unsalted, softened butter
finely grated rind of 1 small lemon (optional)
3 oz (75 g) self raising flour
3 oz (75 g) potato flour
5 oz (150 g) sifted icing sugar plus a little extra for sprinkling
6 separated eggs

Set the oven at 350°F (180°C) or Mark 4.

In a mixing bowl cream the butter, with the lemon rind if using, until pale and fluffy. Sift the 2 flours together and then gradually beat in the icing sugar and about a quarter of the flours. Next beat in 2 egg yolks until well combined. Beat in another quarter of the flours and 2 more egg yolks, and repeat this process until all the flour and egg yolks are incorporated and you have a smooth batter. Stiffly whip the egg whites and fold into the batter. Then beat until combined and no streaks of egg white remain.

Grease and flour a rectangular cake tin measuring 9 by 5 by 3 inches (22×12×8 cm). Turn cake mixture into the prepared tin and smooth the surface, flattening the centre slightly, so it remains flat during baking. Put cake in pre-set oven and cook for 40 minutes. Take out and cool cake in the tin until only just warm. Turn out and sprinkle thickly with icing sugar.

Ice Cream Cake

For swiss rolls
8 oz (225 g) castor sugar
6 eggs
5 oz (150 g) self raising flour

To finish
6 oz (175 g) sieved apricot jam
2 family blocks of multiflavoured ice cream
¼ pt (15 cl) double cream
4 oz (100 g) finely crushed buttered walnuts

Set the oven at 425°F (220°C) or Mark 7.

Make swiss rolls. If you have 2 swiss roll tins, each measuring 10 by 14 by ¾ inches (25 cm×35 cm×19 mm), make the batter in one batch and divide it between them. Otherwise make each one separately as follows. Line the tin with greaseproof paper cut to fit. Smooth paper up the sides, then cover all over with vegetable oil.

Sift half the castor sugar onto a heat resistant plate and heat through in the pre-set oven for about 6 minutes or until very hot. Then tip onto 3 eggs in a mixing bowl and beat hard until very foamy and doubled in volume. Scatter 2½ oz (62 g) flour over the top, then fold in with a spatula until a soft, airy batter is formed.

Pour at once into the prepared tin, spreading it evenly and right into the corners. Then bake in the pre-set oven just above the centre for about 8 minutes or until golden and feathery in texture. Take out and cool. Stiffly whip the cream.

Take both swiss roll rectangles, trim the long edges, reserving the pieces, then cut in half to give 4 rectangles in all. Cover 2 sponge rectangles with apricot jam; then cover them with thin slices cut from two thirds of each block of ice cream, and place one on top of the other on a very cold plate. Continue the layering with another rectangle of sponge, spread with apricot jam, and slices of ice cream remaining from the 2 blocks. Spread apricot jam on the underside of the remaining sponge rectangle and place on top. Coat the ice cream sides with reserved sponge trimmings, crumbled until they resemble fine crumbs.

Fill the whipped cream into a piping bag fitted with a large rosette nozzle and pipe rows of rosettes all over the top of the cake. Sprinkle with finely crushed buttered walnuts. Serve the cake at once or put in coldest part of the refrigerator until required.

Ice Cream Cake.

Victoria Sponge

4 eggs
4 oz (100 g) castor sugar
4 oz (100 g) self raising flour
1 oz (25 g) unsalted butter, melted but not oily

To finish
jam or jelly of choice for filling
icing sugar for sprinkling

Set the oven at 350°F (180°C) or Mark 4.

In a mixing bowl stood over a pan of hot water beat the eggs and sugar together until light and creamy. Remove from the heat and continue beating until cool. Sift the flour over the mixture and lightly fold in, then stir in the melted butter.

Line 2 9 inch (22 cm) diameter sandwich tins with greased and floured greaseproof paper cut to fit. Pour the batter into the prepared tins and bake just below the centre of the pre-set oven for 35 minutes or until golden and just firm to the touch. Take out and cool on a wire rack.

Turn one sponge round bottom side up to give a smooth top; spread rounds with jam or jelly, then sandwich together and sprinkle with icing sugar to finish.

Variations:
Coffee: increase the flour quantity by 1 oz (25 g); stir in 1 tbsp (15 ml) coffee syrup before adding the melted butter; sandwich with coffee butter cream and decorate the top with coffee glacé icing.
Orange or lemon: add finely grated rind of 1 large orange or lemon to mixture before adding melted butter; use the juice to flavour butter cream for the filling and glacé icing for the top.
Cherry: stir in 3 oz (75 g) lightly floured, coarsely chopped glacé cherries, after the flour has been folded in.
Ginger: stir in ½ tsp (2.50 ml) ground ginger after the flour has been folded in. Sandwich with ginger flavoured whipped double cream (blend in 1 oz (25 g) finely chopped glacé ginger per ¼ pt (15 cl) double cream), top with plain glacé icing and decorate with pieces of crystallized or glacé ginger.
Nut: stir in 2 oz (50 g) finely chopped walnuts, pecans, brazils etc. after the flour has been folded in. Sandwich with orange or lemon butter cream and decorate either with orange or lemon glacé icing and a few whole nuts on top or decorate top with plain glacé icing sprinkled with finely ground pistachio nuts and pipe on small rosettes of whipped cream to cover the sides of the cake completely. Finish with a few green leaves, if liked.

Nut Sponge: a variation of Victoria Sponge.

Rich Sponge Cake

4 egg yolks
3¼ oz (82 g) castor sugar
3¼ oz (82 g) self raising flour
icing sugar to finish

Set the oven at 350°F (180°C) or Mark 4.

In a mixing bowl beat the egg yolks well until creamy. Beat in the sugar until the mixture is thick and frothy. Sift the flour and lightly fold in.

Line a 9 inch (22 cm) diameter sandwich tin with greased and floured greaseproof paper cut to fit.

Turn the cake batter into the prepared tin and bake just above the centre of the pre-set oven for 20 minutes or until brown and firm to the touch. Turn out and cool on a wire rack. Sprinkle thickly with icing sugar.

Spanish Fruit and Nut Sponge.

Spanish Fruit and Nut Sponge

5 oz (150 g) softened butter or margarine
finely grated rind of 1 lemon
5 oz (150 g) castor sugar
8 oz (225 g) self raising flour
salt
3 eggs
2 oz (50 g) flaked almonds or pine kernels
2 oz (50 g) roughly chopped glacé cherries
10 sugar lumps

Set the oven at 350°F (180°C) or Mark 4

In a mixing bowl cream together the fat and lemon rind until light and fluffy. Then cream with the sugar until pale coloured and fluffy. Sift the flour with a pinch of salt. Beat in 1 egg, together with 1 oz (25 g) of the flour and the salt. Continue beating in the remaining eggs, one at a time, together with portions of flour, until all are combined.

Line a well greased and floured 9 inch (22 cm) square shallow baking tin with greased and floured greaseproof paper cut to fit.

Turn cake mixture into the prepared tin and spread it over evenly. Sprinkle over the nuts and glacé cherries. Roughly crush the sugar lumps and sprinkle over the top of the cake. Put in the pre-set oven and bake for 35–40 minutes or until golden and the cake is just firm to the touch. Take out and cool in the tin before removing to serve.

HOW TO APPLY CHOPPED NUTS TO THE SIDE OF A CAKE

1. Spread soft butter cream round the side of the cake with a small knife. It must be evenly spread but it does not have to be particularly smooth.

2. Place your hand on the cake, slip a knife underneath and use your other hand to lift the cake. Holding the cake like a vertical wheel on a shallow plate of chopped nuts, turn it round until the sides are completely coated.

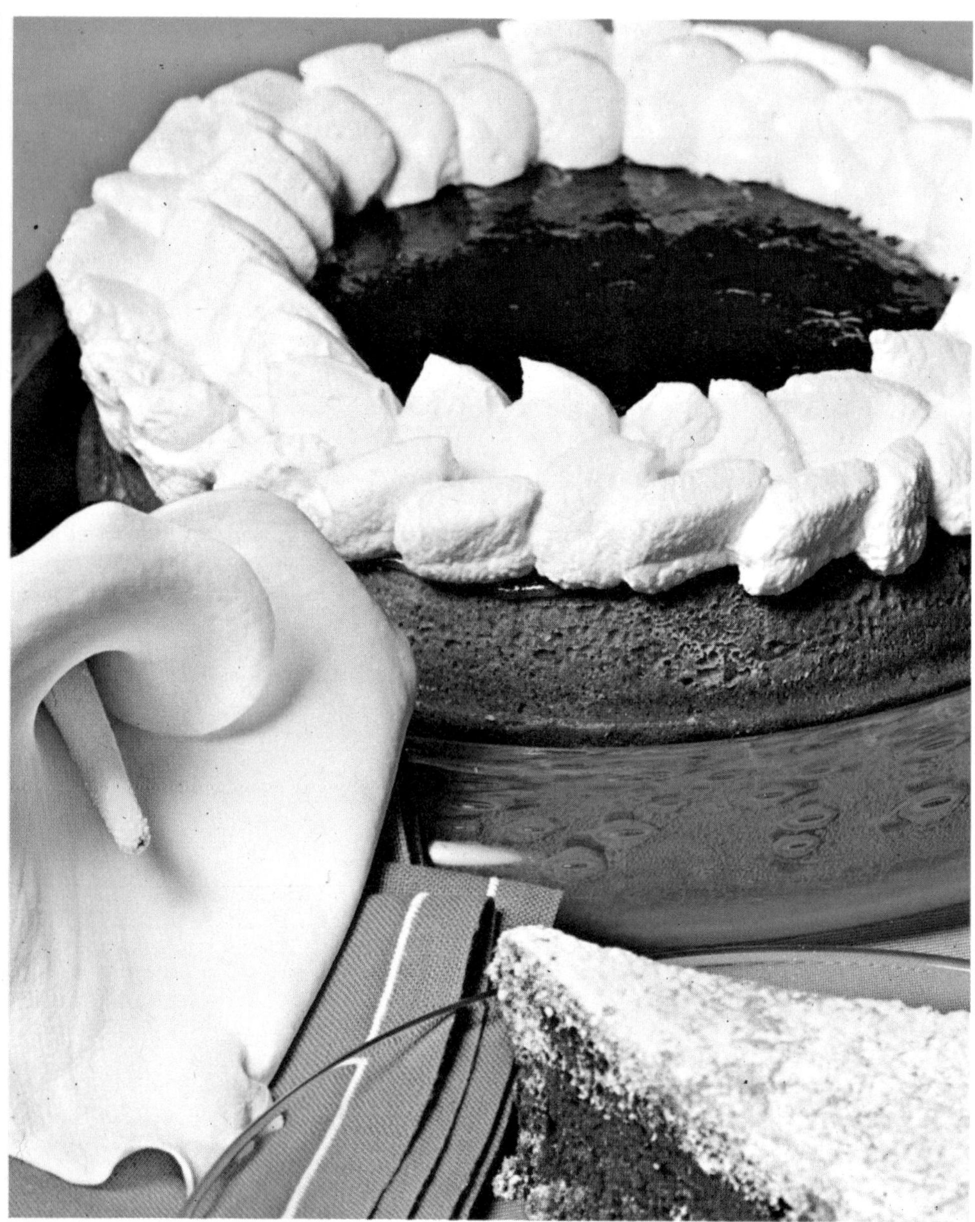

Sachertorte.

Sachertorte

5 oz (150 g) plain dessert chocolate, broken into pieces
1 tbsp (15 ml) water or rum
5 oz (150 g) unsalted, softened butter
5 oz (150 g) sifted icing sugar
6 separated eggs
5 oz (150 g) self raising flour

For chocolate frosting
4 oz (100 g) plain dessert chocolate, broken into pieces
4 oz (100 g) castor sugar
1¾ fl oz (4 cl) water
1 drop of olive oil

To finish
apricot glaze
½ pt (30 cl) stiffly whipped double cream

Set the oven at 350°F (180°C) or Mark 4.

In a small pan over a very low heat, melt the chocolate in the water or rum until it is just liquid. In a mixing bowl cream the butter until light and fluffy, then beat in 4 oz (100 g) icing sugar and the egg yolks only, one at a time. Beat in the softened chocolate.

Sift the flour. In another bowl whisk the egg whites until they stand in a stiff peak, then whisk in the remaining 1 oz (25 g) icing sugar. Fold egg whites, alternating with portions of flour, into the chocolate mixture a little at a time until all are combined.

Line a greased 9 inch (22 cm) diameter tin with greased and floured greaseproof paper cut to fit. Turn the cake mixture into the prepared tin and bake in the pre-set oven for 40 minutes or until firm to the touch. Take out and cool on a wire rack.

Meanwhile make the chocolate frosting. In a pan over a medium heat dissolve the sugar in the water, bring to the boil, then reduce heat and simmer gently until the sugar syrup goes a pale yellow; remove from the heat and cool until tepid. In another pan heat the chocolate until it is just liquid, then stir sugar syrup and olive oil into the chocolate and stir continuously until it forms a spreading consistency. Coat top of the chocolate cake with apricot glaze and spread with chocolate frosting, using a palette knife dipped in hot water. Allow to firm, then pipe or heap on stiffly whipped cream to serve, or sprinkle thickly with icing sugar if preferred.

Sugar Syrup

Basic Recipe

4 lb (approx 2 kg) granulated sugar
6 cups water

Gently heat the sugar and water in a larg heavy based pan over a low heat, withou stirring, until all the sugar is completel dissolved. Increase the heat just enough t bring the syrup to the boil, then reduce th heat immediately and simmer for about minutes. Cool at once. When cold pou into clean, dry, airtight containers an store until required.

Chocolate Gâteau

3¼ oz (82 g) self raising flour
1 oz (25 g) drinking chocolate powder
4 eggs
4 oz (100 g) castor sugar
1 oz (25 g) butter, melted but not oily
icing sugar for sprinkling
chocolate leaves to decorate

For mocha butter cream
4 oz (100 g) icing sugar
3 egg yolks
4 oz (100 g) softened butter
2 tsp (10 ml) coffee syrup
2 oz (50 g) plain dessert chocolate, melted until just liquid

Set the oven at 350°F (180°C) or Mark 4.

Sift the flour and drinking chocolate together. In a mixing bowl stood over a pan of hot water, beat together the eggs and castor sugar until pale and fluffy and almost doubled in volume. Remove from the heat and continue beating until tepid. Scatter over the flour mixture and lightly fold in with a spatula; stir in the butter.

Line a well greased 6 inch (15 cm) square deep cake tin with greased and floured greaseproof paper cut to fit.

Turn cake mixture into the prepared tin and bake just below the centre of the pre-set oven for 35 minutes. Take out and cool on a wire rack.

To make mocha butter cream, put icing sugar and egg yolks in a bowl stood over a pan of hot water. Whisk until the mixture is thick and creamy. Remove bowl from the heat and continue whisking, with the bowl stood in iced water, until cool. In another bowl cream the butter until pale and fluffy, then beat into the egg mixture a little at a time until combined. Beat in the coffee syrup, then the liquid chocolate.

Set the cooled cake on a cake board. Fill mocha butter cream into a piping bag fitted with a small star nozzle and completely cover the cake with rows of little rosettes.

Arrange chocolate leaves in the centre to resemble a rose and lightly sprinkle with icing sugar. Place a few more chocolate leaves at each corner.

Chocolate Gâteau decorated with chocolate leaves.

HOW TO MAKE CHOCOLATE LEAVES

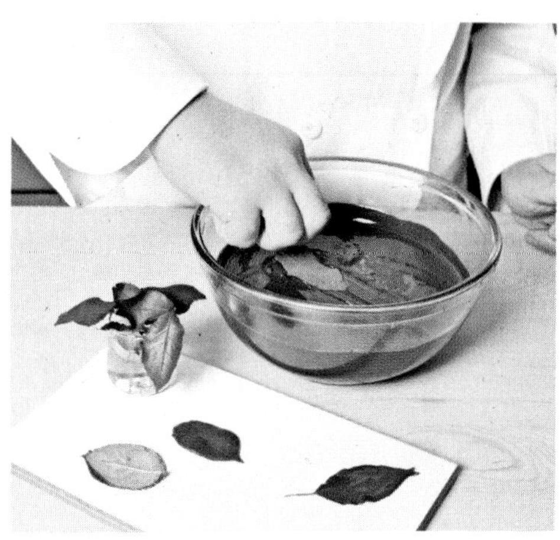

1. Gather a few rose leaves from your garden and wash and dry well. In a bowl over a pan of hot water melt 12 oz (350 g) plain dessert chocolate until liquid. Remove bowl from heat and, holding a leaf at its stalk end, trail it across the chocolate to coat one side.

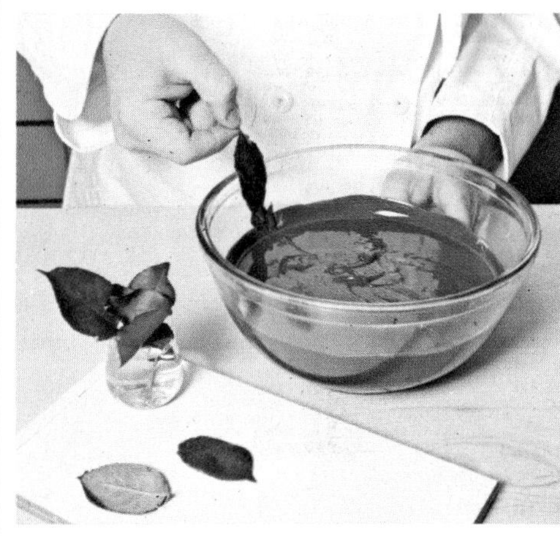

2. Get rid of any surplus chocolate by lightly drawing the leaf against the side of the bowl. Place the leaf, chocolate side uppermost, on a very cold surface to allow the chocolate to set.

3. When completely cold and set, simply peel off the rose leaves to give assorted chocolate leaves. Store in a cool place until required.

Dobos Torte.

Dobos Torte

3 separated eggs
2 oz (50 g) icing sugar
2 oz (50 g) self raising flour

For chocolate filling
4 oz (100 g) plain dessert chocolate, broken into pieces
4 oz (100 g) softened, unsalted butter
4 oz (100 g) sifted icing sugar
2 egg yolks

For topping
6 oz (175 g) castor sugar

Set the oven at 450°F (230°C) or Mark 8.

In a mixing bowl whip the egg whites until very stiff, then beat in the icing sugar. Using a fork whip the egg yolks a little, then blend into the egg white mixture. Sift the flour, sprinkle over the mixture and lightly fold in until well combined. This sponge mixture is enough to make 5 very thin rounds for the layer cake.

Line 2 well greased 9 inch (22 cm) diameter sandwich tins with greased greaseproof paper cut to fit. Pour just enough of the cake batter to cover thinly the prepared tins – if you have more 9 inch (22 cm) sandwich tins prepare them at the same time.

Bake just above the centre in the pre-set oven for no longer than 5 minutes, then turn out onto a wire rack to cool. Prepare tins again as above and continue baking until you have 5 thin rounds of sponge.

When cold place one sponge round on a firm base, then stack up the rounds, with a piece of greaseproof paper between each one and over the top round. Place a flat based tin on top, together with some weights (small cans will do) and leave for 12 hours or overnight. Remove the weights and tin, as well as the greaseproof paper.

Make the filling by melting the chocolate in a pan over a low heat until just liquid. In a bowl cream the butter until soft and pale coloured, then beat in the melted chocolate and icing sugar. Beat in the egg yolks until the mixture is creamy and fluffy. Spread the chocolate filling equally over 4 of the sponge rounds. Put the remaining round on a piece of greaseproof paper.

To make the topping, heat the castor sugar in a heavy based pan over a low heat until it dissolves and eventually turns a deep golden brown liquid. At once remove pan from the heat and quickly pour over the remaining sponge round to cover it completely. Before it has time to set like toffee, dip a sharp knife into boiling water and speedily mark the topping into 8 portions; wet the knife before marking each one. When completely set and brittle, put the round on top of the others to complete the layer cake.

Variation:
A simpler alternative to the sugar topping is to sprinkle finely ground nuts all over the cake.

Coffee Syrup

Basic Recipe

1 pt (60 cl) black coffee, preferably made from ground coffee beans for the best flavour

Despite its name, no sugar is added to the coffee syrup because there will be sufficient natural sweetness in the other ingredients according to the recipe.

Bring coffee to the boil in a pan over a medium heat. Reduce by boiling to about 2 fl oz (5 cl) to concentrate its flavour. Remove the pan from the heat, leave to cool, then pour into clean, dry containers or jars to store and use according to recipe.

Chocolate Layer Cake

2 eggs plus 1 egg yolk
2½ oz (62 g) icing sugar
2 oz (50 g) self raising flour
2 tbsp (30 ml) drinking chocolate powder
2 tbsp (30 ml) coffee syrup
coffee butter cream for filling

For chocolate icing and decoration
4 oz (100 g) castor sugar
1¾ fl oz (4 cl) water
6 oz (175 g) plain dessert chocolate, broken into pieces
1–2 drops of olive oil

Set the oven at 350°F (180°C) or Mark 4.

In a mixing bowl beat together the eggs, egg yolk and sugar until thick and creamy. Sprinkle over the flour together with the drinking chocolate, then fold in lightly. Stir in the coffee syrup.

Line a greased and floured shallow roasting tin with greased greaseproof paper cut to fit.

Turn the mixture into the prepared tin and bake just below the centre of the pre-set oven for about 30 minutes or until risen and the sponge springs back when pressed lightly with a fingertip. Turn out onto a wire rack to cool, then trim the sloping edges.

With a sharp knife cut the sponge in 3 equal pieces lengthways. Cover one piece with coffee butter cream, place the second piece of sponge on top, then cover with more butter cream and top with the third piece of sponge.

Make the chocolate icing by dissolving 4 oz (100 g) castor sugar in the water in a pan over a moderate heat. Bring to the boil, reduce heat at once and simmer until the sugar syrup is a light yellow colour.

Take the pan from the heat and cool until the syrup is tepid. In a heavy based pan heat the chocolate until just liquid. Stir the sugar syrup into the chocolate, add the olive oil and continue stirring until the icing is of a spreading consistency. Spread the icing over the top and sides of the cake to cover them completely and leave to set.

When icing is cold and firm, melt the remaining chocolate in a pan over a low heat until liquid, fill into a piping bag fitted with ¼ inch (6 mm) plain nozzle and pipe thin lines of chocolate at random all over the top and sides. Leave to set.

ocolate Layer Cake.

Ginger Curl Gâteau

For ginger curls
3 oz (75 g) golden syrup
3½ oz (82 g) castor sugar
3 oz (75 g) butter or margarine
3½ oz (82 g) plain flour
finely grated rind of 1 lemon
1 tsp (5 ml) ground ginger

For sponge cake
3 separated eggs
2 oz (50 g) icing sugar
2 oz (50 g) self raising flour

For chocolate filling
4 oz (100 g) plain dessert chocolate, broken into pieces
4 oz (100 g) softened, unsalted butter
4 oz (100 g) sifted icing sugar
2 egg yolks

To finish
¼ pt (15 cl) stiffly whipped double cream
1 chocolate finger biscuit
2 tiny pieces of glacé cherry
2 very thin strips of angelica

Set the oven at 350°F (180°C) or Mark 4.

First make the ginger curls (you need 10 for this cake). In a heavy based pan over a low heat heat all the ginger curl ingredients together, except the flour and the ginger, until all are dissolved and blended. Take the pan off the heat. Sift the flour and blend in with ginger until smooth. Grease a baking sheet, then spoon 4–5 small heaps of mixture at a time onto it, leaving plenty of space between them. Bake just above the centre of the pre-set oven for 12 minutes, then remove at once and cool. Continue baking in batches until all the ginger curl mixture is used up. While they are still warm, trim the edges of 8 ginger curls with scissors to give a straight edge.

To make the sponge cake, increase the oven heat to 450°F (230°C) or Mark 8. Line 2 greased 9 inch (22 cm) diameter sandwich tins with greased greaseproof paper, cut to fit. In a mixing bowl whisk the egg whites until stiff, then beat in the icing sugar. Lightly beat the egg yolks, then blend into the egg white mixture. Sift the flour, sprinkle over and lightly fold in.

Pour just enough of the batter to cover thinly the prepared tins and bake just above the centre of the pre-set oven for no longer than 5 minutes. Turn out onto a wire rack to cool. Bake 3 more sponge rounds with the remaining mixture, then stack with pieces of greaseproof paper between each round and weight down for about 12 hours or overnight.

To make the chocolate filling: heat the chocolate in a pan over a low heat until liquid. In a bowl cream the butter until soft, then beat in the melted chocolate and icing sugar. Beat in the egg yolks until the mixture is light and fluffy. Spread over 4 rounds of sponge and sandwich them together, leaving the top plain. Press down so some of the chocolate filling squeezes out and smear it round the sides. Take the 8 trimmed ginger curls and press them firmly onto the sides of the cake, rounded sides rising above the cake, in a circle. Fill the whipped cream into a piping bag fitted with a small rosette nozzle and cover the top of the sponge with rosettes. Place another ginger curl flat in the centre, pipe a thick band of rosettes on top and press into this, at an angle to resemble wings, a halved ginger curl.

Take the chocolate finger biscuit and soften each end slightly; attach a piece of glacé cherry at either tip to resemble eyes, then stick on the angelica strips to resemble antennae. When the chocolate has hardened, place in the middle of the 2 wings to resemble a dragonfly.

Cheesecake

3½ oz (82 g) unsalted butter or margarine
4 oz (100 g) crushed digestive biscuits
12 oz (350 g) curd cheese
1 egg
juice and finely grated rind of ½ lemon
2 tbsp vanilla flavoured icing sugar

For choux pastry topping
2 oz (50 g) unsalted butter
4¾ fl oz (13 cl) cold water
2½ oz (62 g) self raising flour
2 eggs

Set the oven at 350°F (180°C) or Mark 4.

Line a rectangular metal flan case measuring 4½ by 11 inches (12×30 cm) with well greased and floured greaseproof paper so that it stands at least 1 inch (2.50 cm) above the rim.

In a pan over a moderate heat melt the fat and stir in the biscuit crumbs until they bind together. Press the biscuit mixture into the prepared case.

In a mixing bowl work the curd cheese until soft, then beat in the egg, lemon juice and rind and the flavoured icing sugar. When well blended turn into a biscuit lined case and smooth the top.

Make the choux pastry. In a heavy based pan over a moderate heat melt the butter in the water until dissolved and the mixture comes to the boil. Add the flour at once and as the mixture bubbles up turn off the heat immediately. Using a wooden spoon beat until the mixture forms a smooth paste and comes away cleanly from the sides of the pan. Beat in 1 egg, until the mixture becomes smooth again, then beat in the remaining egg. Cover the pan and leave until cold.

When cold fill choux paste into a piping bag fitted with ¼ inch (6 mm) plain nozzle and pipe a trellis pattern over the top. Bake cheesecake in the pre-set oven for 20 minutes, take out and cool. Then refrigerate for about 6 hours before serving. To serve, carefully remove metal case and peel away the paper.

Variations:
Instead of covering the top with a trellis of choux pastry leave cheesecake plain, then after baking spread over ¼ pt (15 cl) soured cream, top with rosettes of stiffly whipped cream and sprinkle with either icing sugar or browned almonds.

Cheesecake.

Large cakes

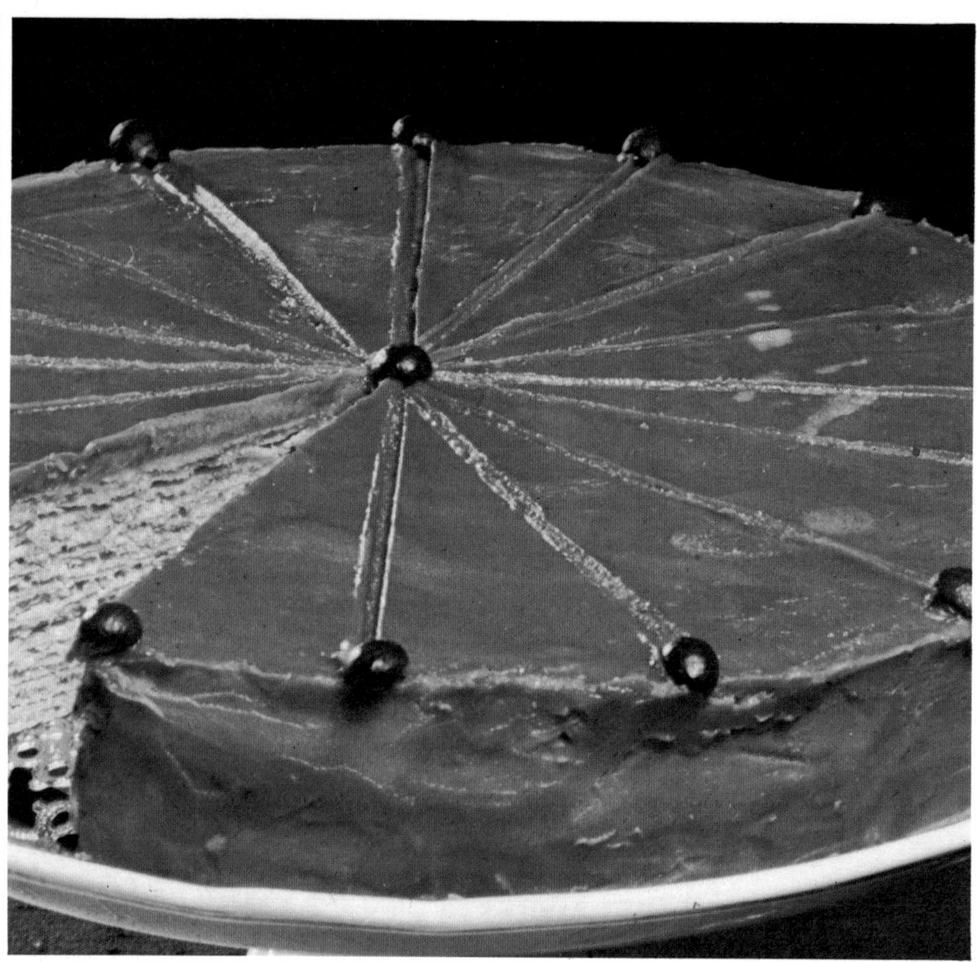

Viennese Torte.

Viennese Torte

1 packet round Vienna wafer biscuits
13 coffee beans for decoration

For coffee butter cream
2½ oz (62 g) softened, unsalted butter
5 oz (150 g) sifted icing sugar
1–2 tsp (5–10 ml) coffee liqueur
2–3 drops of coffee syrup

For coffee glacé icing
8 oz (225 g) sifted icing sugar
2 tbsp warmed coffee syrup

Make the coffee butter cream by creaming the butter in a mixing bowl until soft and light, then beat in the icing sugar and the coffee liqueur. Gradually stir in enough coffee syrup to flavour it delicately and still retain a fairly firm mixture. Spread butter cream over all the wafers except for one. Carefully sandwich them together, topping with the remaining plain wafer.

Make the coffee glacé icing. Sift the icing sugar into a bowl and gradually add coffee syrup. Mix until smooth and of a thick spreading consistency. Smooth glacé icing over the top and sides of the wafer cake, using a palette knife dipped in hot water.

Before the icing sets, mark off 12 portions with a sharp knife and place a coffee bean at the edge of each one; place remaining coffee bean in the centre.

Mocha Refrigerator Cake

For swiss roll mixture
4 oz (100 g) castor sugar
3 lightly beaten eggs
2½ oz (62 g) self raising flour

For chocolate filling
4 oz (100 g) softened, unsalted butter
12 oz (350 g) sifted icing sugar
1 egg yolk
1 tsp (5 ml) orange flower water
1 tsp (5 ml) rose water
8 oz (225 g) plain dessert chocolate, broken into pieces
1 tbsp (15 ml) coffee syrup
1 tbsp (15 ml) coffee liqueur
1 tbsp (15 ml) brandy

To decorate
¼ pt (15 cl) stiffly whipped double cream
chocolate rolls or leaves

Set the oven at 425°F (220°C) or Mark 7.

Line a swiss roll tin measuring 10 by 14 by ¾ inches (25 cm × 35 cm × 19 mm) with greased greaseproof paper cut to fit.

Make the swiss roll. Sift the castor sugar onto a foil plate and heat through in the pre-set oven for about 6 minutes or until hot. Then tip at once onto the lightly beaten eggs in a mixing bowl and beat hard until the mixture is foamy and almost doubled in volume. Sprinkle the flour over the top, then fold in, using a spatula.

Pour into the prepared tin and bake for 8–10 minutes or until golden and feathery in texture. Take out and cool on a wire rack.

When cold cut out 2 circles each 7 inch (18 cm) in diameter from the sponge (cut round a saucepan lid or dish of the same size). Put one round into 7 inch (18 cm) diameter springform cake tin with a removable base; reserve the other round for the top.

Make chocolate filling by creaming the butter in a mixing bowl until light and soft. Then gradually beat in the icing sugar, egg yolk and flavoured waters. Heat the plain dessert chocolate in a pan over a low heat until just liquid, then stir into the butter mixture. Beat in the coffee syrup, coffee liqueur and brandy until well combined. Leave the mixture for a few minutes to settle, then fill into the prepared tin and smooth over the top. Place the reserved sponge round on top, cover with foil and chill in the refrigerator until firm. When completely firm, unclip the tin and carefully remove the cake. Decorate with whipped cream and chocolate rolls.

Variation:
Cut sponge rectangle in half, then trim to fit a rectangular baking tin measuring about 9 by 5 by 3 inches (22×12×8 cm). Put one piece of sponge in the tin, then line the sides with either cats' tongues or Savoy biscuits, trimmed to fit. Fill with chocolate mixture and top with remaining piece of sponge. Chill as above, then turn out. Pipe a border of cream rosettes around the bottom of the cake and decorate with milk chocolate rolls.

Lemon Refrigerator Cake

For swiss roll mixture
4 oz (100 g) castor sugar
3 eggs
2½ oz (62 g) self raising flour

For lemon soufflé mixture
1 oz (25 g) powdered gelatine
juice and finely grated rind of 2 large lemons
5 eggs plus 5 egg yolks
7 oz (200 g) sifted icing sugar
½ pt (30 cl) double cream

Set the oven at 425°F (220°C) or Mark 7.

Line a swiss roll tin measuring 10 by 14 by ¾ inches (25 cm × 35 cm × 19 mm) with greased greaseproof paper cut to fit.

Make the swiss roll. Sift the castor sugar onto a foil plate and heat through for 6 minutes just above the centre of the pre-set oven. When hot tip at once onto the lightly beaten eggs in a mixing bowl and beat hard until the mixture is foamy and almost doubled in volume. Sprinkle the flour over the top and fold in.

Pour into the prepared tin and bake for –10 minutes or until golden and feathery in texture. Take out and cool on a wire rack. When cold cut in 2 equal pieces.

Make lemon soufflé mixture. In a pan over a low heat dissolve the gelatine in the lemon juice, take off the heat and leave for about 5 minutes or until spongy. In a mixing bowl beat together the eggs, egg yolks and icing sugar until thick and fairly stiff, and almost white in colour. Add the gelatine liquid a little at a time together with the lemon rind. Stir in the cream and blend until the mixture no longer looks streaky. Beat hard until the mixture starts to pull away from the sides of the bowl and to gel together.

Line a polythene box, similar in size to the cut pieces of sponge, with greaseproof paper cut to fit and with enough to hang out over the ends of the box (this will make it easier to turn the frozen cake out of the box). Place one piece of sponge in the box, then cover with the setting soufflé mixture and top with the other piece of sponge. Cover with foil and put the box in the ice making compartment of the refrigerator and leave until firm.

To serve, remove cake from the box and, for a special occasion, cover either end with rosettes of plain whipped cream, filling in the centre with piped coffee butter cream. Decorate with sugared oranges and lemons.

Almond Paste

☆ Basic Recipe

4 oz (100 g) ground almonds
8 oz (225 g) sifted icing sugar
1 lightly whipped egg white
½ tsp (2.50 ml) each orange flower water and rose water
cornflour for dusting

Knead together the ground almonds and icing sugar. Make a well in the centre and pour in half the egg white and the flavoured waters. Knead until a smooth paste is formed.

Turn paste onto work surface, dusting with cornflour, and knead until it resembles a soft but not sticky pastry dough. Only add more egg white if the paste is still crumbly. Wrap in foil and store in refrigerator.

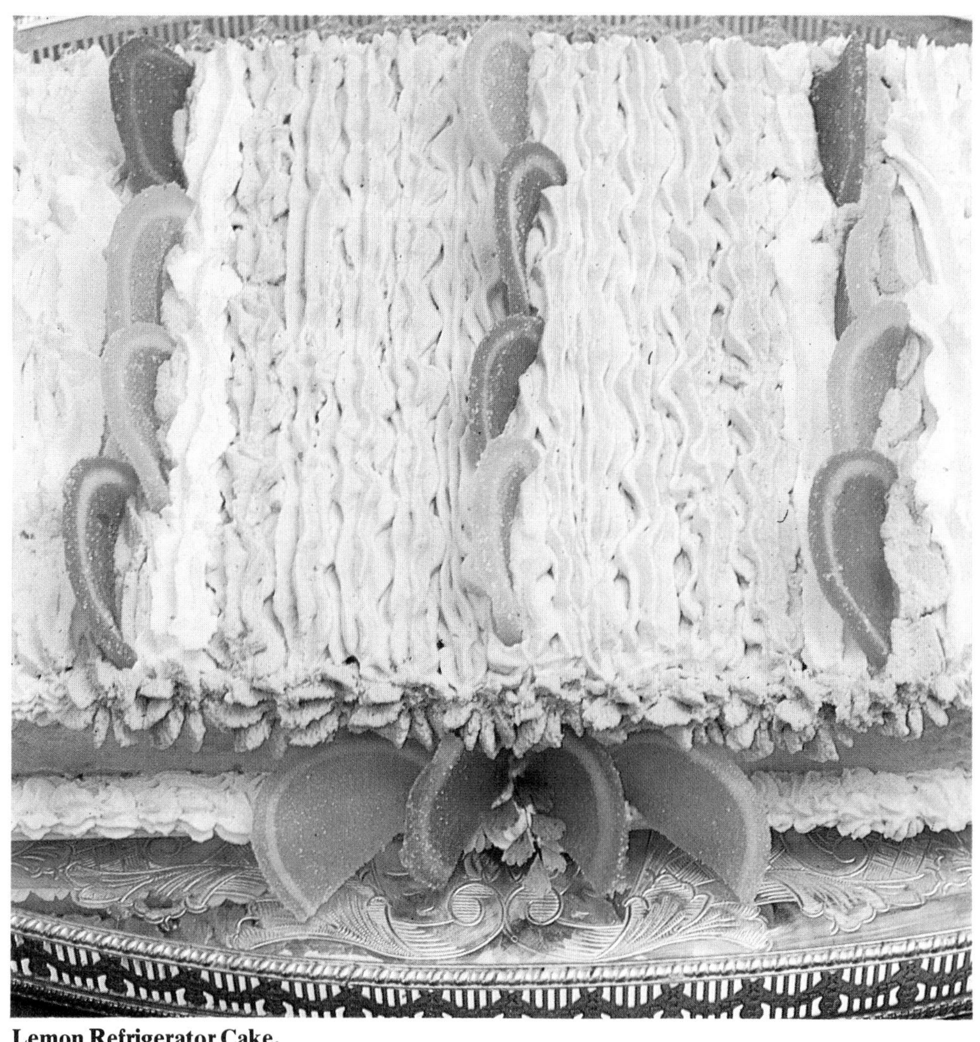

Lemon Refrigerator Cake.

Large cakes

Fruit Loaf Cake.

Fruit Loaf Cake

1 lb (450 g) mixed dried fruits or sultanas
8 oz (225 g) soft brown sugar
½ pt (30 cl) cold tea
1 lb (450 g) self raising flour
salt
1 lightly beaten egg
plain glacé icing to finish

Set the oven at 375°F (190°C) or Mark 5.

In a mixing bowl stir together the dried fruits or sultanas and the sugar. Stir in the strained tea. Sift the flour with a pinch of salt. Add to the mixture with the egg. Combine together until the mixture forms a soft dough, then turn into a greased and floured, 9 by 5 by 3 inches (22×12×8 cm), loaf tin. Bake in the pre-set oven fo 1 hour, then take out and cool slightly on wire rack before removing from the tin. I liked, cover loaf with a thin topping c plain glacé icing.

Cherry Cake

6 oz (175 g) softened unsalted butter
finely grated rind of 1 small lemon
8 oz (225 g) castor sugar
1 lb (450 g) self raising flour
4 eggs
12 oz (350 g) glacé cherries

Set the oven at 325°F (160°C) or Mark 3.

In a mixing bowl cream the butter with the lemon rind until very soft. Sift the flour, stir in 1 oz (25 g) and 1 egg, beat well. Continue adding the flour a little at a time, with an egg each time, and beating well. Then beat in the remaining flour until a smooth, creamy mixture is formed.

Put the glacé cherries in a sieve with a little flour and shake over a bowl; this will prevent them from sticking to each other. Fold them into the cake mixture.

Line the bottom and sides of a loose ottomed deep 8 inch (20 cm) cake tin vith a piece of greased and floured reaseproof paper cut to fit. Turn the mixure into the tin. Bake in the pre-set oven or about 1½ hours or until well risen and olden. Take out and cool in the tin for a vhile before turning out onto a wire rack o cool completely.

Note:

ruit tends to sink to the bottom of light ruit cakes and cherry cake is particularly otorious for having all the cherries lying n the base of the cooked cake. This is sually because the cake texture is not trong enough to support the weight of the ruit. The recipe above should result in venly distributed cherries, however, bear n mind the following points:

Do not wash the cherries unless they are specially sticky; dry thoroughly before sing.

Coat the cherries lightly in flour. Do this y turning the fruit with a little flour in a eve, then shaking off the surplus flour.

Lastly, do not open the oven door durg cooking. Draughts can also cause nking.

Carrot Cake

4½ oz (112 g) castor sugar
finely grated rind of 1 lemon
3 separated eggs
4½ oz (112 g) grated raw carrot
1 tbsp (15 ml) kirsch
4½ oz (112 g) ground almonds
2 oz (50 g) potato flour
2 oz (50 g) melted butter or margarine
icing sugar for sprinkling
almond paste carrots for decoration

Set the oven at 350°F (180°C) or Mark 4.

In a mixing bowl beat together the castor sugar, lemon rind and egg yolks until light and creamy. Stir in the grated carrots and kirsch; mix together the ground almonds and potato flour, then stir into the egg mixture and blend well. Stir in the melted butter or margarine.

In another bowl whisk the egg whites until stiff; then carefully and lightly fold them into the cake mixture to retain as much air as possible. Turn into a greased and floured 9 by 5 by 3 inches (22×12×8 cm) loaf tin and bake in the pre-set oven for 50 minutes or until golden.

Turn out and cool on a wire rack. Sprinkle with icing sugar and decorate with almond paste carrots if liked.

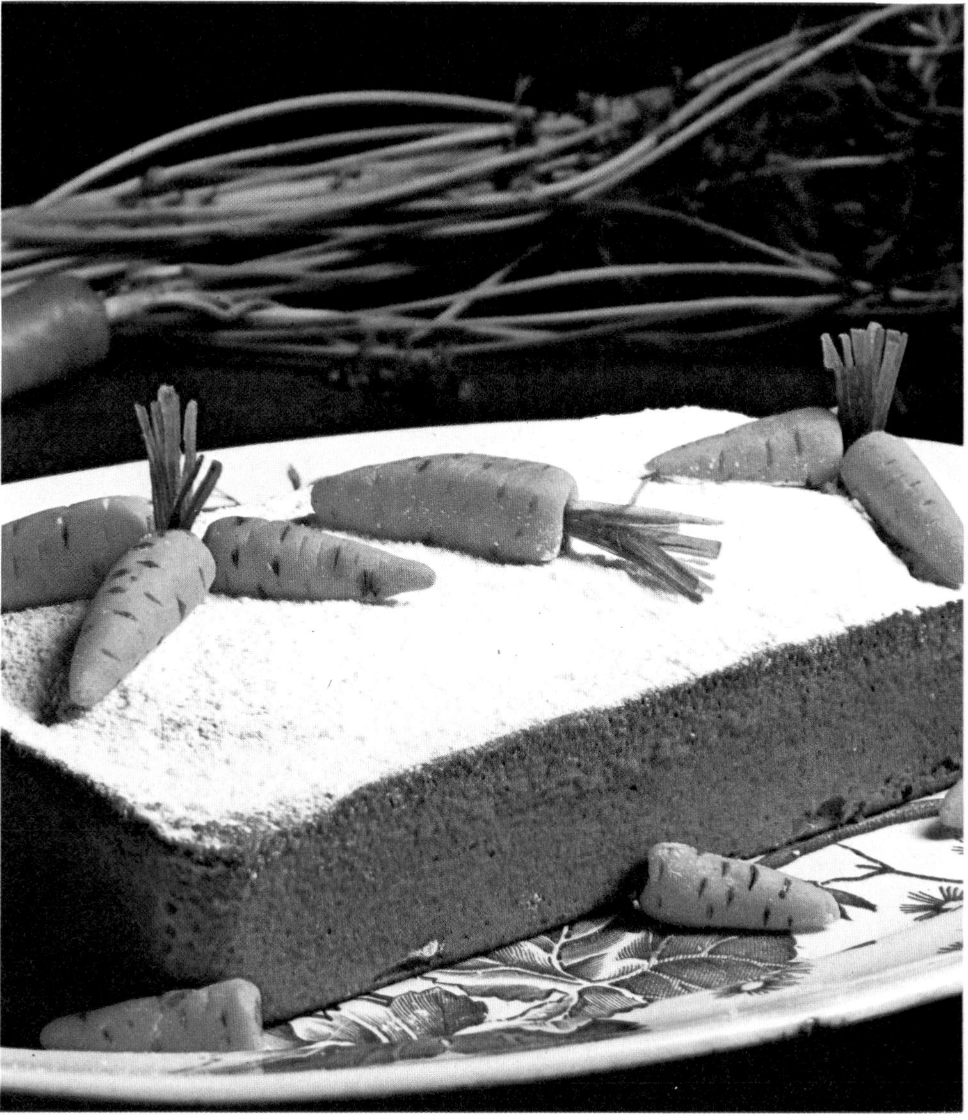

Carrot Cake.

Large cakes

Brown Ale Cake

11 oz (300 g) black treacle
2½ oz (62 g) butter or margarine
12 fl oz (35 cl) brown ale
9 oz (250 g) seedless raisins
13½ oz (387 g) self raising flour
salt
1 tsp (5 ml) cinnamon
grated nutmeg
ground cloves
1 tbsp (15 ml) baking powder
2 oz (50 g) chopped walnuts
icing sugar for sprinkling

Set the oven at 350°F (180°C) or Mark 4.

In a pan over a moderate heat melt the treacle and butter or margarine in the brown ale, then stir in the raisins. Take the pan off the heat and cool until tepid.

Sift together the flour, a pinch of salt, a pinch of each of the spices and the baking powder and stir into the treacle mixture. Stir in the walnuts, then turn the mixture into a greased and floured 9 inch (22 cm) ring mould or savarin tin and bake in the pre-set oven for 50 minutes. Take out and cool in the tin. Sprinkle with icing sugar.

Spicy Gingerbread

5 oz (150 g) lard
5 tbsp (75 ml) black treacle
7 oz (200 g) self raising flour
2 tsp (10 ml) ground ginger
1 egg
2½ oz (62 g) soft brown sugar
bicarbonate of soda
2 tbsp (30 ml) milk

Set the oven at 350°F (180°C) or Mark 4.

In a pan over a very low heat gently melt the lard in the treacle, then beat well. Sift the flour and ginger together, and in another bowl beat the egg with the brown sugar. Dissolve a pinch of bicarbonate of soda in the milk in a cup.

Pour the treacle mixture into the flour and ginger mixture, add the sugar mixture then the milk and bicarbonate of soda; blend together until smooth. Pour the mixture into a greased and floured 9 by 5 by 3 inch (22×12×8 cm) loaf tin and bake in the pre-set oven for about 30 minutes.

Take out of the oven, ease the gingerbread away from the sides of the tin and leave to cool completely.

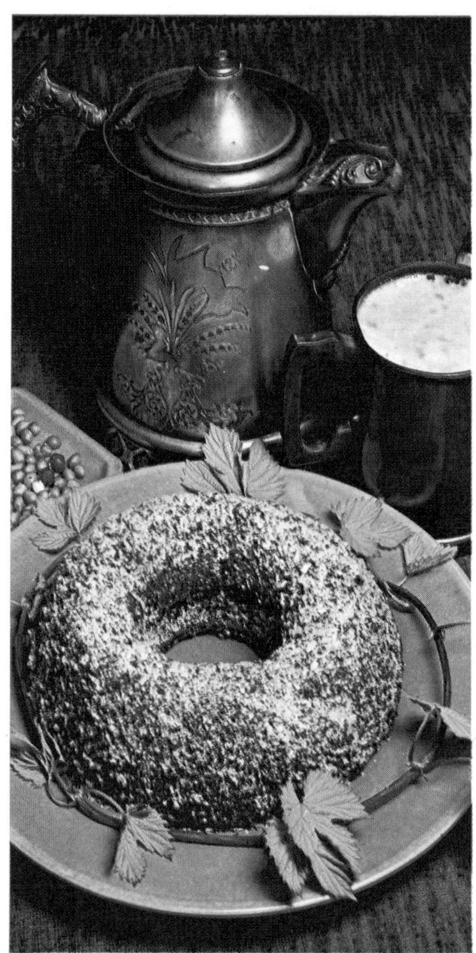

Brown Ale Cake.

Fruit and Nut Bread

6 small eggs
8 oz (225 g) castor sugar
7 oz (200 g) self raising flour
1 oz (25 g) potato flour
4 oz (100 g) sultanas
2 oz (50 g) chopped blanched almonds
2 oz (50 g) chopped hazelnuts
2 oz (50 g) candied lemon peel
2 oz (50 g) candied orange peel
2 tbsp (30 ml) dark rum
1 tsp (5 ml) lemon juice

For topping
4–6 oz (100–175 g) crushed sugar lumps or apricot glaze, 8 oz (225 g) crystallized fruits and 4 oz (100 g) roughly chopped walnuts

Set the oven at 325°F (160°C) or Mark 3.

In a mixing bowl work the eggs and sugar together until light and creamy. Sift the flours into another bowl and mix in the sultanas, nuts, candied peels and ground cinnamon. Mix the rum and lemon juice.

Add portions of flour mixture alternately with the rum and lemon juice to the egg mixture until all are incorporated. Blend together, then turn into a greased and floured 6–7 inch (15–18 cm) diameter deep cake tin.

Bake in the pre-set oven for about 1 hour or until a skewer comes away clean. Take out of the oven, turn out, upside down, and cool on a wire rack. When cold either cover with a topping of crushed sugar lumps and caramelize under a hot grill, or brush with warmed apricot glaze and cover with crystallized fruits and walnuts.

Moist Tea Bread

2 eggs
6 oz (175 g) castor sugar
10 oz (275 g) self raising flour
1 oz (25 g) butter or margarine
4 oz (100 g) chopped candied peel
2 oz (50 g) currants
1 tsp (5 ml) ground mixed spice
2 tsp (10 ml) baking powder
milk to mix

For topping
4–6 oz (100–175 g) sugar lumps, or apricot glaze, 8 oz (225 g) crystallized fruits and 4 oz (100 g) chopped walnuts

Set the oven at 325°F (160°C) or Mark 3.

In a mixing bowl beat the eggs and suga together until well blended. Sift the flou into another bowl. Rub the butter or mar garine into the flour until the mixtur resembles fine breadcrumbs, then stir i the rest of the ingredients except the milk.

Beat portions of the flour mixture int the egg mixture, together with just enoug milk to form a soft dropping consistency Turn into greased and floured 6–7 inc (15–18 cm) diameter deep cake tin an bake for about 1 hour or until a skewe comes away clean. Take out of the over turn out of the tin, upside down, on a wir rack to cool.

When cold either cover with a toppin of crushed sugar lumps and carameliz under a hot grill or brush with warme apricot glaze and cover with fruit and nut

picy Gingerbread in the foreground, Fruit and Nut Bread and, at the back, Moist Tea Bread.

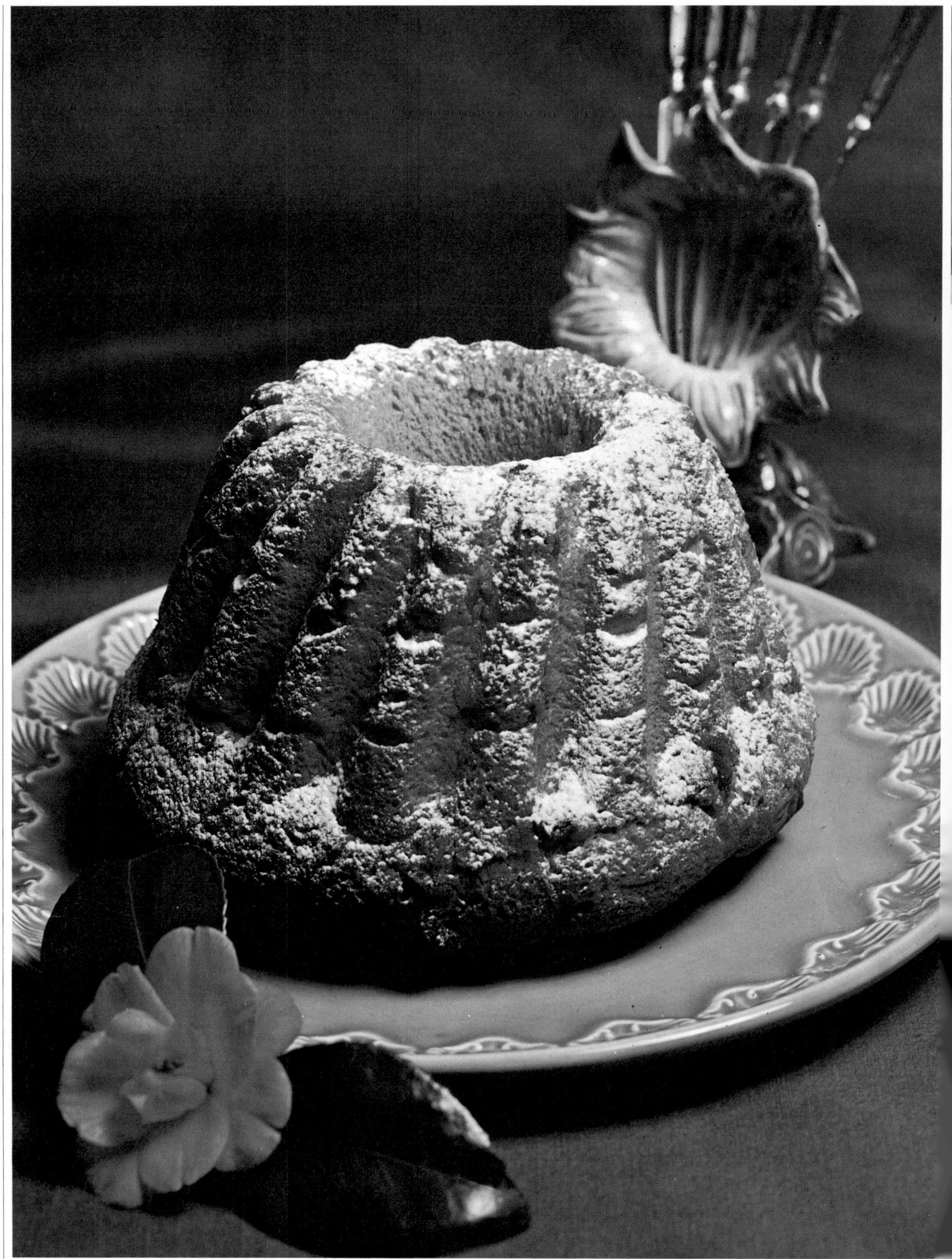

Kugelhopf.

Kugelhopf

½ oz (12 g) fresh yeast
9 oz (250 g) castor sugar
2 fl oz (5 cl) lukewarm water
1 lb 11 oz (750 g) self raising flour
1 tsp (5 ml) salt
1 tsp (5 ml) vanilla powder
4 oz (100 g) seedless raisins
3 oz (75 g) blanched, flaked almonds
finely grated rind of 1 lemon
2 beaten eggs
2½ oz (62 g) melted butter or margarine
10 fl oz (30 cl) warm milk
icing sugar for sprinkling

In a basin blend together the yeast and 2 tbsp (30 ml) castor sugar until completely dissolved and liquid. Stir in the lukewarm water and set aside yeast mixture to prove in a warm place for 30 minutes. Well grease a kugelhopf tin.

Warm a mixing bowl and sift the flour and salt into it. Stir in the remaining castor sugar, vanilla powder, raisins, almonds and lemon rind. Make a well in the centre of the mixture, tip in the yeast liquid and blend. Stir in the eggs a little at a time, then add the melted butter or margarine. Blend in enough of the warm milk to form a smooth dough. Lightly sprinkle with flour, cover with a warm cloth and stand the bowl in a warm place so the dough can prove for about 2 hours or until doubled in size.

Place the risen dough on a floured work surface. Using your fist, knock down the dough several times, then place in the prepared tin. Cover again with a warm cloth, put in a warm place and leave to rise for about 1 hour. Set the oven at 350°F (180°C) or Mark 4.

When risen put the cake into the pre-set oven and bake for about 1 hour or until a rich brown. If the top browns too quickly cover with a piece of greased greaseproof paper. When baked take out of the oven and cool on a wire rack.

Leave for 24 hours before cutting and sprinkle with icing sugar before serving.

Rum Coffee Cake

1 oz (25 g) fresh yeast
3¼ oz (82 g) castor sugar
1 lb (450 g) self raising flour
salt
1 tbsp (15 ml) milk
8 oz (225 g) softened butter or margarine
4 egg yolks plus 1 egg
1 tbsp (15 ml) dark rum
2 oz (50 g) sultanas

To finish
icing sugar for sprinkling
crystallized fruits
glacé cherries

Mix the yeast with 1 oz (25 g) sugar until it goes liquid, then stir in the milk and reserve. Sift the flour with a pinch of salt into a bowl.

In a mixing bowl cream the butter or margarine until soft and light and blend in the yeast liquid. Beat in the egg yolks one at a time, then beat in the whole egg, the remaining sugar and rum, together with about 2 oz (50 g) of the flour and blend well. Then carefully beat in the remaining flour a little at a time until incorporated. Fold in the sultanas and work the mixture with your hand until it forms a smooth dough. Stand the bowl in a warm place, cover with a warm cloth and leave the dough to prove for about 2 hours or until doubled in size.

Place the risen dough on a floured work surface and knock down with your fist a few times. Then put the dough into a greased kugelhopf or large brioche tin, cover with a warm cloth and leave to rise again in a warm place for about 30 minutes or until doubled in size.

Meanwhile set the oven at 350°F (180°C) or Mark 4

Bake the cake in the pre-set oven for 1 hour or until well risen and a rich brown. Take out of the oven and cool on a rack.

Turn out, then sprinkle with icing sugar and decorate with crystallized fruits and glacé cherries if liked.

Rum Coffee Cake.

Large cakes

Vanilla Coffee Cake.

Vanilla Coffee Cake

¼ oz (6 g) fresh yeast
9 oz (250 g) castor sugar
10 oz (275 g) softened butter or margarine
3 separated eggs
4 fl oz (10 cl) double cream
9 oz (250 g) self raising flour
vanilla powder

For cream topping
1½ oz (37 g) butter or margarine
5½ oz (162 g) soft brown sugar
vanilla powder
1 egg yolk
1½ tbsp (22 ml) orange liqueur or fresh orange juice
¼ oz (6 g) powdered gelatine
3-4 tbsp (45-60 ml) hot water
2 fl oz (5 cl) stiffly whipped double cream
finely ground pistachio nuts

Mix the yeast with 1 oz (25 g) sugar until it turns to a liquid, then set aside.

In a mixing bowl cream the butter or margarine until very soft and light, then work with the remaining sugar until light and fluffy. In another bowl beat the egg yolks with the cream.

Sift the flour and a pinch of vanilla powder into a mixing bowl, make a well in the centre and pour in the yeast liquid; work in just enough of the flour to absorb the liquid. Add the egg yolk mixture and blend well; cover the bowl with a warm cloth and stand in a warm place to prove for about 30 minutes. Set the oven at 350°F (180°C) or Mark 4.

Whisk the 3 egg whites until very stiff, then lightly fold into the proven yeast mixture. Turn the cake mixture into a greased and floured 8–9 inch (20–22 cm) loose bottomed, deep cake tin and bake in the pre-set oven for about 1 hour or until a skewer comes out clean. Take out of the oven, turn out, upside down, onto a wire rack to cool.

To make the cream topping: in a mixing bowl cream the butter or margarine until very soft, then cream with the sugar and a pinch of vanilla powder. Beat in the egg yolk, then the orange liqueur or juice. In a small pan dissolve the gelatine in the water over a very low heat and when clear and spongy (about 5 minutes) beat into the egg mixture. Fold in the stiffly whipped egg whites, then the whipped cream, then spread thickly over the top of the cake. Sprinkle with ground pistachio nuts to finish.

Dried Fruit Coffee Cake.

Dried Fruit Coffee Cake

5 oz (150 g) dried apple rings
5 oz (150 g) chopped dates
5 oz (150 g) dried figs
3 oz (75 g) chopped walnuts
2 oz (50 g) seedless raisins
2 tsp (30 ml) cinnamon
1 tbsp (15 ml) chopped candied peel
finely grated rind of 1 small lemon

4 fl oz (10 cl) brandy
½ oz (12 g) fresh yeast
8 fl oz (22 cl) lukewarm milk
1¼ oz (30 g) butter or margarine
9½ oz (262 g) castor sugar
1 egg
14 oz (400 g) self raising flour
salt

To finish
apricot glaze
about 8 dried apple rings, soaked in sugar syrup
about 16 seedless raisins, soaked in sugar syrup

Soak 5 oz (150 g) dried apple rings in water for about 6 hours, then simmer gently in a pan until tender; drain and chop finely. In a bowl mix them with the dried fruits, cinnamon, candied peel, lemon rind and brandy. Set aside.

In a small bowl dissolve the yeast in the milk and set aside for 5 minutes. In a mixing bowl cream the butter until soft, then cream with the sugar until pale and fluffy. Beat in the egg, then beat in the yeast liquid.

Sift the flour with a pinch of salt, then gradually blend into the yeast mixture until a smooth dough is formed. Turn the dough onto a floured work surface and knead for about 10 minutes. Put back in the bowl, cover with a warm cloth and stand in a warm place for about 2 hours or until the dough has doubled in size.

Turn the dough onto a floured surface, punch down with your fist a few times, then return to the bowl, cover again and stand in a warm place to prove for a further 45 minutes. Set the oven at 350°F (180°C) or Mark 4.

When proven cut a third of the dough and knead the dried fruits mixture into it. Grease and flour a deep cake tin. Roll the remaining dough into a round large enough to line the tin and overlap to form a lid. Put the dried fruits dough into the plain dough lined tin; brush the edges of the dough with a little cold water and fold over the flap of dough to cover it completely. Press the edges together where the doughs meet to seal.

Leave for about 20 minutes to prove, then bake just above the centre of the pre-set oven for about 45 minutes or until a light brown. Take out of the oven and turn out, upside down, on a wire rack to cool.

To finish, brush cooled cake with warmed apricot glaze, then place drained apple rings and raisins on top; brush again with apricot glaze.

Large cakes

Traditional Lardy Cake.

Traditional Lardy Cake

1 oz (25 g) fresh yeast
1¾ oz (45 g) castor sugar
1 lb 1½ oz (500 g) strong white flour
salt
6 oz (175 g) lard, cut in tiny pieces
4 oz (100 g) currants
3 oz (75 g) sultanas
9½ fl oz (29 cl) water
½ fl oz (12 ml) milk

For topping
1½ oz (32 g) butter or margarine
3 oz (75 g) soft brown sugar

Set the oven at 325°F (160°C) or Mark 3.

Put the yeast in a small bowl and work with the sugar until it becomes liquid. Add 5 fl oz (15 cl) tepid water to the yeast liquid and mix the remaining water with the milk.

Sift the flour and a pinch of salt into a mixing bowl then rub in 2 oz (50 g) lard until the mixture resembles fine breadcrumbs. Stir in the currants and raisins. Make a well in the centre and pour in the yeast liquid. Gradually blend in the flour mixture, using as much of the milk and water as is necessary to form a soft dough. Cover with a warm cloth and stand the bowl in a warm place to prove for about an hour or until the dough has approximately doubled in size.

Turn out onto a floured work surface, knead well, then roll out into a rectangle 9 by 3 inches (12 × 8 cm). Leave a border of about 1 inch (2.50 cm) all round and place tiny pieces of remaining lard all over as for puff pastry. Fold into a parcel by lifting one edge into the centre and folding the sides into the centre so they overlap; then fold other edge into the centre. Half turn the dough and roll out to the same sized rectangle as before.

Wrap in waxed paper and leave to rest for 30 minutes in a cool place. Repeat rolling, folding and turning process 3 times. The final dough should be about ¾–1 inch (19–25 mm) thick and about 2 inches (5 cm) wide. Cut the dough in 3 pieces, roll up and sit side by side in a greased and floured 6–7 inch (16–18 cm) square tin. Stand in a cold place to prove so the lard does not soften until the dough has risen enough just to fill the tin. Bake just above the centre of the pre-set oven for 35–40 minutes or until a light brown.

Meanwhile make the topping by creaming the butter or margarine with the sugar in a mixing bowl until creamy. As soon as the cake is baked, take out, remove from the tin and turn over; spread with the topping.

Variations:
For alternative shapes, bake lardy cake dough in a kugelhopf tin and sprinkle with icing sugar or using a 1 inch (2.50 cm) plain cutter stamp out rounds of dough and bake on a greased baking sheet; cover with topping while still hot.

Saffron Coffee Cake or Buns

¼ envelope of saffron
4 fl oz (10 cl) boiling water
¼ oz (6 g) fresh yeast
1 lb 2 oz (500 g) self raising flour
salt
4 oz (100 g) lard
2 oz (50 g) butter or margarine
2 oz (50 g) castor sugar
4 fl oz (10 cl) lukewarm milk
1 egg
3 oz (75 g) currants
3 oz (75 g) sultanas
1 oz (25 g) chopped candied peel

To decorate
icing sugar
citron peel

Put the saffron in a small basin, pour over the boiling water and infuse for 10 minutes; cool until tepid, then blend in the yeast. In a mixing bowl sift the flour with the salt, then rub in the fats until the mixture resembles fine breadcrumbs. Blend in the sugar. Make a well in the centre and pour in 3 tbsp (45 ml) warm milk, then the yeast liquid and cover with a little of the flour mixture.

Set aside until the yeast bubbles through the flour, then work to a soft dough, using more milk if required. Beat the egg and work into the dough, together with the dried fruits and candied peel. Cover with a warm cloth and stand the bowl in a warm place for the dough to prove and double in size – about 1½ hours. Set the oven at 400°F (200°C) or Mark 6.

Turn the dough into a greased and floured 9 inch (22 cm) diameter deep cake tin or bun tins and leave to rise for a further 15–20 minutes. Then bake in the pre-set oven for about 1 hour for the cake 45 minutes for the buns. Take out of the oven, turn out of the tin(s) and cool on a wire rack.

Sprinkle with icing sugar and decorate the large cake with pieces of citron peel.

affron Coffee Cake and Saffron Buns.

Special occasion cakes

The test of a really good cook is often whether he or she can produce a truly spectacular cake for a special occasion. Many of the cakes in this chapter could double as a dinner party dessert when you really want to impress your guests, and there are also cakes for Christmas, Easter, childrens' parties, weddings and any other occasion when you feel like celebrating. Naturally the cakes in this section require more time and effort but none of them are too difficult for a confident and competent cook. If you are doubtful, try your hand at something deceptively simple like Strawberry Shortcake.

Strawberry Mille Feuilles.

Strawberry Mille Feuilles

8 oz (225 g) quantity puff pastry
¼ pt (15 cl) double cream
1–1½ lb (450–700 g) strawberries, wiped, hulled and cut in half except for a few whole ones to be reserved for decoration
sifted icing sugar

For confectioners' custard
¼ pt (15 cl) milk
½ vanilla pod
1 egg yolk
½ oz (12 g) plain flour
2 oz (50 g) castor sugar

Set the oven at 400°F (200°C) or Mark 6.

On a cool floured surface roll out the puff pastry to a rectangle measuring about 15 by 11 inches (37 × 27 cm); it should be wafer thin and almost transparent. Cut out 5 rectangles each measuring 3 by 11 inches (8 × 28 cm), place on dampened baking sheets, spacing them fairly wide apart, and bake just above the centre of the pre-set oven for 10–12 minutes or until a light brown. Take out of the oven and cool slightly before carefully transferring to a wire rack. Stiffly whip the cream.

Make confectioners' custard. In a pan over a very low heat gently bring milk, together with the vanilla pod, just to simmering point; do not allow to boil. Remove pan from the heat and take out vanilla pod (wash and dry ready for re-use), then set milk aside. In a mixing bowl beat together the egg yolk, flour and sugar, then stir in the flavoured milk. Pour into a bain marie or into a basin stood over a pan of hot water. Using a wooden spoon, stir until the custard becomes thick and creamy and evenly coats the back of the spoon. Remove from heat and cool.

Choose one piece of pastry for the base and cover with cold confectioners' custard; put a second strip of pastry on top. Cover with halved strawberries, then whipped cream. Top with third strip of pastry, cover with confectioners' custard and follow with the fourth strip of pastry. Cover with more halved strawberries, then whipped cream and sprinkle with icing sugar. Top with remaining strip of pastry, propped on its side like an open lid, and arrange the whole reserved strawberries on top. Pipe on rosettes of cream if liked to decorate.

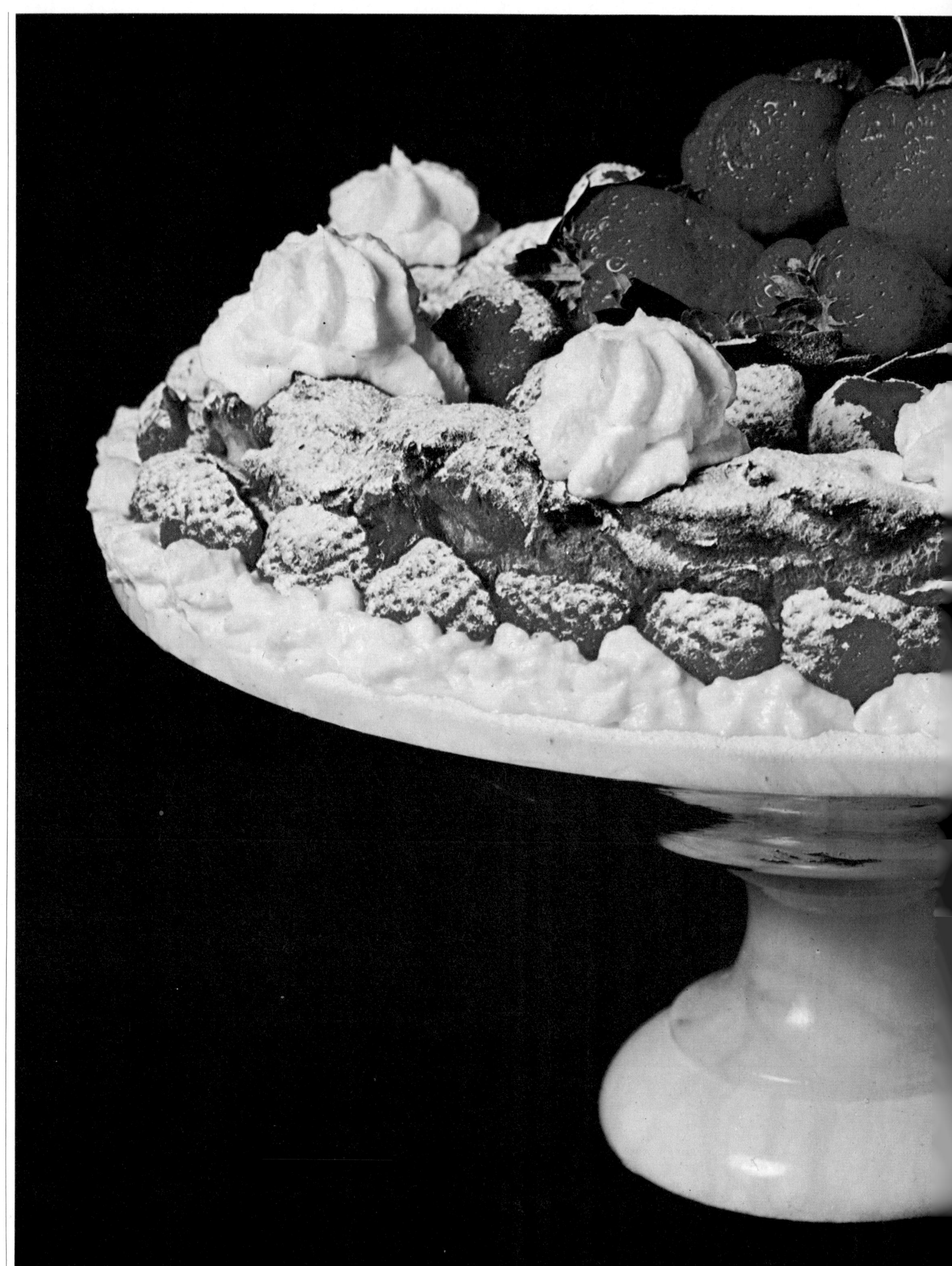

Strawberry Ring.

Special occasion cakes

Strawberry Ring

2½ egg quantity sweet choux paste
1 pt (60 cl) chantilly cream
2 lb (1 kg) strawberries
icing sugar for dusting

Set the oven at 425°F (210°C) or Mark 7.

Make the choux paste and put in a piping bag, fitted with a large rosette nozzle. Pipe an 8 inch (20 cm) ring onto a floured and greased baking sheet. Bake in the pre-set oven for 20 minutes.

Reduce the oven temperature to 350°F (175°C) or Mark 4 and remove the cake from the oven. Quickly cut some slits in the inner edge to allow steam to escape, then return to the oven for a further 10 minutes. Cool on a wire rack.

When cold, split and fill with chantilly cream and a few crushed strawberries. Decorate with more cream, piped in rosettes if liked, and whole strawberries. At the moment of serving, dust with sifted icing sugar.

Strawberry Shortcake

1½ lb (700 g) strawberries
icing sugar

For shortcake
8 oz (225 g) unsalted butter
4 oz (100 g) castor sugar
8 oz (225 g) plain flour
4 oz (100 g) rice flour

For chantilly cream
¼ pt (15 cl) chilled double cream
2 tsp (10 ml) castor sugar
1–2 drops of vanilla essence
1 egg white

Set the oven at 350°F (180°C) or Mark 4.

Wipe over the strawberries, pick out about 16 for the final decoration and set aside; hull the remainder and sprinkle with icing sugar.

Make the shortcake. Work the butter with the sugar with 2 knives on a work surface until soft; blend in the flours, again using the 2 knives, until a smooth dough is formed. Knead gently, then cut into 2 equal pieces.

Well grease and flour 2 7 inch (18 cm) diameter flan rings and place on a greased baking sheet.

Gâteau Rosamund.

Roll out each piece of shortcake to a round to fit the prepared flan rings. Bake in the pre-set oven for 10 minutes, then reduce heat to 325°F (160°C) or Mark 3, and continue baking until the shortcake is golden. Take out, cut one round carefully into half whilst still hot.

When cold place the whole shortcake round on the serving dish or platter; pile on enough whole strawberries to support the shortcake halves, arranged like wings.

Make the chantilly cream. In a bowl whip the cream until just thick but not firm; stir in the sugar and vanilla essence. In another bowl whip the egg white until very stiff and lightly fold into the cream. Fill chantilly cream into a piping bag fitted with a rosette nozzle and pipe rosettes of cream all round the edges of the shortcake and across the wings.

Gâteau Rosamund

oz (100 g) crushed Petit Beurre biscuits
fl oz (45 ml) kirsch
separated eggs
oz (100 g) plain dessert chocolate
tbsp (30 ml) water
oz (100 g) unsalted butter
oz (100 g) sifted icing sugar
oz (50 g) grapes
fl oz (45 ml) double cream

o decorate (optional)
oloured almond paste roses
aidenhair fern

n a small bowl soak the crushed biscuits in e kirsch. In a mixing bowl whip the egg hites until very stiff.

In a pan over a low heat dissolve the nocolate in the water and stir until mooth; take the pan off the heat and stir the butter, cut into tiny flakes, until elted and blended. Beat in the egg yolks ntil the mixture is smooth, then blend in e sugar, followed by the stiffly whipped g whites. Blend well. Peel and halve the apes, and discard the pips. Fold in the scuit mixture together with the grapes d the cream.

Line a well greased 5 inch (12 cm) ameter loose bottomed or springform ke tin with a piece of greased greaseoof cut to fit. Turn the cake mixture into e prepared tin and chill in the regerator until firm. Turn out carefully d remove paper on the bottom and derate according to choice.

Kirsch Cake.

Kirsch Cake

1¾ fl oz (45 ml) kirsch
3 fl oz (75 ml) sugar syrup
8 oz (225 g) quantity butter cream
1–2 drops of pink food colouring
3 oz (75 g) nibbed browned almonds

For Genoese sponge
2½ oz (62 g) sifted icing sugar
2 eggs
salt
2½ oz (62 g) self raising flour
2½ oz (62 g) melted butter

For hazelnut meringue
5 egg whites
8 oz (225 g) castor sugar
3 oz (75 g) finely ground hazelnuts

Set the oven at 350°F (180°C) or Mark 4.

Mix 1 fl oz (25 ml) kirsch with the sugar syrup; beat the remaining kirsch into the butter cream and add food colouring.

Make the Genoese sponge. In a mixing bowl stood over a pan of hot water beat together the sugar, eggs and salt until thick and foamy. Remove the bowl from the heat and continue beating until the mixture cools to about blood temperature. Sift the flour over the egg mixture and carefully fold in; stir in the melted butter.

Well grease 8 inch (20 cm) diameter sandwich tin and line with greased and floured greaseproof paper cut to fit. Turn into the prepared tin and bake in the pre-set oven for 20 minutes or until golden and the sponge springs back when lightly pressed with a fingertip. Take out and cool on a wire rack. When cold cut sponge in 2 equal halves. Reduce oven heat to 275°F (140°C) or Mark 1.

Make the hazelnut meringue. In a mixing bowl stiffly whip the egg whites until they stand in a peak. Sprinkle over 2 oz (50 g) of the sugar and whip again for about 3 minutes. Sprinkle over the remaining sugar and fold in lightly with a spatula, then fold in the ground hazelnuts. Spread the meringue in 2 large circles. Bake in the pre-set oven for 45 minutes. Take out and cool on a rack.

When cold spread one meringue round with a thin layer of butter cream and top with a sponge round. Sprinkle over half the kirsch and sugar syrup liquid to moisten, then cover with another thin layer of butter cream and the second sponge round. Sprinkle again with remaining kirsch liquid, then spread thinly with butter cream.

Put second meringue round on top and coat the sides of the completed gâteau with butter cream. Slide a cake slice under the gâteau to help you lift it cleanly and then turn it sideways on and roll through the nibbed almonds to coat the sides. Place gâteau on serving dish, spread more butter cream over the top and fill the rest into a piping bag fitted with a small rosette nozzle and pipe rosettes on top.

Gâteau St Honoré

For sweet shortcrust pastry
1 lb 2 oz (500 g) plain flour
salt
11 oz (300 g) butter
2 oz (50 g) sifted icing sugar
1 lightly beaten egg
¼ pt (15 cl) cold water

For sweet choux paste
1 oz (25 g) unsalted butter
¼ pt (15 cl) milk
1 sugar lump
3 oz (75 g) plain flour
2½ eggs

To finish
3 oz (75 g) castor sugar
3 tbsp (45 ml) water
½ pt (30 cl) confectioners' custard
½ pt (30 cl) chantilly cream

Set the oven at 350°F (180°C) or Mark 4.

Make the shortcrust pastry. Sift the flour and a pinch of salt onto your work surface, make a well in the centre and into this put the butter, sugar and egg. Using 2 knives, gradually blend the flour into the other ingredients, adding a little water from time to time, until a soft but not sticky dough is formed. Wrap in waxed paper and chill in the refrigerator for 30 minutes before rolling out to 8 inch (20 cm) diameter, ½ inch (12 mm) thick, round. Put on a greased and floured baking sheet and bake in the pre-set oven for 20–25 minutes or until golden. Take out and cool.

Increase the oven temperature to 400°F (200°C) or Mark 6. Make the sweet choux pastry. In a heavy based pan over a low heat melt the butter in the milk and heat until the milk starts to bubble. At once add the sugar and stir until it is dissolved. Increase the heat and bring the mixture to the boil, then stir in the flour at once and let the mixture bubble up quickly. Take off the heat immediately and beat in the eggs until a smooth paste is formed and it comes away cleanly from the sides of the pan. Set aside to cool.

When cold fill the choux paste into a piping bag fitted with a medium or small plain round nozzle and pipe about 16–18 choux buns onto greased and floured baking sheets, spacing them wide apart. Bake in the pre-set oven for 10–15 minutes or until puffed and golden. Take out and cool on a wire rack. Split in half when cold and fill with a little confectioners' custard. To finish the cake, place pastry base on a serving dish. In a heavy based pan over a low heat dissolve the sugar in the water, then bring to the boil and boil until the syrup starts to go straw coloured at the edges. Remove from the heat at once.

Dip the choux buns in the syrup, using a pair of kitchen tongs, and arrange in 2 circles, one on top of the other, around the pastry base. Use the syrup to anchor them in position. Spoon confectioners' custard into the centre of the cake, then cover with about two thirds of the chantilly cream. Fill the remaining chantilly cream into a piping bag fitted with a rosette nozzle and pipe rosettes on top and over the cake.

La Religieuse.

La Religieuse

For sweet shortcrust pastry
8 oz (225 g) plain flour
4 oz (100 g) softened unsalted butter
2 oz (50 g) castor sugar
1 egg yolk
4 fl oz (5 cl) cold water

For sweet choux paste
2 oz (50 g) unsalted butter
½ pt (30 cl) milk
2 sugar lumps
6 oz (175 g) plain flour
5 eggs

For flavoured confectioners' custard
½ pt (30 cl) milk
1 vanilla pod
3 egg yolks
1 oz (25 g) plain flour
4 oz (100 g) castor sugar
1 tbsp (15 ml) coffee syrup
2 oz (50 g) plain dessert chocolate, broken into pieces and softened until just liquid
4 fl oz (5 cl) stiffly whipped double cream

To finish
4 oz (100 g) plain dessert chocolate
1¼ oz (32 g) unsalted butter
5 oz (150 g) sifted icing sugar
1 tbsp (15 ml) coffee syrup
½ pt (30 cl) double cream

Set the oven at 350°F (180°C) or Mark 4.

Make the shortcrust pastry. Sift the flou onto your work surface, make a well in the centre and into this put the fat, sugar an egg yolk. Using 2 knives, gradually blen the flour into the other ingredients adding a little water from time to time, until a sof but not sticky dough is formed. Wrap i waxed paper and chill in the refrigerato for 30 minutes before rolling out to 8 inc (20 cm) diameter, ¼ inch (6 mm) thick round. Put on a greased and floured bak ing sheet and bake in the pre-set oven fo 20–25 minutes or until golden. Take ou and cool on a wire rack.

Grease 2 baking sheets and increase th oven temperature to 400°F (200°C) o Mark 6. Make the sweet choux paste. In heavy based pan over a low heat melt th butter in the milk and heat until the mil starts to bubble. At once add the sugar an stir until it is dissolved. Increase heat an bring mixture to the boil, then sift in th flour, stirring at once and let the mixtur bubble up quickly. Take off the heat im mediately and beat in the egg until smooth paste is formed and it comes awa cleanly from the sides of the pan. Set asid to cool completely.

When cold fill the choux paste into piping bag fitted with a large plain roun nozzle and pipe 8 large éclairs onto one c the prepared baking sheets. Pipe 2 chou buns, one 2 inch (5 cm) in diameter, th other 1 inch (2.50 cm) in diameter, on th other baking sheet. Bake in the pre-se oven for about 15 minutes or until puffe and golden. Take out and cool on a rack

Make the flavoured confectioners' cus-
ard. In a pan over a very low heat gently ring the milk, together with vanilla pod, ust to simmering point; do not allow to oil. Remove pan from the heat, take out anilla pod (wash and dry ready for re-se), then set milk aside. In a mixing bowl eat together the egg yolks, flour and ugar, then stir in the flavoured milk. Pour ıto a bain marie or into a basin stood over pan of hot water. Using a wooden spoon, ir until the custard thickens and becomes reamy and evenly coats the back of the ɔoon. Remove from the heat and divide ıto 2 portions. Beat the coffee syrup into ne half, the melted chocolate into the ther (this half must be still fairly hot or mps can form). When the chocolate cus-rd is lukewarm, beat in half the whipped eam. When the coffee custard is cold, eat in the remaining cream.

Split the éclairs and choux buns in half d fill half the éclairs and the small bun th coffee custard; reserve any custard ft over. Fill chocolate custard into the maining éclairs and choux bun, again serving any custard left over. Beat to-ther the leftover custards and spread er the sweet shortcrust pastry round to thin 1 inch (2.50 cm) of its edge.

To finish and assemble the gâteau, first elt the chocolate pieces and butter in a avy based pan over a low heat and stir nstantly until blended. Cool a little, en dip the chocolate filled éclairs and n into this icing to cover the tops. Stand a wire rack to set. Blend the icing sugar h the coffee syrup, adding a few drops warm water to thin the icing if too thick spread. Dip the remaining éclairs and n in this icing to coat the tops and set on ire rack to firm.

Press the éclairs, alternating coffee with ocolate flavours, almost vertically into butter cream topped pastry base so y lean slightly inwards at the top and m a circle. Place the chocolate choux n on top, anchoring it with a little am, then top with the coffee choux bun, in securing it with cream. Fill remain-cream into a piping bag fitted with ious decorative nozzles and pipe roset-and other shapes around the bottom e, vertically between the éclairs and at points where the choux buns sit on one other.

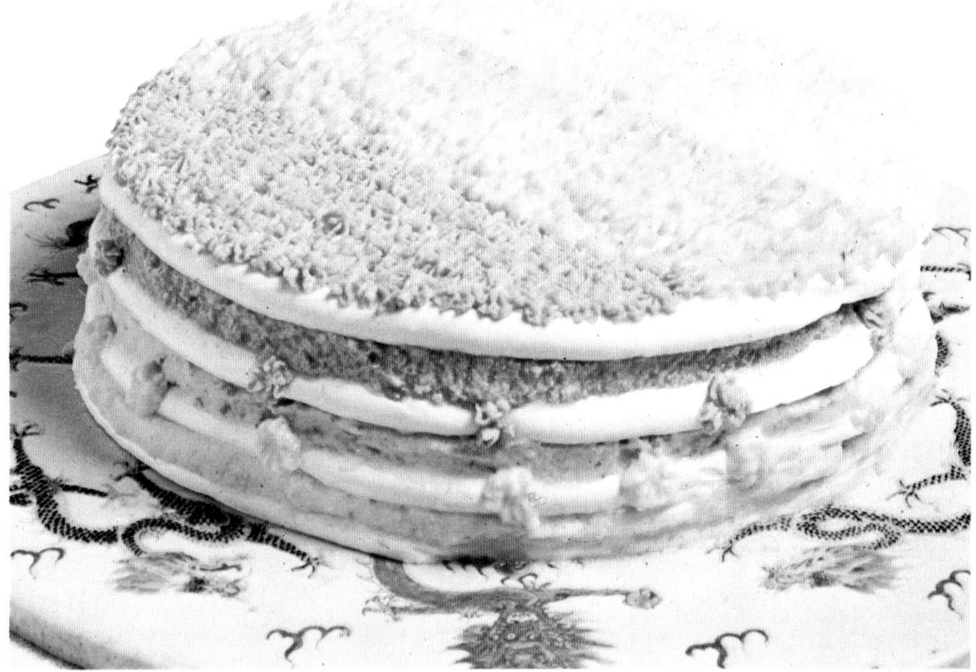

Neopolitan Meringue Cake.

Neopolitan Meringue Cake

4 egg white quantity of basic Italian meringue
½ pt (30 cl) stiffly whipped double cream
14 oz (400 g) softened unsalted butter
coffee syrup
kirsch
3 oz (75 g) finely ground pistachio nuts
1–2 drops of green edible food colouring

For confectioners' custard
1 pt (60 cl) milk
1 vanilla pod
6 egg yolks
2 oz (50 g) plain flour
8 oz (225 g) castor sugar

Faintly trace 4 circles, each 8 inches (20 cm) in diameter, on the reverse side of a large sheet of waxed paper, spread on a baking sheet. Spread the meringue equally over the circles, starting from the centre of each one and easing the meringue out towards the edge with a palette knife. Leave over-night to dry out, then stand above a warm stove to complete the drying if necessary. Peel off the paper.

Make the confectioners' custard. In a large pan over a very low heat gently bring the milk, together with the vanilla pod, just to simmering point; do not allow to boil. Remove pan from heat, take out vanilla pod (wash and dry ready for re-use), then set the milk aside. In a mixing bowl beat together the egg yolks, flour and sugar, then stir in the flavoured milk. Pour into a bain marie or a basin stood over a pan of hot water. Using a wooden spoon, stir until the custard thickens and becomes creamy and evenly coats the back of the spoon. Remove from the heat and leave until cold.

Beat the whipped cream into the cold custard; cream the butter until light and soft, then beat into the custard mixture. Split into 3 equal portions. Flavour one portion with coffee syrup, one with kirsch and blend the other into the ground pistachio nuts; then colour this pastel green.

Spread a little of the kirsch flavoured cream over one meringue round and make this the base of the cake; reserve remaining cream. Top with a second meringue round and spread with the green cream, again reserving enough cream for piping on top of the finished cake. Place the third meringue round on top and cover with a little of the coffee flavoured cream. Top with the remaining meringue.

Fill the reserved creams, separately, into a piping bag fitted with a small rosette nozzle and pipe 3 bands of cream rosettes over the top to decorate, as well as a few rosettes around the sides. Leave in a cool place for a few hours before serving so the meringue softens a little.

If serving immediately, dip a sharp knife into boiling water so the blade cuts cleanly through without shattering the meringue.

Paradise Meringue

4 egg white quantity of basic Italian meringue
2 ripe pears
2 peaches
4 slices of canned pineapple
redcurrant or apricot glaze
2 oz (50 g) finely ground pistachio nuts

For confectioners' custard
½ pt (30 cl) milk
1 vanilla pod
3 egg yolks
1 oz (25 g) plain flour
4 oz (100 g) castor sugar

For chantilly cream
¼ pt (15 cl) chilled double cream
2 tsp (10 ml) castor sugar
1–2 drops of vanilla essence
1 egg white

Make the confectioners' custard. In a pan over a very low heat gently bring the milk, together with the vanilla pod, just to simmering point; do not allow to boil. Remove pan from the heat, take out the vanilla pod (wash and dry ready for re-use), then set the milk aside. In a mixing bowl beat together the egg yolks, flour and sugar, then stir in the flavoured milk. Pour into a bain marie or into a basin stood over a pan of hot water. Using a wooden spoon, stir until the custard thickens and becomes creamy and evenly coats the back of the spoon. Remove from the heat and leave to cool.

On the reverse side of a large piece of waxed paper draw 9 inch (22 cm) diameter circle; place paper, waxed side up, on a baking sheet. Spoon about three quarters of the meringue into the outlined circle, spreading it out towards the edges with a palette knife, until you have a meringue round about ¾ inch (19 mm) thick. Leave in a warm place to dry out until the top of the meringue is firm. Fill remaining meringue into a piping bag fitted with large nozzle and pipe a 'rope' border all around the meringue circle; on a tiny piece of waxed paper, pipe a small meringue whirl or pyramid, finishing with a peak, and leave to dry until firm. Then carefully peel off the paper from the meringues and lift the round onto a serving dish.

Wash, peel, halve and core the pears; wipe, skin and halve the peaches. Spread confectioners' custard over the meringue

Paradise Meringue.

base. Arrange peach and pear halves alternately in a circle on the custard; stack the pineapple rings in the centre. Brush thickly with chosen glaze. Place meringue whirl on top of the pineapple and sprinkle pistachio nuts over the pears.

Make the chantilly cream. In a bowl whisk the cream until just thick, stir in the sugar and vanilla essence. In another bowl stiffly whip the egg white and fold into the cream. Fill into a piping bag fitted with a rosette nozzle and pipe rosettes all round inside the meringue case, between each piece of fruit and around the base of the pineapple rings.

Basic Italian Meringue

Basic Recipe

1¼ lb (456 g) granulated sugar
17½ fl oz (406 ml) water
4 egg whites

This type of meringue needs no cooking; instead it is left to dry out for at least 12 hours until it becomes firm.

In a large pan over a low heat put the sugar in the water and leave, unstirred, until the sugar is completely dissolved. Bring to the boil and allow to boil for about 4 minutes. Keep it at a rolling boil and, using a perforated metal spoon, lift in and out of the syrup, gently blowing through the holes until clear bubbles of liquid slip from the spoon.

While this is being done, enlist another pair of hands to whip the egg whites until very stiff. As soon as the syrup is ready, pour it at once onto the egg whites and continue beating hard until the meringue forms a very stiff mixture again. Use according to recipe. If covered with a damp cloth, the meringue will remain soft enough to pipe if required.

Meringue Pavé

8 oz (225 g) browned flaked almonds
icing sugar for sprinkling

For Swiss meringue
10 egg whites
1 lb (450 g) castor sugar

For coffee butter cream
6 oz (175 g) softened unsalted butter
12 oz (350 g) sifted icing sugar
3–4 tbsp (45–60 ml) coffee syrup

Set the oven at 275°F (140°C) or Mark 1

Make the meringue in 2 batches (halve th ingredients given above). In a mixing bow stiffly whip the egg whites until they stan in a peak. Sprinkle over 2 oz (50 g) of th sugar and whip again for about 3 minute Sprinkle over remaining sugar and fold in

Line 2 baking sheets with a piece of we greased greaseproof paper cut to fit. Dro spoonfuls of meringue onto the prepare baking sheets, spacing them fairly wid apart, and bake in the pre-set oven f about 55 minutes or until pale brown ar crisp. Take out and cool on a rack.

Make the coffee butter cream. In a mi ing bowl cream the butter until pale an soft, then gradually beat in the icing suga and enough coffee syrup to blend to smooth mixture.

Crumble the cold meringues into a mi ing bowl and blend in just enough of t butter cream to form a smooth ball paste, working the mixture in your hand Divide the paste in half, then place ea one on a piece of waxed paper and roll o into 2 equal narrow strips. Cover one str with butter cream. Top with the remaini strip, using 2 palette knives to lift it, th cover the top and sides with butter crea Sprinkle thickly with browned almond then icing sugar. Pipe rosettes of coff butter cream around the base.

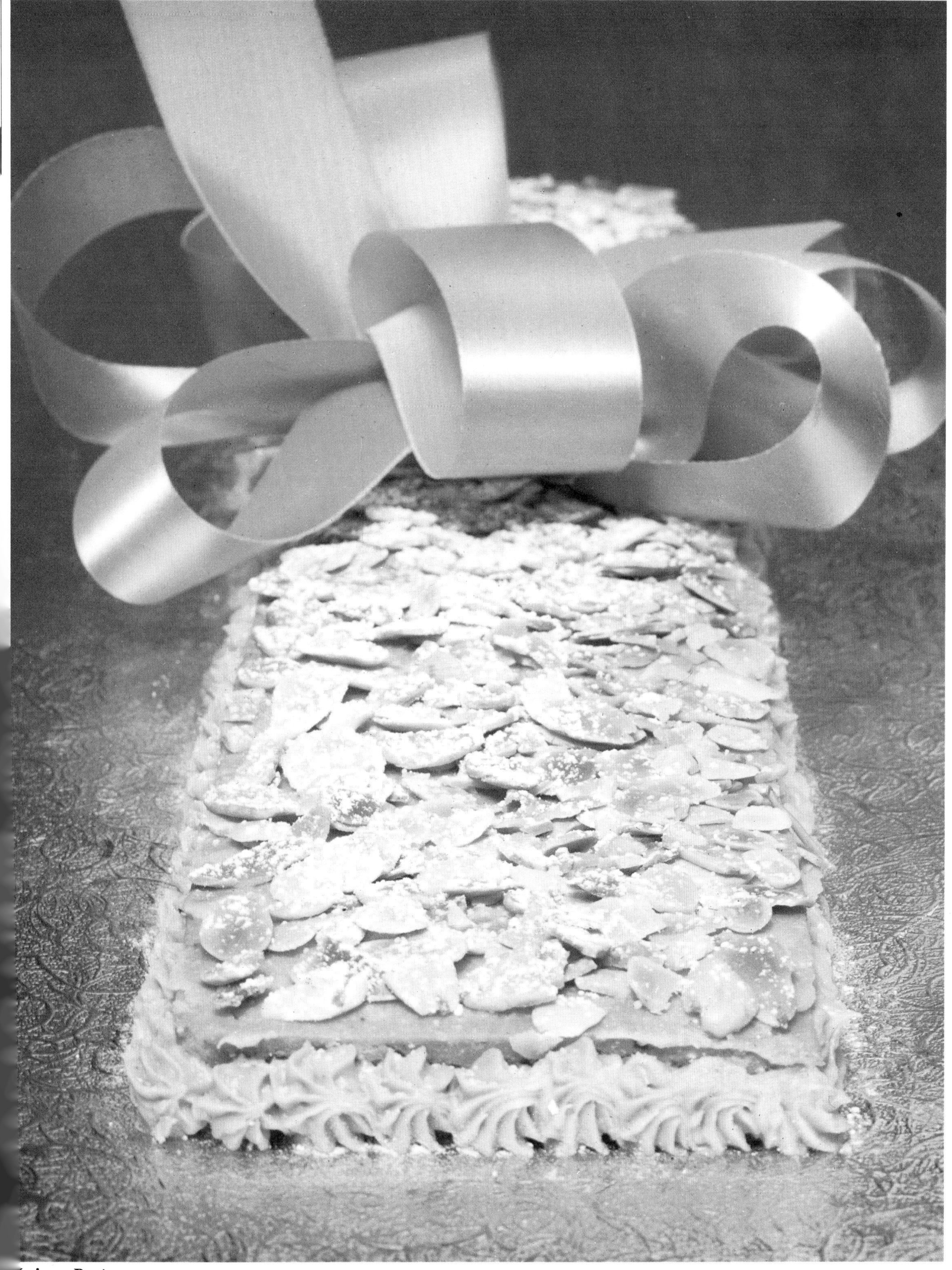

Meringue Pavé.

Special Chocolate Gâteau

8 oz (225 g) softened butter or margarine
8 oz (225 g) castor sugar
4 eggs
7½ oz (212 g) self raising flour
½ oz (12 g) cocoa powder

For filling and decoration
6 oz (175 g) butter quantity coffee butter cream
chocolate flakes

Set the oven at 350°F (180°C) or Mark 4.

Put the fat and sugar into a mixing bowl and cream until pale coloured and fluffy. Using a metal spoon, fold in a quarter of the flour, then carefully beat in 1 egg, a little at a time to avoid curdling the cake batter. Continue folding in portions of flour, including the cocoa powder with the last one and followed by an egg each time, until all are incorporated.

Well grease 2 8 inch (20 cm) diameter sandwich tins and line with greased and floured greaseproof paper cut to fit. Pour cake batter into tins.

Bake cakes in the pre-set oven for 20 minutes or until well risen and firm to the touch, and they just pull away from the sides of the tins. Take out and cool on a wire rack.

When cold, sandwich sponge rounds with half the coffee butter cream, then spread remainder over the top. Decorate with chocolate flakes.

Chocolate and Chestnut Gâteau

1 lb (450 g) can of unsweetened chestnut purée
4 oz (100 g) plain dessert chocolate
1 tbsp (15 ml) coffee syrup
4 oz (100 g) butter or margarine
4 oz (100 g) sifted icing sugar

To decorate
¼ pt (15 cl) double cream

Stand the opened can of chestnut purée in a pan of hot water and heat through until warm to the touch.

Break the chocolate into tiny pieces and melt in a bowl over a pan of hot water until it is just liquid. Remove from the heat and beat in the coffee syrup. Cut the butter or margarine into tiny pieces and stir into the chocolate mixture. When absorbed, blend in the icing sugar and then add the chestnut purée. Beat well until smooth.

Pour the mixture into a greased 8 by 2 inches (20 × 5 cm) square cake tin or a large shallow rectangular tin. Chill in the refrigerator for 24 hours.

Turn onto a serving dish. Whip the cream until stiff, then fill into a piping bag fitted with a large nozzle. Carefully pipe a border of cream around the cake and in the centre.

HOW TO MAKE CHOCOLATE ROLLS

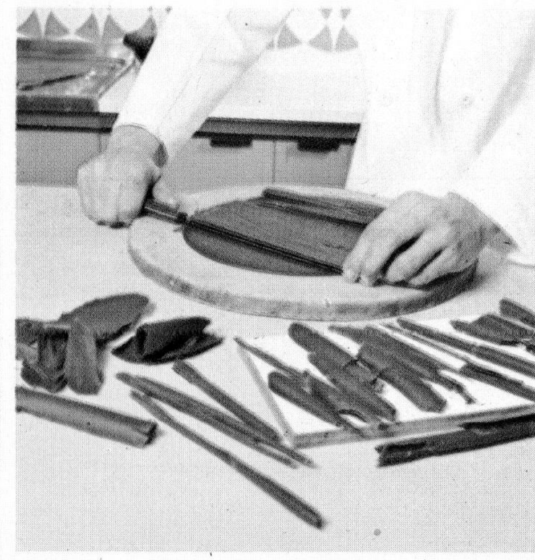

Melt plain dessert chocolate in a pan over a low heat. Pour onto a very cold work surface (marble is best), spreading it out smoothly and evenly with a spatula. When almost firm but not hard, take a broad bladed knife and hold it at either end with the blade horizontal to the chocolate at the edge furthest away from you. With the cutting edge at an angle to the chocolate, draw the blade across the chocolate towards you and shave off thin rolls. Leave until firm before using.

Mocha Cake.

Mocha Cake

3 eggs plus 1 egg yolk
5 oz (150 g) castor sugar
2¼ oz (56 g) self raising flour
4 oz (100 g) plain dessert chocolate, broken into pieces and melted until just liquid

For coffee almond paste
4 oz (100 g) ground almonds
8 oz (225 g) sifted icing sugar
1 lightly whipped egg white
1 tsp (5 ml) coffee syrup
cornflour for dusting

To decorate
apricot glaze
chocolate flakes
drinking chocolate powder for sprinkling

Set the oven at 350°F (180°C) or Mark 4.

In a mixing bowl stood over a pan of hot water whisk together the eggs, egg yolk and sugar until thick, creamy and almost doubled in volume. Remove the bowl from the heat and continue whisking until just tepid. Sprinkle over the flour, then fold in lightly with a metal spoon, until blended. Stir in the melted chocolate.

Well grease and flour sides of 8 inch (20 cm) diameter sandwich tin and line with greased and floured greaseproof paper cut to fit. Turn the mixture into the prepared tin and bake in the pre-set oven for about 25 minutes or until risen and the cake just pulls away from the sides of the tin. Take out and turn onto a wire rack to cool; remove paper from the base.

Meanwhile make the almond paste. In a mixing bowl work together the ground almonds and the icing sugar with your hand. Make a well in the centre and pour in half the egg white and the coffee syrup. Work again until a smooth paste is formed. Turn onto a work surface dusted with cornflour and knead to a soft dough. Only add remaining egg white or part of it if the paste stays stiff and crumbly. Roll out to a round large enough to cover the top and sides of the chocolate cake.

To decorate: brush the cake with warmed apricot glaze, then cover with the almond paste. Tie a satin ribbon around the sides of the cake. Pile chocolate flakes on top and sprinkle with drinking chocolate powder.

Croquembouche with Spun Sugar.

HOW TO SPIN SUGAR

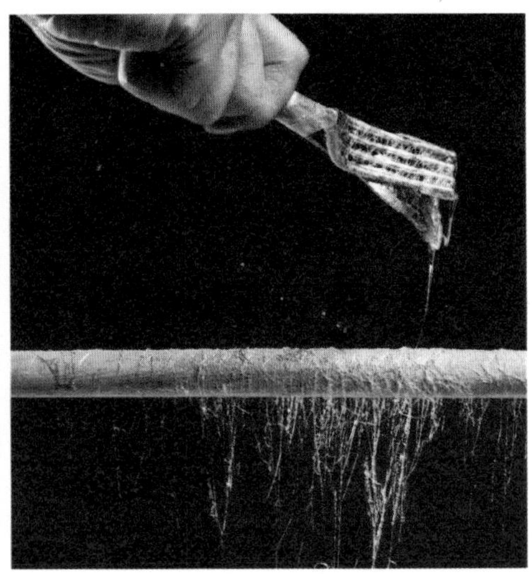

1. Practice the technique first on a clean broom handle or pole, balanced between 2 chairs. Spread newspaper on the floor below. Hold 2 forks back to back, dip the prongs in the sugar mixture and flick over the broom handle.

2. This is the effect you will achieve: long, hairlike strands of spun sugar falling from the broom handle to the floor. When you feel confident, apply the same technique to making a sugar veil for the cake.

Croquembouche with Spun Sugar

several batches of basic sweet choux paste
1½ lb (700 g) sugar quantity of royal icing
chantilly cream

For spun sugar syrup
14 oz (400 g) granulated sugar
¼ pt (15 cl) cold water
½ tsp (2.5 ml) liquid (not powdered) glucose
2 tsp (10 ml) cream of tartar

A croquembouche gâteau can be as large or as small as you want to make it, so it is not really possible to specify exact quantities of choux pastry. Stand the croquembouche on a cake board, the size being dependent, of course, on the diameter of the base of the gâteau; the completed croquembouche should lean slightly inwards as it tapers off towards the top, the diameter of which should be no more than 5 inches (12 cm).

Set the oven at 400°F (200°C) or Mark 6.

Fill the cold choux paste into a piping bag fitted with ½ inch (12 mm) plain nozzle and pipe into rounds of decreasing sizes, spacing them well apart, on greased baking sheets. The largest rounds will form the base of the croquembouche, and the tiers of choux buns should go down in size gradually as the pyramid rises. Bake in the pre-set oven for 10–15 minutes or until puffed and golden. Take out and cool on a wire rack.

Make the spun sugar syrup. In a heavy based pan over a very low heat dissolve the sugar in the water and glucose. Meanwhile prepare close at hand a large heat resistant bowl, filled with enough crushed ice to come halfway up, and a pastry brush. When the sugar has dissolved increase the heat so the syrup comes to a steady boil. At once sprinkle over the cream of tartar, then stir in. Then begin dipping the brush into the ice and brush around the 'water' line where the syrup bubbles break against the sides of the pan. The water on the brush prevents any crystals of sugar forming. When the sugar syrup turns a dark yellow colour (but not brown), remove from the heat at once and push down the pan into the bowl of ice to stop the syrup cooking and darkening any further and to thicken it. After about 3 minutes the syrup should be thick enough to coat lightly a slice of fruit without being tacky. If it is still tacky, return the pan of syrup to the stove and boil for about 3 minutes longer.

Dip the largest choux buns in the syrup and place in a circle on the cake board to within about ½ inch (12 mm) of the edge. Continue building up the tiers until all the choux buns are used up. Fill in the tiny gaps between them with piped rosettes of royal icing, using a small rosette nozzle, and leave to harden. Then fill the centre of the croquembouche with as much chantilly cream as it takes to come right to the top. Leave for about an hour to settle in a cool place. If decorating with flowers, gently ease a slim plastic flower holder into the cream filling then refrigerate if possible.

Just before serving, spin the sugar syrup into wispy strands as follows: hold 2 forks back to back; dip the tips of the prongs into the sugar syrup, then flick them lightly from side to side so the syrup falls in wispy thin strands over the croquembouche. This is very tricky indeed so first practice spinning the sugar over a thin cylindrical object like a clean mop or broom handle suspended between 2 chairs, and with plenty of newspaper on the floor.

Arrange the flowers in the concealed holder and decorate with a long trail of ribbon if liked. Serve at once.

The Croquembouche is traditionally served at weddings in France. Its origins are shrouded in the mists of time, but are believed to be connected with fertility rites.

Without the spun sugar veil, ribbon and floral decoration, the croquembouche can be served at special occasions other than weddings.

HOW TO DECORATE A THREE TIER WEDDING CAKE

Wedding Cake

3 lb (1.35 kg) softened butter
3 lb (1.35 kg) soft brown sugar
3 lb (1.35 kg) self raising flour
2 tbsp (30 ml) grated nutmeg
2 tbsp (30 ml) cinnamon
2 tbsp (30 ml) ground cloves
2 tbsp (30 ml) ginger
1½ lb (675 g) roughly chopped, glacé cherries
1½ lb (675 g) chopped mixed peel
1½ lb (675 g) chopped seedless raisins
4½ lb (2 kg) currants
4½ lb (2 kg) sultanas
12 oz (350 g) ground almonds
6 oz (175 g) chopped walnuts
18 eggs
12 fl oz (35 cl) brandy
1 bottle (75 cl) port
4 tbsp (60 ml) orange flower water
finely grated rind and juice of 6 oranges
finely grated rind and juice of 6 lemons
6 tbsp (90 ml) golden syrup
6 tbsp (90 ml) black treacle

To decorate
apricot jam glaze
almond paste
royal icing

These quantities are too large to mix in one batch, so divide ingredients into 2 or 3 and make up shallow batches. Quantities given above are enough for 3 round tiers, measuring 9 by 4 inches (22×10 cm), 11 by 4 inches (28×10 cm) and 13 by 4½ inches (32×11 cm) respectively.

Set the oven at 325°F (160°C) or Mark 3.

In a mixing bowl cream the butter until light and soft, then gradually beat in the brown sugar. In another bowl mix together the flour, spices, glacé cherries, mixed peel, dried fruits and nuts. In a third bowl beat the eggs, then beat in the brandy and port, orange flower water, fruit juices and rinds.

In a pan over a low heat gently warm the syrup and treacle until blended, then stir into the egg mixture. Beat the flour mixture into the creamed butter and sugar, gradually blending in the egg and syrup mixture from time to time until a smooth mixture is formed.

Line the well greased cake tins (sizes as above) with greaseproof paper cut to fit. Turn into the prepared cake tins having same depth of mixture in 9 and 11 inch tins and a little greater depth in the largest tin. Bake just below the centre of the pre-set oven for 1 hour for the 9 inch (22 cm) cake, 1½ hours for the 11 inch (28 cm) cake, and 2 hours for the 13 inch (32 cm) cake; then reduce the oven temperature to 300°F (150°C) or Mark 2 and bake for a further 3–4 hours, according to the size of the cake, until dark brown (but not burnt) and a heated thin skewer inserted in the centre comes away clean. Take out of the oven and cool on a wire rack.

This mixture can be kept overnight, in the tin in the refrigerator, when it is not possible to cook all cakes on the same day.

To complete the wedding cake, first brush the top and sides of each cake with warmed apricot glaze, then cover with almond paste. To ice the cakes, stand the largest cake on a silver cake board about 16 inches (40 cm) in diameter; thickly coat the top and sides with royal icing and smooth off; leave to harden before proceeding with the decoration. Stand the other 2 cakes on cake boards or an icing table if you have one and coat with royal icing as for the base cake. Leave to harden before proceeding with the decoration as given below. When the icing is hard, put the 3 tiers together, the smallest cake being the top tier, and decorate the top according to choice.

1. On a large piece of paper trace 3 11-pointed stars, their diameters equalling those of each of the cakes to be decorated ie. 13 inch (32 cm) for the 13 inch (32 cm) cake. Place the paper star on top of the cake and, using a fine needle, prick round the star shape.

3. Fill in a side outline of linked half circles, using the same nozzle. Each half circle meets directly below each star point and these half circles should arc to a depth of 1 inch (2.50 cm) on the 13 inch (32 cm) cake, ¾ inch (19 mm) on the 11 inch (28 cm) cake, and ½ inch (12 mm) on the 9 inch (22 cm) cake.

5. Change the nozzle for a finer one. Then pipe directly on top of the first series of arcs that formed the basis of the trellis pattern to give a raised effect and make the lines stand out.

2. Fill a quantity of royal icing into a piping bag fitted with a plain nozzle and pipe a thin line along the pin pricks to form the frame of the star design.

4. The next step is to fill in the triangular spaces between the points of the star with a simple trellis pattern. Using the same nozzle, pipe a series of fine arcs across each space, and complete the trellis effect.

6. Fill royal icing into a piping bag fitted with a rosette nozzle and pipe tiny rosettes along the outline of the star, so concealing the beginnings of the trellis pattern. Repeat this overall pattern on the 2 smaller cakes and when completely hard, assemble the tiers.

Wedding Cake.

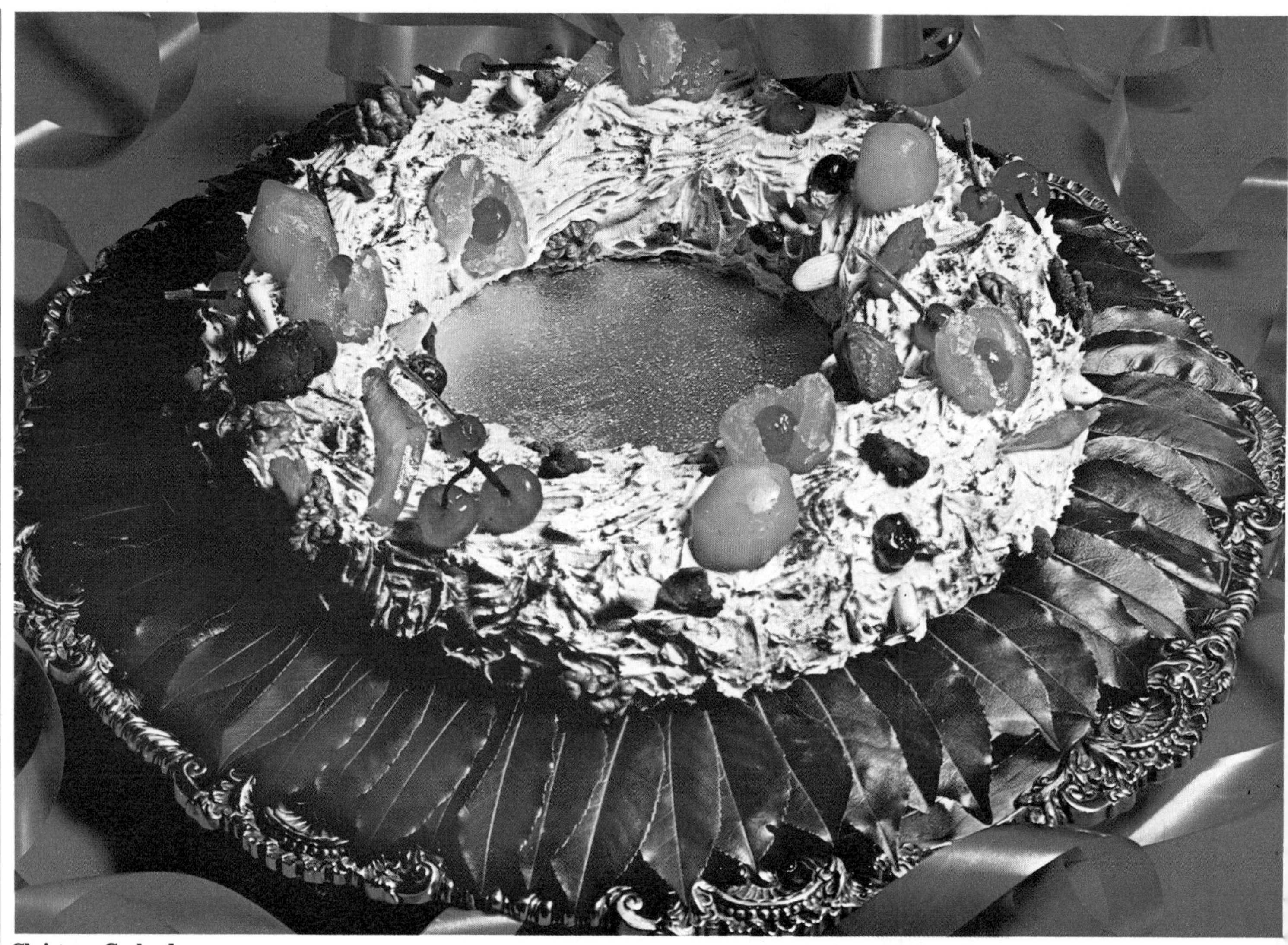

Christmas Garland.

Christmas Garland

For 3 swiss rolls
3 × 4 oz (100 g) castor sugar
3 × 3 lightly beaten eggs
3 × 1 tbsp (15 ml) coffee syrup
3 × 2½ oz (62 g) self raising flour
coffee butter cream for filling

To finish
coffee butter cream
glacé fruits
marrons glacés
halved walnuts
angelica strips
artificial green leaves brushed with colourless chocolate varnish

Set the oven at 425°F (220°C) or Mark 7.

Line a swiss roll tin measuring 10 by 14 by ¾ inches (25 cm × 35 cm × 19 mm). Make each swiss roll separately. Sift the castor sugar onto a foil plate and heat through just above the centre of the pre-set oven. When hot tip at once onto the eggs and coffee syrup in a mixing bowl and beat hard until the mixture is foamy and almost doubled in volume. Sprinkle the flour over the top, then fold in. Turn the mixture into the prepared tin and bake in the pre-set oven for 8–10 minutes or until golden and feathery in texture. Take out and cool on a wire rack.

Sift a little flour over a piece of greaseproof paper about 3 inches (8 cm) larger than the sponge. Trim the ends of the 3 sponges, then spread each one with coffee butter cream; roll up each sponge, then arrange on chosen serving dish in a circle.

Spread thickly with remaining coffee butter cream to cover the sponges completely and roughen the surface with a fork. Decorate with a mixture of glacé fruits, marrons glacés, halved walnuts and strips of angelica. Arrange a border of artificial green leaves around the outer edge of the circle. Finish with red ribbon.

Rich Christmas Cake

8 oz (225 g) softened butter
8 oz (225 g) soft brown sugar
8 oz (225 g) self raising flour
1 tsp (5 ml) grated nutmeg
1 tsp (5 ml) cinnamon
1 tsp (5 ml) ground cloves
1 tsp (5 ml) ginger
4 oz (100 g) roughly chopped, glacé cherries
4 oz (100 g) chopped mixed peel
4 oz (100 g) chopped seedless raisins
12 oz (350 g) currants
12 oz (350 g) sultanas
2 oz (50 g) ground almonds
1 oz (25 g) chopped walnuts
3 eggs
2 fl oz (5 cl) brandy
¼ pt (15 cl) Madeira or Marsala
2 tsp (10 ml) orange flower water
finely grated rind and juice of 1 orange
finely grated rind and juice of 1 lemon
1 tbsp (15 ml) golden syrup
1 tbsp (15 ml) black treacle

Set the oven at 325°F (160°C) or Mark 3.

In a mixing bowl cream the butter until light and soft, then gradually beat in the brown sugar. In another bowl mix together the sifted flour, spices, glacé cherries, mixed peel, dried fruits and nuts. In a third bowl beat the eggs, then beat in the brandy, Madeira or Marsala, orange flower water, fruit juices and rinds.

In a pan over a low heat gently warm the syrup and treacle until blended, then stir into the egg mixture. Beat the flour mixture into the creamed butter and sugar, gradually blending in the egg and syrup liquid from time to time, until a smooth mixture is formed.

Well grease a 12 inch (30 cm) diameter cake tin and line with greaseproof paper cut to fit. Turn into the prepared cake tin and bake just below the centre of the pre-set oven for 1 hour, then reduce the oven temperature to 300°F (150°C) or Mark 2 and bake for a further 3 hours or until the cake is dark brown (but not burnt) and a skewer inserted in the centre comes away clean. Take out and cool on a wire rack.

HOW TO APPLY ALMOND PASTE

1. Brush the top of the cake generously with sieved apricot jam.

2. Roll out the almond paste and place the cake, jam side down, in the middle.

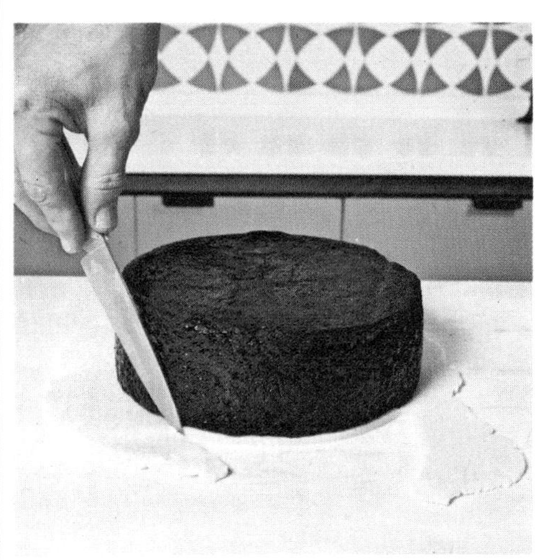

3. Cut off the almond paste round the cake, using a sharp knife.

4. The neat almond paste top will adhere to the jammy cake.

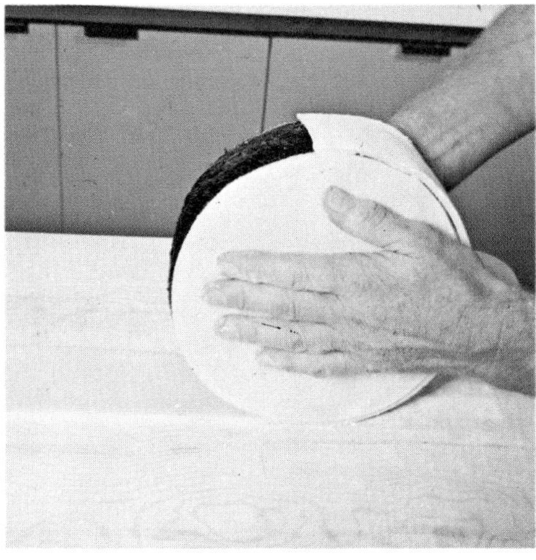

5. Gather up the trimmings and roll out the paste again in a strip which is slightly longer than the circumference of the cake and exactly the depth. Brush the cake sides with jam and roll the cake over the paste to coat the sides.

HOW TO APPLY ROYAL ICING

Royal Icing

1½ lb (675 g) sifted icing sugar
juice of ½ lemon
several egg whites
edible food colouring if required

In a mixing bowl work the icing sugar with the lemon juice and 1 egg white; continue adding egg white until the mixture is smooth, free from any air bubbles and of a thick spreading consistency. Too much egg white will make the icing runny, in which case add more icing sugar; too little egg white will make the icing stiff and dry to work.

To colour royal icing, spoon a little of the mixture on to the work surface; work in a few drops of chosen colour so icing is vividly coloured, then blend this into the main quantity of icing, which will tone down the brightness and the icing will gradually assume a pastel shade.

Variation:
An alternative method of making royal icing is to dissolve 1½ tbsp (22 ml) albumen based powder in 3 fl oz (7 cl) tepid water. Then work this liquid into 1½ lb (675 g) sifted icing sugar until a smooth mixture is formed and holds a soft peak.

1. Put the almond paste covered cake on a turntable. Spoon a dollop of icing on it.

2. Work it round smoothly with a spatula moving the wrist backwards and forwards.

3. Keep spreading until the top begins to look smooth. The wrist action with the spatula expells the air bubbles.

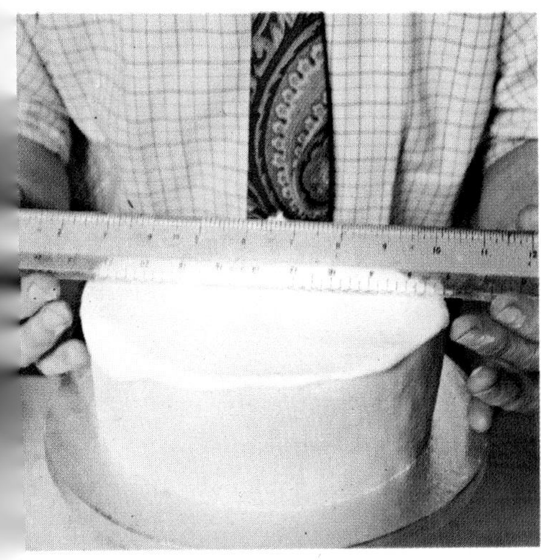

4. Finish off the smoothing process by skimming the top with a ruler.

5. Apply more icing to the sides of the cake with a spatula.

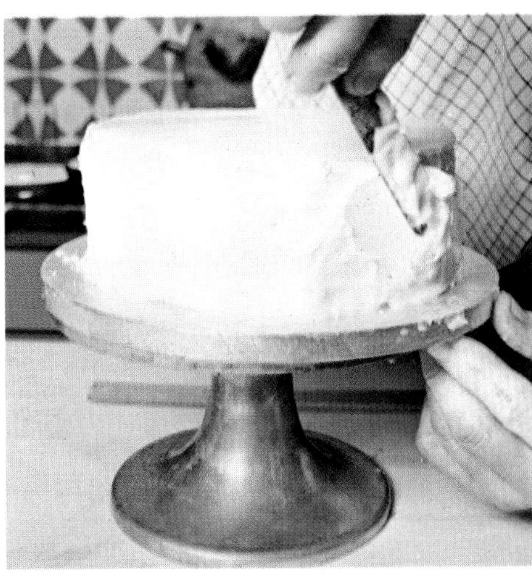

6. Thickly cover the sides with icing.

7. Take a piece of perspex, cross your hands, hold the edge of the turntable with one hand and the perspex with the other. Pull the turntable round, holding the perspex still, so that the sides of the cakes are skimmed with the perspex.

8. As you turn, the hands uncross and the cake sides become smooth all round.

Iced Christmas Cake.

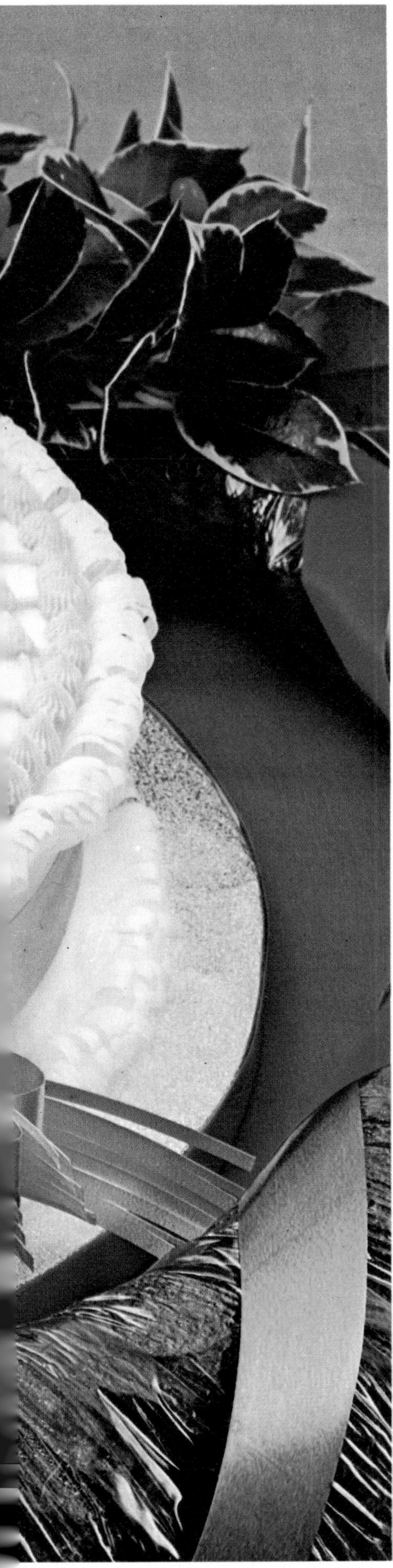

Iced Christmas Cake

8 oz (225 g) softened butter
8 oz (225 g) soft brown sugar
8 oz (225 g) self raising flour
1 tsp (5 ml) grated nutmeg
1 tsp (5 ml) cinnamon
1 tsp (5 ml) ground cloves
1 tsp (5 ml) ginger
4 oz (100 g) roughly chopped, glacé cherries
4 oz (100 g) mixed chopped peel
4 oz (100 g) chopped seedless raisins
12 oz (350 g) currants
12 oz (350 g) sultanas
2 oz (50 g) ground almonds
1 oz (25 g) chopped walnuts
3 eggs
2 fl oz (5 cl) brandy
¼ pt (15 cl) Madeira or Marsala
2 tsp (10 ml) orange flower water
finely grated rind and juice of 1 orange
finely grated rind and juice of 1 lemon
1 tbsp (15 ml) golden syrup
1 tbsp (15 ml) black treacle

To finish
apricot glaze
½ lb (225 g) sugar quantity of royal icing
green butter cream
paper cake frill

Set the oven at 325°F (160°C) or Mark 3.

Line a well greased 12 inch (30 cm) diameter cake tin with greaseproof paper cut to fit.

In a mixing bowl cream the butter until light and soft, then gradually beat in the brown sugar. In another bowl mix together the flour, spices, glacé cherries, mixed peel, dried fruit and nuts. In a third bowl beat the eggs, then beat in the brandy, Madeira or Marsala, orange flower water, fruit juices and rinds.

In a pan over a low heat gently warm the syrup and treacle until blended, then stir into the egg mixture. Beat the flour mixture into the creamed butter and sugar, gradually blending in the egg and syrup liquid from time to time, until a smooth mixture is formed.

Turn into the prepared cake tin and bake just below the centre of the pre-set oven for 1 hour, then reduce the oven temperature to 300°F (150°C) or Mark 2 and bake for a further 3 hours or until the cake is dark brown (but not burnt) and a skewer inserted in the centre comes away clean. Take out and cool on a wire rack.

To finish the cake: when cold brush with apricot glaze, then cover the top and sides with almond paste. Cover the top and sides with plain royal icing, smooth off and leave to harden. When hard, pipe a trellis pattern of green butter cream on top, using a piping bag fitted with a plain nozzle for the trellis lines, and medium rosette nozzle for piping rosettes all round the top edge of the cake and at the points where the lines of the trellis cross each other. Put round the paper frill and tie with ribbon.

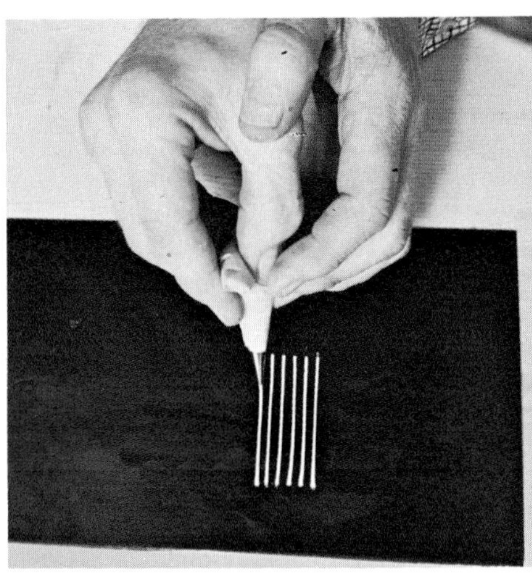

1. Practise piping on a work surface before attempting to decorate the cake. Note the correct position of the hands for plain piping. The pipe is held slightly above the work surface, not on it.

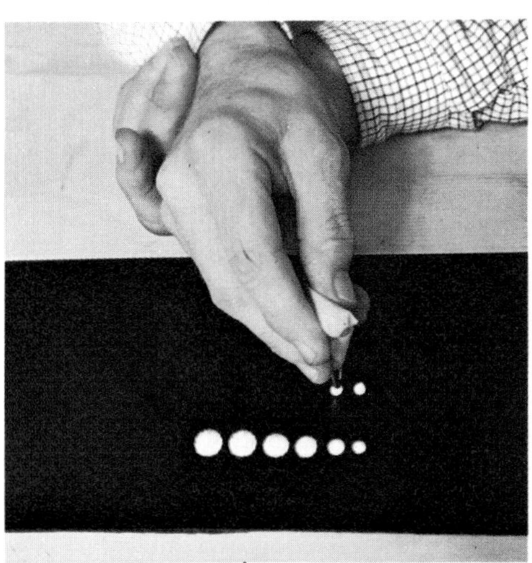

2. This is the correct position for the hands when piping rosettes. The thumb pushes the icing out – the greater the pressure, the larger the rosette.

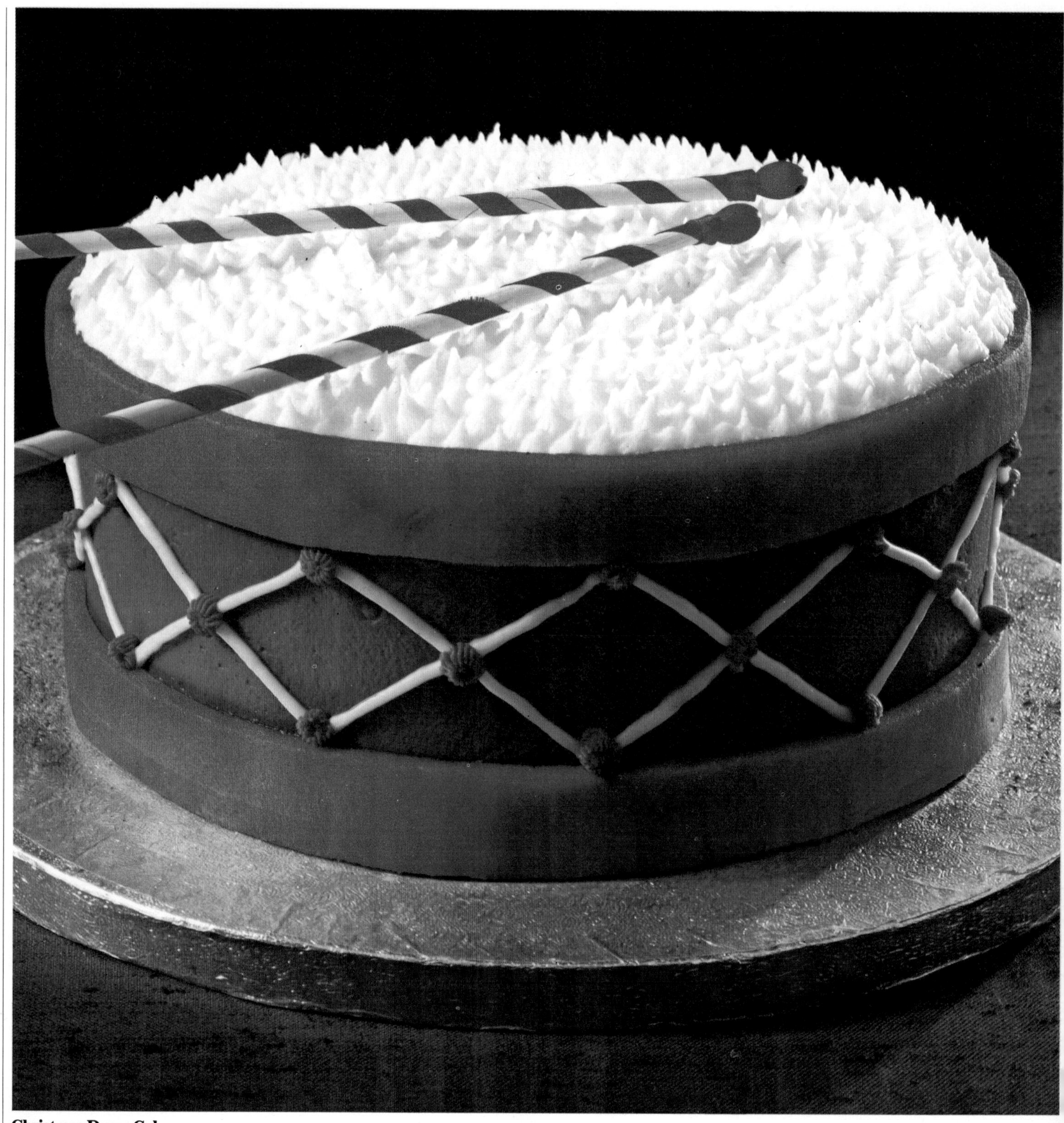

Christmas Drum Cake.

Christmas Drum Cake

pricot glaze
lue and pink edible food colourings
lb (450 g) almond paste
little cornflour
yal icing

or sponge cake
oz (225 g) softened butter or margarine
oz (225 g) castor sugar
eggs
oz (200 g) self raising flour
oz (25 g) cornflour
fl oz (9 cl) milk

r fondant icing
fl oz (10 cl) liquid glucose
b (900 g) sifted icing sugar
gg whites

t the oven at 350°F (180°C) or Mark 4.

ake the sponge cake. In a mixing bowl eam together the fat and sugar until pale d fluffy. Fold in a quarter of the flour xture, then beat in 1 egg, a little at a ne to avoid curdling the mixture. Con- ue adding portions of flour, with an egg ch time, until all are incorporated.

Well grease an 8 inch (20 cm) diameter ke tin and line with greased and floured easeproof paper cut to fit. Beat the milk o the cake mixture until it is smooth. en pour into the prepared tin and bake he pre-set oven for about 30 minutes or til golden, firm to the touch and the nge just pulls away from the sides of tin. Take out and cool on a wire rack.

Make the fondant icing. In a bowl stood r a pan of boiling water, heat the glu- e for a few minutes. In a mixing bowl ke a well in the centre of the icing ar, then pour in the egg whites and cose. Work to a stiff paste, then turn on work surface lightly dusted with icing ar and knead. Cut off two thirds of the dant and colour a deep blue as for royal g; knead the small ball of blue fondant k into the main piece until the colour- is evenly distributed. Colour the re- ining fondant bright red in the same . Set aside.

urn the cooled sponge cake upside vn, brush the top with apricot glaze, cover the top with almond paste. On a k surface dusted with cornflour roll the blue fondant icing into a strip long ugh to go round the cake and wide ugh to equal the depth of the cake.

Light Christmas Cake.

Brush the sides of the cake with apricot glaze and mould the fondant around it, pressing the ends together to join them. Place the cake on 10 inch (22 cm) diameter cake board.

Roll out the red fondant to a thin strip long enough to go round the cake and 2 inches (5 cm) wide. Cut in half to give 2 1 inch (2.50 cm) strips. Brush one side of each strip with apricot glaze and stick them around the top and bottom of the cake respectively.

Fill three quarters of the royal icing into a piping bag fitted with a small rosette nozzle and cover the top of the cake with white rosettes. Then pipe criss cross lines on the blue fondant icing to resemble the side cords on a drum. Colour the remaining royal icing a deep blue, fill into a piping bag fitted with a plain writing nozzle and put a tiny dot of blue icing to resemble the knots where the white drum cords meet each other. Dip 2 artificial holly berries in a little glue and stick each to the end of a 8 inch (20 cm) drinking straw to make the drum sticks; place them on top of the cake when the icing is hard.

Light Christmas Cake

7 oz (200 g) self raising flour
3¼ oz (82 g) cornflour
9 oz (250 g) roughly chopped, glacé cherries
8 oz (225 g) roughly chopped, glacé pineapple
4 oz (100 g) chopped mixed peel
8 oz (225 g) sultanas
4 oz (100 g) chopped walnuts
2 oz (50 g) chopped angelica
2 fl oz (5 cl) brandy
finely grated rind and juice of 1 orange
2 tsp (10 ml) orange flower water
4 separated eggs
8 oz (225 g) softened unsalted butter
8 oz (225 g) sifted icing sugar

To decorate
icing sugar or almond paste and royal icing

Set the oven at 325°F (160°C) or Mark 3.

In a mixing bowl sift the flour and cornflour together; toss the glacé cherries in a little flour to keep the pieces separate during mixing and add to the flours, together with the pineapple, mixed peel, sultanas, walnuts and angelica. In a basin mix together the brandy, orange juice and flower water, then beat in the egg yolks. In another mixing bowl cream the butter with the orange rind until light and soft, then beat in the icing sugar.

Beat in the flour and fruit mixture, a little at a time, and add some of the brandy liquid at the same time, until all are combined to form a smooth mixture.

In a bowl whip the egg whites until they stand in a stiff peak, then fold into the cake mixture.

Line a well greased and floured 10 inch (22 cm) diameter loose bottomed cake tin with greased greaseproof paper cut to fit. Turn into the prepared tin and stand on 4 thicknesses of brown paper on a baking sheet; bake just below the centre of the pre-set oven for about 2½–3 hours or until a rich brown and a skewer inserted in the centre comes out clean. Take out and cool in the tin, then turn out. Sprinkle with icing sugar or cover with almond paste, then royal icing.

Easter Cake.

Easter Cake

For sponge cake
8 oz (225 g) softened butter or margarine
8 oz (225 g) castor sugar
4 eggs
7 oz (200 g) self raising flour
1 oz (25 g) cornflour
$3\frac{1}{2}$ fl oz (9 cl) milk

For filling
2 fl oz (5 cl) double cream
1 egg yolk
1 tsp (5 ml) plain flour
$1\frac{1}{4}$ oz (30 g) unsalted butter
$1\frac{1}{4}$ oz (30 g) sifted icing sugar

To decorate and finish
a little icing sugar
12 oz (350 g) almond paste
2–3 drops of green edible food colouring
4 oz (100 g) plain dessert chocolate, broken into pieces
1 length of thin plaited liquorice stick

Set the oven at 350°F (180°C) or Mark 4.

Make the sponge cakes. In a mixing bowl cream together the fat and sugar until pale and fluffy. Fold in a quarter of the flour mixture, then beat in 1 egg, a little at a time to avoid curdling the mixture. Continue adding portions of flour, with an egg each time, until all are incorporated. Beat in the milk until the mixture is smooth.

Well grease 2 8 inch (20 cm) diameter sandwich tins and line with greased and floured greaseproof paper cut to fit. Pour into the prepared tins and bake in the pre-set oven for about 20 minutes or until golden, firm to the touch and the sponge just pulls away from the sides of the tin. Take out and cool on a wire rack.

Have ready a bowl half filled with icec water. Make the filling. In a double saucepan over a moderate heat beat togethe the cream, egg yolk and flour until thick Plunge the pan holding the cream mixtur into the iced water and continue beatin until cold. In a mixing bowl cream th butter and icing sugar together until pal and fluffy, then beat into the cold crean mixture a little at a time until we blended. Put one sponge round on you serving dish and spread with about tw thirds of the cream, top with the othe sponge round and coat the sides with th remaining cream. Sprinkle the top wit icing sugar.

Colour the almond paste a bright greer then cut off about a quarter and roll into sausage about $\frac{1}{4}$ inch (6 mm) thick. Cu into short lengths matching the depth c the cake and stick them around the side about 1 inch (2.50 cm) apart, in the butte cream. Roll out the remaining almon paste to a thickness of about $\frac{1}{8}$ inc (3 mm). Cut into 2 inch (5 cm) length each $\frac{1}{2}$ inch (12 mm) wide. Place on th sides of the cakes to resemble basketwo weave in 4 rows, alternating the positic of the strips in each row. To make th handle for the basket, melt the chocola in a pan over a low heat until just liqui then draw the liquorice stick through and leave on a piece of greased greas proof paper until almost firm; careful bend round into a loop about 7 inch (18 cm) long. Leave to firm completely.

To assemble the cake, put a circle florists' foam on a cake board. Wrap th ends of the liquorice handle with foil an push them down into the foam on eith side. Twist a ribbon around the handl then stud the foam with a few spri flower heads to conceal it. Carefully pla on top of the sponge cake; simply lift c and set aside to cut the cake.

Hedgehog Cake

For sponge
4 egg yolks
3½ oz (82 g) castor sugar
3½ oz (82 g) self raising flour

For coffee butter cream
4 oz (100 g) softened unsalted butter
8 oz (225 g) sifted icing sugar
coffee syrup to taste

To finish
2 chocolate chips or drops (for eyes)
6 oz (175 g) halved, blanched flaked almonds
a little softened chocolate
chocolate leaves (optional)

Set the oven at 350°F (180°C) or Mark 4.

Make the sponge. In a mixing bowl beat the egg yolks until creamy. Beat in the sugar until the mixture is thick and foamy. Lightly fold in the flour.

Line 2 greased and floured 6 inch (15 cm) square cake tins with greased and floured greaseproof paper cut to fit. Turn the mixture into the prepared tins. Bake just above the centre of the pre-set oven for 20 minutes or until brown and firm to the touch. Take out and cool on a rack.

Make the butter cream. In a mixing bowl cream the butter until light and soft, then gradually beat in the icing sugar until smooth, adding a little coffee syrup at a time until the desired flavour is reached. Spread some of the butter cream over one sponge cake, then top with the remaining sponge cake.

Using a sharp knife, trim the sponge cake into a dome shape to resemble the hedgehog's body, shaping at the corners and paring away at one end to form a snout. Spread the remaining butter cream all over. Put on the chocolate 'eyes' and spread a little softened chocolate for the snout. Then stick the almonds all over to resemble the prickles and scatter round chocolate leaves if liked.

edgehog Cake.

Petits fours and candies

Petits fours and candies are impressive additions to the good cook's repertoire. Petits fours are normally served as the last of many courses at a formal dinner, and the emphasis is on appearance as they must look tempting to revive the flagging appetite. However, they can be handed round at parties as a sweet toothed equivalent of canapés and cocktail snacks. Petits fours take their name from the little ovens in which they were originally made. Candies are for eating any time you feel like something sweet. Attractively wrapped they make ideal gifts.

Rosettes, Iced Petits Fours, Glazed Strawberries and Macaroon Balls.

Iced Petits Fours

4 oz (100 g) castor sugar
3 lightly beaten eggs
2½ oz (62 g) self raising flour
liqueur- or fruit-flavoured butter cream
glacé icing in various colours

To decorate
silver sugar balls or crystallized rose petals and violets

Set the oven at 425°F (220°C) or Mark 7.

Make the sponge. Sift the sugar onto a foil plate and heat through for about 6 minutes in the pre-set oven. Then tip at once onto the eggs in a mixing bowl and beat hard until foamy and almost doubled in volume. Sprinkle over the flour, then fold in with a spatula.

Line a swiss roll tin measuring 10 by 14 by ¾ inches (25 cm × 35 cm × 19 mm) with greased greaseproof paper cut to fit.

Pour the mixture into the prepared tin and bake in the pre-set oven just above the centre for about 8 minutes or until golden and feathery in texture. Take out and cool on a wire rack.

Using a 1½ inch (3 cm) diameter plain pastry cutter stamp out tiny rounds. Fill the butter cream into a piping bag fitted with a small rosette nozzle and pipe a single rosette, doming it well, on each round. Chill in the refrigerator for about 15 minutes to firm.

Place rounds on a wire rack. Spoon a little of the coloured glacé icings over the rounds to cover; the icing needs to be thicker than usual to ensure it doesn't slip off. Decorate with a mixture of sugar balls, crystallized violets and rose petals. Leave in a cool place to set. Put in paper sweet cases if liked.

Petits fours and candies

Rosettes

1 oz (25 g) sifted icing sugar
4 oz (100 g) softened unsalted butter
4 oz (100 g) self raising flour
6 oz (175 g) plain dessert chocolate, broken into pieces

To decorate
silver or lemon sugar balls

Set the oven at 375°F (190°C) or Mark 5.

In a mixing bowl blend the sugar and butter together. Sift and work in the flour and beat until a stiff paste is formed. Fill the mixture into a piping bag fitted with a small rosette nozzle and pipe walnut sized shapes on a greased and floured baking sheet. Decorate with sugar balls if liked. Bake in the pre-set oven for about 8 minutes or until just set. Take out and cool on a wire rack.

In a heavy based pan over a low heat melt the chocolate until just liquid. Use to sandwich the rosettes together; put in paper sweet cases if liked.

Variation:
Instead of melted chocolate, sandwich the rosettes with flavoured and coloured butter cream or glacé icing.

Chocolate Nut Petits Fours

4 oz (100 g) plain flour
mixed spice
baking powder
2 oz (50 g) ground hazelnuts
1 small beaten egg
2 oz (50 g) melted butter
1½ oz (37 g) castor sugar
2 oz (50 g) plain dessert chocolate, broken into pieces and melted until just liquid

To finish
flaked blanched almonds
a little melted chocolate

Sift the flour, a pinch of mixed spice and a pinch of baking powder into a mixing bowl. Make a well in the centre and pour in the hazelnuts, beaten egg, butter, castor sugar and melted chocolate.

Using 2 knives, work the flour into the other ingredients until blended and a smooth dough is formed. Wrap in waxed paper and chill for at least 12 hours before rolling out very thinly on a floured surface.

Grease and flour a baking sheet and set the oven at 350°F (180°C) or Mark 4. Using 1½ inch (3 cm) plain pastry cutter, stamp dough into rounds. Place them on the prepared baking sheet and bake in the pre-set oven for about 8 minutes or until firm.

Take out and cool on a wire rack. Put a blob of melted chocolate in the middle of each one and top with a flaked almond.

HOW TO PIPE ROSETTES

Hold the piping bag almost vertically above the baking sheet and squeeze out the paste (it must be stiff for it to hold its shape when piped) into walnut sized shapes, spacing them fairly wide apart. The forefinger of the hand holding the piping bag should be directly above the end of the nozzle to help guide the paste as it is squeezed out. Jerk the nozzle as you finish piping a shape to ensure a clean break and to leave a tiny point in the centre of the rosette.

Half and Half

8 oz (225 g) shortbread dough
8 oz (225 g) plain dessert chocolate, broken into pieces

Set the oven at 350°F (180°C) or Mark 4.

Roll out the shortbread to about ¼ inch (6 mm) thickness. Using a small sharp knife cut out a decorative leaf shape, an oak leaf for example, each about 2½ inch (6 cm) long. Place them on a greased and floured baking sheet and bake in the pre-set oven for about 6 minutes or until golden and just set. Take out and cool on the baking sheet.

In a heavy based pan heat the chocolate until it is just liquid. Dip one half of each shortbread in the chocolate to coat it, then place on a sheet of waxed paper and leave to set. Store in an airtight container.

Macaroon Balls

6 oz (175 g) granulated sugar
1 oz (25 g) powdered glucose
4 fl oz (10 cl) water
4 oz (100 g) ground almonds
4–6 oz (100–175 g) plain dessert chocolate, broken into pieces

In a heavy based pan over a moderate hea dissolve the sugar and glucose in th water, then bring to the boil. Reduce th heat and simmer the syrup until a drop set to a soft ball when dropped into ice water. Remove pan from the heat, an beat in the ground almonds until the mixture is smooth and cold. Turn out onto cold, floured surface and knea thoroughly.

Roll the mixture into tiny balls, eac weighing about ½ oz (12 g), put them ont a greased and floured baking sheet, cove with waxed paper and stand in a warn place for several hours. Set the oven a 400°F (200°C) or Mark 6.

Bake the macaroons just above th centre of the pre-set oven for about minutes or until tinged a light brown. Thi mixture is very delicate and the bakin time can vary by at least 2 minutes eithe way, depending on the accuracy of th oven thermostat. Take out and cool on th baking sheet. In a pan over a low heat me the chocolate until it is just liquid, then us to sandwich the macaroon biscuits tc gether. Put in paper sweet cases.

Little Coffee Meringues

1 egg white
2 oz (50 g) castor sugar
1 tsp (5 ml) instant coffee powder
½ oz (12 g) softened butter
1 oz (25 g) sifted icing sugar

Set the oven at 250°F (130°C) or Mark ½.

Make the meringue. In a mixing bowl whip the egg white until just stiff, then sprinkle over ½ oz (12 g) castor sugar and half of the coffee powder. Whip again for 3 minutes, then fold in the remaining castor sugar. Fill the meringue mixture into a piping bag fitted with ½ inch (12 mm) plain nozzle and pipe an equal number of small blobs of meringue onto a greased and floured baking sheet, spacing them fairly wide apart. Bake in the pre-set oven for 20–25 minutes or until firm and crisp. Take out and cool on a wire rack.

Make the coffee butter cream. Cream the butter until light and soft, then beat in the remaining coffee powder. Sprinkle over the icing sugar, then beat in. Sandwich together with butter cream.

Little Chocolate Sponges

2 egg whites
2 oz (50 g) softened unsalted butter
2 oz (50 g) castor sugar
2 oz (50 g) self raising flour
2 tsp (10 ml) drinking chocolate powder
4–6 oz (100–175 g) plain dessert chocolate, broken into pieces

Set the oven at 375°F (190°C) or Mark 5.

Whip the egg whites until stiff.

Make the sponge. In a mixing bowl cream the butter until light and soft, then beat in the sugar. Sprinkle over the flour and drinking chocolate powder and stir in. When blended, fold in the stiffly whipped egg whites. Spoon an equal number of tiny blobs of mixture onto a greased and floured baking sheet and bake in the pre-set oven for about 5 minutes or until firm. Take out and cool on a wire rack.

In a heavy based pan over a low heat melt the chocolate until just soft; spoon a little onto half of the sponges, then sandwich together with the remainder. Place the biscuits close together on a wire rack, then trail thin trickles of melted chocolate all over them.

Sablés, Chocolate Nut Petits Fours, Little Fingers, Mini Macaroons – chocolate tipped and plain, and Chocolate Delights.

Half and Half, Almond Crunchies, Cherry Rosettes, Little Coffee Meringues, Little Chocolate Sponges, Shortbread Swirls and Ginger Petits Fours.

Petits fours and candies

Shortbread Swirls

4 oz (100 g) shortbread dough
2–3 oz (50–75 g) apricot jam
4–6 oz (100–175 g) green glacé cherries
tiny strips of angelica

Set the oven at 325°F (160°C) or Mark 3.

Roll out the shortbread to about ¼ inch (6 mm) thickness. Using a 1¼ inch (3 cm) plain pastry cutter stamp out into an equal number of rounds. Using a ¼ inch (6 mm) plain nozzle, stamp out a circle from the centre of half the shortbread rounds to form rings. Place all the shortbread shapes on a greased and floured baking sheet and bake in the pre-set oven for about 6 minutes or until pale coloured and set. Take out and cool on a wire rack.

Spread the rounds with a little jam, put a ring on top of each one, then dab a little more jam into the centre. Put a halved glacé cherry and strip of angelica in the middle of each ring.

Sablés

4 oz (100 g) plain flour
baking powder
1 small beaten egg
2 oz (50 g) melted butter
1½ oz (37 g) castor sugar

To finish
2–3 tbsp (30–45 ml) sugar syrup
1–2 oz (25–50 g) nibbed almonds
4 oz (100 g) plain dessert chocolate, broken into pieces and just melted

Set the oven at 350°F (180°C) or Mark 4.

Sift the flour and a pinch of baking powder into a mixing bowl. Make a well in the centre and pour into it the beaten egg, butter and castor sugar. With 2 knives, work the flour into the ingredients until blended and a smooth dough is formed.

Turn dough onto a floured surface and roll out to about ¼ inch (6 mm) thickness. Using 1¼ inch (3 cm) plain pastry cutter stamp into rounds. Place them on a greased and floured baking sheet, brush with sugar syrup, sprinkle with almonds, lightly push in the top of each biscuit with a spoon handle, then bake in the pre-set oven for 8 minutes or until pale gold. When cold, put a blob of melted chocolate in the middle of each one.

Mini Macaroons

6 oz (175 g) granulated sugar
1 oz (25 g) powdered glucose
4 fl oz (10 cl) water
4 oz (100 g) ground almonds

To finish
4 oz (100 g) plain dessert chocolate, broken into pieces
6 oz (175 g) glacé cherries
2–3 oz (50–75 g) granulated sugar
1 egg white

Set the oven at 400°F (200°C) or Mark 6.

In a heavy based pan over a moderate heat dissolve the sugar and glucose in the water, then bring to the boil. Reduce the heat and simmer the syrup until a drop sets to a soft ball when dropped into iced water. Remove the pan from the heat, and beat in the ground almonds until the mixture is smooth and cold. Turn out onto a cold, floured surface and knead.

Roll out to about ¼ inch (6 mm) thickness. Using 1¼ inch (3 cm) plain pastry cutter, stamp into rounds. Place them on a greased and floured baking sheet, brush with a little egg white and bake in the pre-set oven for about 5 minutes or until tinged a light brown. This mixture is very delicate and baking time can vary by at least 2 minutes either way, depending on the accuracy of the oven thermostat. Take out and cool on the baking sheet.

In a pan over a low heat melt the chocolate until just liquid, then coat the top of each macaroon. Roll as many cherries as you need for each macaroon in the sugar and place on top of each one while the chocolate is still soft. Leave to set.

Glazed Fruits

8 oz (225 g) granulated sugar
½ pt (30 cl) water
fresh strawberries, segments of orange, green grapes, whole stemmed cherries or mirabelle plums

In a heavy based pan over a very low heat dissolve the sugar in the water. When completely dissolved increase the heat to bring the syrup to a gentle rolling boil. Hold the syrup at this rolling boil until smothered in bubbles, then take off the heat.

Take a fresh strawberry or other chosen fruit, hold in a pair of tweezers or tong and dip into the syrup to coat completely Put the sugar glazed fruit straight into a paper sweet case and leave to set; the syrup should set almost immediately. I not, continue boiling the syrup, then tes with another piece of fruit. Return the pa of syrup to the stove and bring back to a gentle rolling boil as many times as i necessary to glaze all the fruit.

Glazed fruits do not keep well becaus exposure to air softens the coating, s make them only a short while before the are required.

Almond Crunchies

4 oz (100 g) shortbread dough
1 tbsp (15 ml) egg white
2 oz (50 g) blanched flaked almonds

Set the oven at 350°F (180°C) or Mark 4

Roll out the shortbread to about ¼ inc (6 mm) thickness. Using a 1¼ inch (3 cm plain pastry cutter, stamp out into round Brush with a little egg white, scatter over few flaked almonds, place on a grease and floured baking sheet and bake in th pre-set oven for about 7 minutes or until light brown and just set.

Take out and cool on a wire rack. Thes store well in an airtight container.

Ginger Petits Fours

3 tbsp (45 ml) golden syrup
3½ oz (85 g) castor sugar
3 oz (75 g) butter or margarine
grated rind of 1 lemon
3½ oz (85 g) plain flour
ground ginger

Set the oven at 350°F (180°C) or Mark

In a heavy based pan over a low he gently heat together until complete melted the syrup, sugar, butter and lemc rind. Take the pan off the stove and beat the flour and a pinch of ground ginger. S aside to cool until the mixture is of dropping consistency.

Spoon tiny blobs of mixture on greased baking sheets, spacing them wi apart. Bake just above the centre of t pre-set oven for 12 minutes, then take o and, using a palette knife, lift onto a wi rack to cool.

HOW TO MAKE CANDIES

Chocolate Cream Mixture

12 oz (350 g) plain dessert or cooking chocolate, broken into pieces
6 fl oz (17 cl) double cream

In a large pan over a low heat, melt the chocolate until just liquid.

In a heavy based pan over a moderate heat bring the cream to a steady rolling boil. At once pour onto the softened chocolate and beat hard until the cream is absorbed and the chocolate mixture glistens and is dark. Return pan to the stove and heat gently until the mixture reaches a soft dropping consistency. Take off the heat and cool a little.

Grease the sides of a rectangular metal or wooden baking frame, about 1 inch (2.50 cm) deep, and stand on a greased baking sheet.

Pour the mixture into the prepared frame. Chill in the refrigerator until set. The canache can then be cut into various shapes with a knife or fancy cutters, dipped in hot water to make clean cuts. Store in waxed paper in a cool dry place.

Variation:
Cut the firm canache into triangles and coat with drinking chocolate powder.

Chocolate Truffles

While chocolate cream mixture is still soft and warm, roll into tiny balls about the size of a walnut. Quickly dip in drinking chocolate powder or roll in chocolate vermicelli.

Liqueur Chocolates

1 lb (450 g) plain dessert chocolate, broken into pieces
glacé cherries
2 tbsp (30 ml) cherry brandy to 1 tbsp (15 ml) sugar syrup

In a large pan over a low heat melt the chocolate until just liquid. Pour a little into metal sweet cases and twist them round to coat the insides, then pour back any surplus chocolate. Put the lined cases onto a baking sheet or tray and chill in the refrigerator for about 5 minutes or until the chocolate is set. Then take out and place a glacé cherry inside each one.

In a bowl mix the cherry brandy with cold sugar syrup. Spoon a little of the brandy liquid into each chocolate lined case so the cherry just rises above it. Spoon the remaining softened chocolate over each one to cover it completely, swirling it to the edges. Put a tiny piece of glacé cherry on top of each chocolate before completely hard.

1. Make fondant shrimps from fondant icing. Simply press into shrimp moulds.

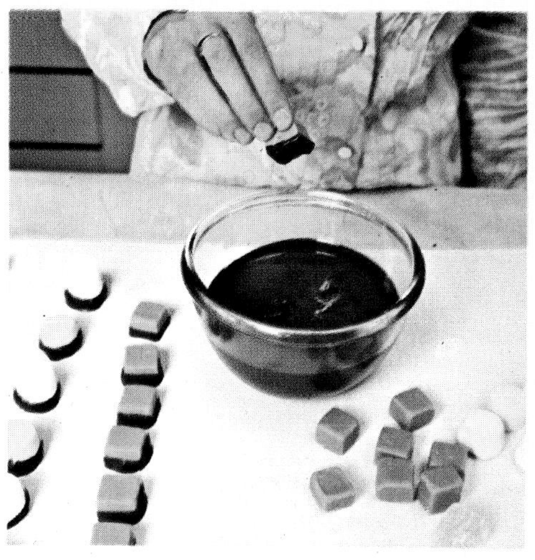

2. Dip squares of fudge and marshmallows in melted chocolate so that they are half covered with chocolate.

3. Dip triangles of the chocolate cream mixture into drinking chocolate powder.

4. Roll pieces of the chocolate cream mixture into small balls, then roll the balls in chocolate vermicelli.

A selection of candies.

Petits fours and candies

Assortment of candies including Peppermint Fondants, Raspberry Fondants, Liqueur Chocolates, Chocolate Orange Twiglets, Stuffed Dates

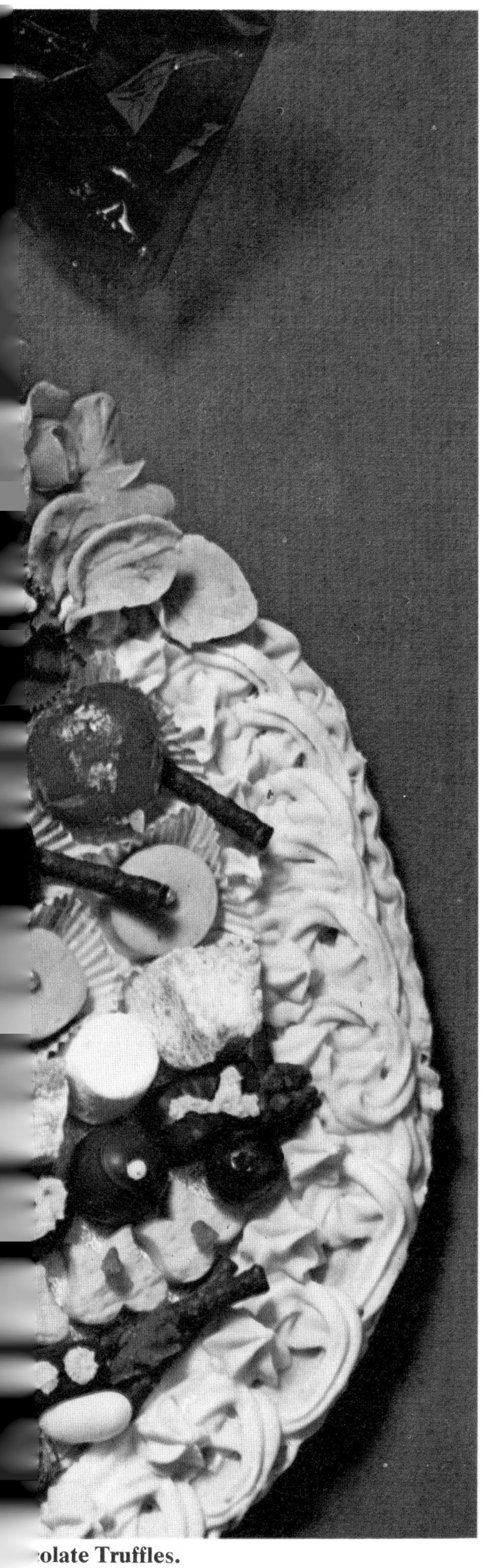

Chocolate Orange Twiglets

freshly pared orange peel
1 pt (60 cl) sugar syrup
½ pt (30 cl) water
6 oz (175 g) plain dessert chocolate, broken into pieces

Cut orange peel into strips to look like little twigs and place in a pan of cold water to cover and bring to the boil. Drain immediately, then replace the orange peel in the pan with a fresh quantity of cold water to cover and boil again. Repeat this process 3 times more to ensure all bitterness is extracted from the peel.

In a large pan heat the pieces of peel in the sugar syrup and water and simmer until the syrup begins to thicken. Lift out the peel with tweezers or tongs and place on a wire rack to drip and leave overnight to harden.

In a pan over a low heat melt the chocolate until just liquid, then using tweezers or tongs, draw each piece of peel through the chocolate to cover them completely, then set on a sheet of waxed paper to set. When hard trim away any surplus chocolate. Store in layers between sheets of waxed paper in an airtight container.

Little Fingers

1 oz (25 g) sifted icing sugar
4 oz (100 g) softened unsalted butter
4 oz (100 g) self raising flour

Set the oven at 375°F (190°C) or Mark 5.

In a mixing bowl blend the sugar and butter together, then sift and work in the flour and beat until a stiff paste is formed. Fill the mixture into a piping bag fitted with a small rosette nozzle and pipe into 2½ inch (6 cm) lengths, on a greased and floured baking sheet, spacing them fairly wide apart. Bake in the pre-set oven for about 8 minutes or until golden and just set. Take out and cool on a wire rack.

Variation:
Bake the fingers as above. When cold spread each one with flavoured butter cream (orange, lemon, coffee or liqueur) and sprinkle thickly with finely ground pistachio nuts.

Chocolatines

15 oz (400 g) plain dessert or cooking chocolate, broken into pieces
6 fl oz (17 cl) double cream

To decorate
sugar balls, pieces of glacé cherry or angelica, chopped or halved nuts, or crystallized violets and rose petals

In a large pan over a low heat melt 12 oz (300 g) chocolate until just liquid. In a heavy based pan over a moderate heat bring the cream to a steady rolling boil. At once pour onto the softened chocolate and beat hard until the cream is absorbed and the chocolate mixture glistens and is dark. Return the pan to the stove and heat gently until the mixture reaches a soft dropping consistency.

Grease the sides of a rectangular metal or wooden baking frame, about 1 inch (2.50 cm) deep, and stand on a greased baking sheet. Pour the mixture into the prepared frame. Chill until set.

Put the remaining chocolate in a pan over a low heat and melt until just liquid. Cut the canache into fancy shapes, then dip each one into the softened chocolate, using a pair of tweezers or tongs. Place on a sheet of waxed paper and while the chocolate is still soft decorate with sugar balls, glacé cherries, angelica, crystallized violets and rose petals, or nuts.

When the chocolate is set, trim the edges, then place each chocolate in a metal or paper sweet case.

Cherry Rosettes

1 oz (25 g) sifted icing sugar
4 oz (100 g) softened unsalted butter
4 oz (100 g) self raising flour
6 oz (175 g) plain dessert chocolate, broken into pieces
3–4 oz (75–100 g) glacé cherries

Set the oven at 375°F (190°C) or Mark 5.

In a mixing bowl blend the sugar and butter together, then sift and work in the flour and beat until a stiff paste is formed. Fill the mixture into a piping bag fitted with a small rosette nozzle and pipe walnut sized shapes onto a greased and floured baking sheet. Put a halved glacé cherry on top of each one and bake in the pre-set oven for about 8 minutes.

olate Truffles.

Petits fours and candies

Chocolate Delights

2 oz (50 g) softened butter
2 oz (50 g) castor sugar
1½ oz (36 g) plain flour
½ oz (12 g) cornflour
1 beaten egg
1 tsp (5ml) milk

To decorate
4 oz (100 g) plain dessert chocolate, broken into pieces and melted until just liquid
icing sugar

Set the oven at 350°F (180°C) or Mark 4.

Make the sponge. In a mixing bowl cream the butter and sugar together until pale and fluffy. Sprinkle over half the flour and fold in, adding a little of the egg. Fold in remaining flour and egg until blended, then beat in just enough of the milk to form a soft but not sticky dough. Spoon an equal number of small blobs of the mixture onto a greased and floured baking sheet and bake in the pre-set oven for about 5 minutes or until a pale brown.

When cold put a blob of melted chocolate on half the biscuits, then sandwich with the remainder. When the chocolate is firm, sprinkle with icing sugar.

Mocha Creams

4 oz (100 g) softened unsalted butter
8 oz (225 g) sifted icing sugar
1 egg yolk
2 tsp (10 ml) orange flower water
coffee liqueur to taste
8 oz (225 g) plain dessert chocolate, broken into pieces

In a mixing bowl cream the butter until light and soft. Then gradually beat in the icing sugar with the egg yolk. When blended beat in the orange flower water and enough liqueur to give the mixture a strong coffee taste. Melt the chocolate pieces in a pan over a low heat until just liquid, then beat into the butter cream mixture until it holds a soft peak.

Fill the mixture into a piping bag fitted with a large crown nozzle and pipe rosettes of the mixture straight into paper sweet cases and decorate with either sugar balls, crystallized violets or rose petals, angelica, finely ground, nibbed or flaked nuts, glacé cherries or citron peel.

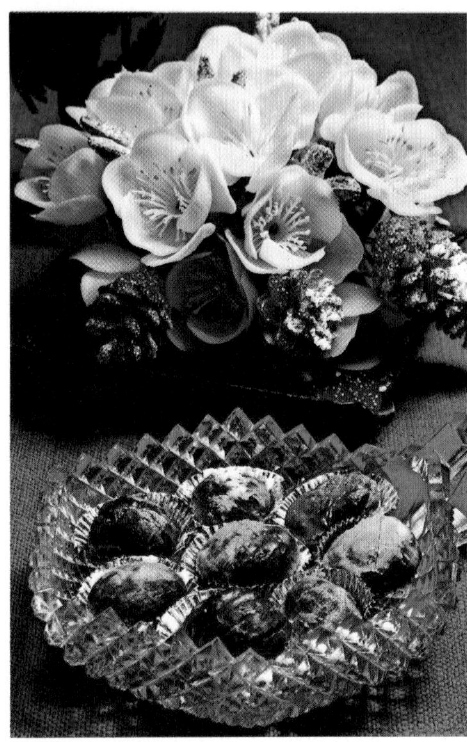

Marrons Glacés.

Marrons Glacés

1 lb (450 g) chestnuts
vanilla pod
sugar syrup

Fry the chestnuts, a few at a time, in a deep frying pan. Within a few moments, the chestnuts will split. Take them out, drain and leave to cool.

Remove the shells and the inner skin. When all the chestnuts are skinned, put them in a pan, cover with boiling water, and simmer with a vanilla pod until tender.

Pack the drained chestnuts into a clean bottling jar, and pour in enough sugar syrup to cover – the amount will depend on your jar. Place the lid loosely on the jar and stand the jar in a sterilizer. Pour water in to come halfway up the side of the jar and simmer until the chestnuts and the syrup turn a rich red-brown colour. Remove jar and tighten lid.

Leave the marrons glacés in the bottling jar until ready to serve.

Vanilla Fudge

½ pt (30 cl) evaporated milk
1 lb (450 g) castor sugar
1½ oz (37 g) butter
vanilla essence

Place the milk, sugar and butter in a heavy based pan and heat very gently until the sugar dissolves. Bring the mixture to the boil and raise to a temperature of 240°F (116°C), stirring to prevent sticking.

Remove the pan from the heat, add a few drops of vanilla essence and beat thoroughly until the mixture thickens.

Pour the fudge into a greased square or rectangular baking tin. Leave until almost cold, then mark into squares with a sharp knife. Cut into squares when firmly set.

Coconut Ice

1 lb (450 g) granulated sugar
¼ pt (15 cl) milk
5 oz (150 g) desiccated coconut
pink food colouring

Dissolve the sugar in the milk in a heav based pan over a low heat. Do not stir Bring to the boil, and boil gently for abou 10 minutes or until a temperature o 240°F (116°C) is reached.

Remove from the heat and stir in th coconut. Pour half the mixture into greased square or rectangular tin. Tint th rest of the mixture with pink colouring and pour it over the mixture in the tin.

Leave until half set, mark into bars wit a sharp knife. Cut into bars when cold.

Treacle Toffee

1 lb (450 g) demerara sugar
1 pt (60 cl) water
¼ level tsp (1 ml) cream of tartar
4 tbsp (60 ml) black treacle
4 tbsp (60 ml) golden syrup

Dissolve the sugar in the water in a heav based pan over a very low heat. Stir little as possible. Add the cream of tarta butter treacle and syrup, and bring th mixture to the boil. Raise the temperatu to 290°F (145°C), without stirring.

Pour into a square or rectangular ti Leave for about 5 minutes, then mark in squares with a sharp knife and leave to se

Fondants

2 fl oz (5 cl) liquid glucose
1 lb (450 g) sifted icing sugar
1 egg white
flavouring and colouring

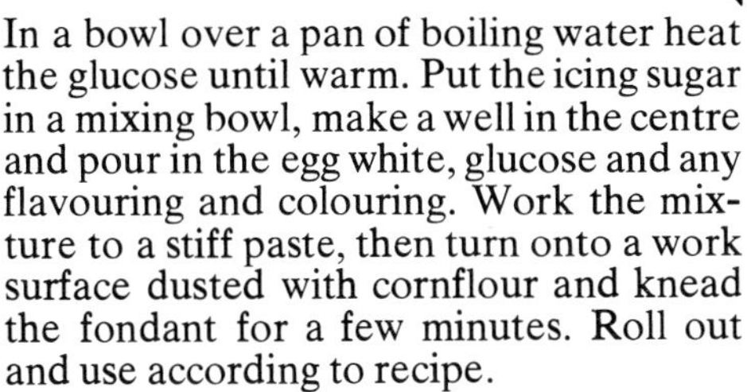

In a bowl over a pan of boiling water heat the glucose until warm. Put the icing sugar in a mixing bowl, make a well in the centre and pour in the egg white, glucose and any flavouring and colouring. Work the mixture to a stiff paste, then turn onto a work surface dusted with cornflour and knead the fondant for a few minutes. Roll out and use according to recipe.

Peppermint Fondants

2 fl oz (5 cl) liquid glucose
1 lb (450 g) sifted icing sugar
1 egg white
3–4 drops of oil of peppermint
1–2 drops of green food colouring

In a bowl over a pan of boiling water, heat the glucose until warm. Put the icing sugar into a mixing bowl, make a well in the centre and pour in the egg white, glucose, flavouring (add oil of peppermint sparingly because it is very strong and costly as well) and colouring. Work to a stiff paste, taste and add more oil of peppermint if required, then turn onto a work surface dusted with cornflour. Knead fondant for a few minutes, then roll out to about ⅛ inch (3 mm) thickness and, using a 1 inch (2.50 cm) plain pastry cutter, stamp into rounds. Place on a baking sheet and leave to dry out. Store in layers between sheets of waxed paper in an airtight container.

Variation:
For Raspberry Fondants, make the fondant as above and substitute framboise liqueur for the oil of peppermint, and pink food colouring for green if liked. Complete as the recipe above.

Stuffed Dates

ates
lmond paste
irsch to flavour

Remove the stones from the dates and fill he cavities generously with kirsch avoured almond paste.

Chocolate Bonbons

1 egg yolk
2 oz (50 g) sifted icing sugar
2 oz (50 g) softened butter
1 tsp (5 ml) coffee syrup
4 oz (100 g) plain dessert chocolate, broken into pieces and melted until just liquid
1 tsp (5 ml) brandy
1 tsp (5 ml) coffee liqueur
1–2 oz (25–50 g) finely ground pistachio nuts

Make mocha butter cream by whisking the egg yolk and icing sugar together in a bowl over a pan of hot water until thick. Remove the pan from the heat, stand in a bowl of ice and continue whisking until the mixture is cool.

In another bowl cream the butter until light and soft, then beat into the egg mixture a little at a time. Beat in the coffee syrup, then 1 tbsp (15 ml) of just melted chocolate, the brandy and coffee liqueur. Then beat in enough of the remaining melted chocolate to turn the butter cream mixture into a stiff paste. Fill into a piping bag fitted with a rosette nozzle and pipe swirls of the mixture into paper or metal sweet cases. Sprinkle with pistachio nuts.

Chocolate Bonbons.

Index

Index